Cheap Rents

I CAME TO TENTH STREET LOOKING FOR
      TO GET STARTED, A LOFT TO LIVE IN AND

NOT WANTING SUBURBS, ACADEMIA, UPTO
ADVERTISING AGENCIES OR GREENWICH
JUST TO BE SOMEWHERE. IT BECAME

I VISITED ROBERT FRANK ON THIRD AVE…5
FROM PERU. THERE WAS A SIGN NEXT
I GOT THE LOFT AND MOVED IN, WITH NO
NEIGHBORHOOD IT WAS OR WHAT ELSE W
THERE WAS CHEAP RENT, NICE LIGHT, HE

PLACE

AKE ART

,

AGE BOHEMIA_
NG ADVENTURE.

ED HIM MY WORK

R "SPACE FOR RENT"

EA OF WHAT
ON THE BLOCK

Y TRUCK TRAFFIC.

For my children and their children

John Cohen

Cheap Rents

... and de Kooning

**The downtown art world
New York, 1957–63**

Introduction by John Elderfield

Steidl

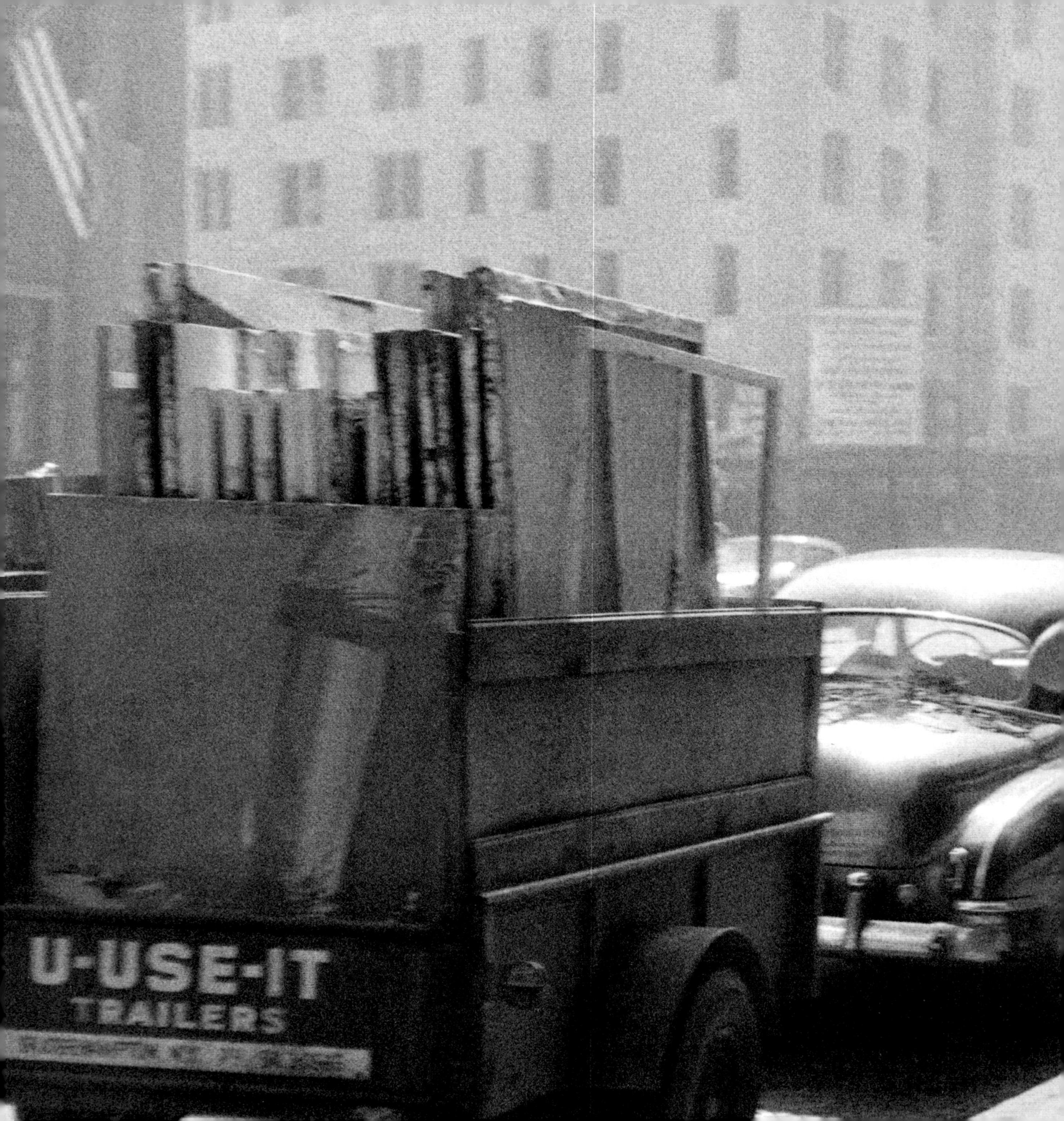
U-USE-IT
TRAILERS

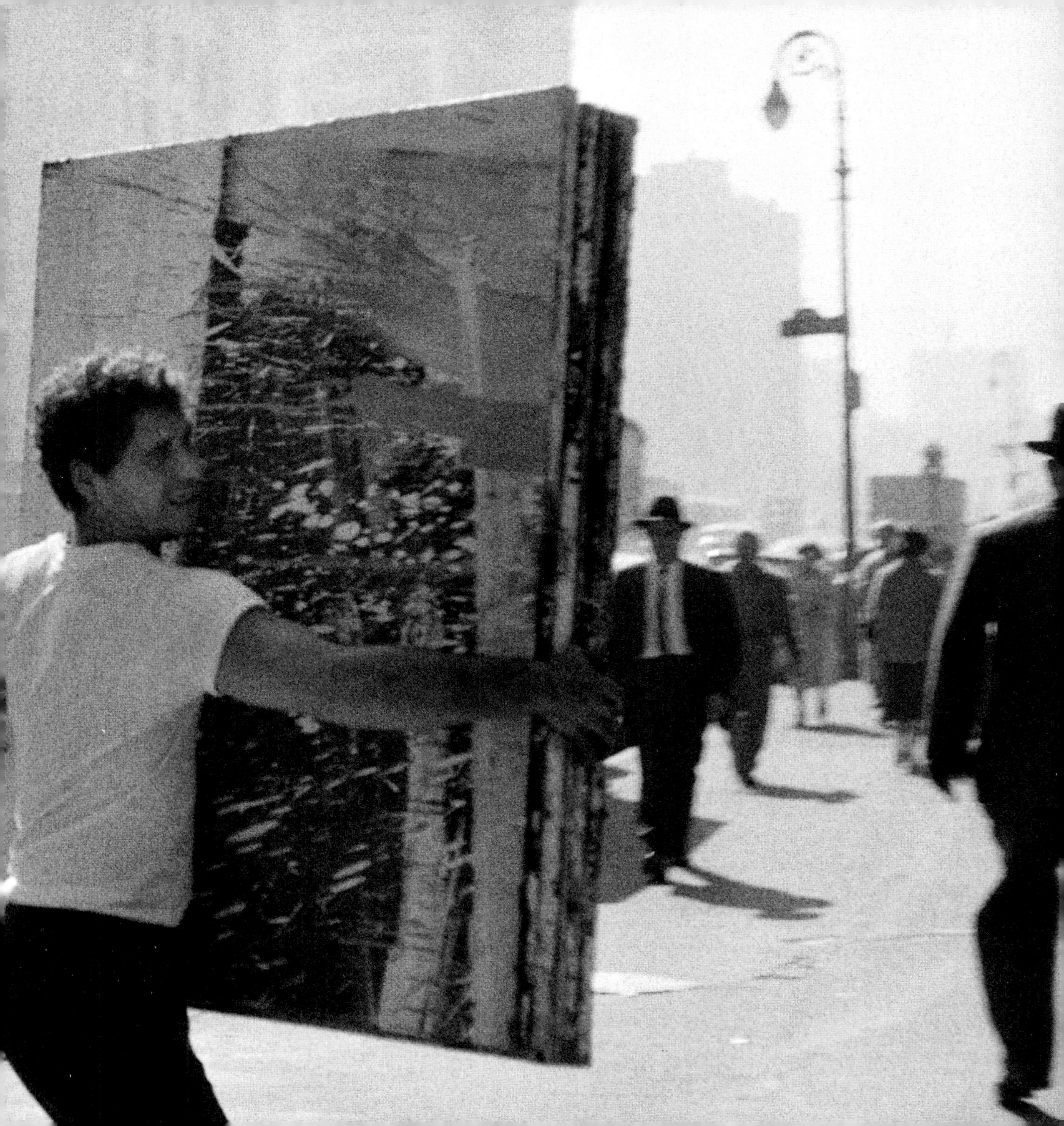

INTRODU

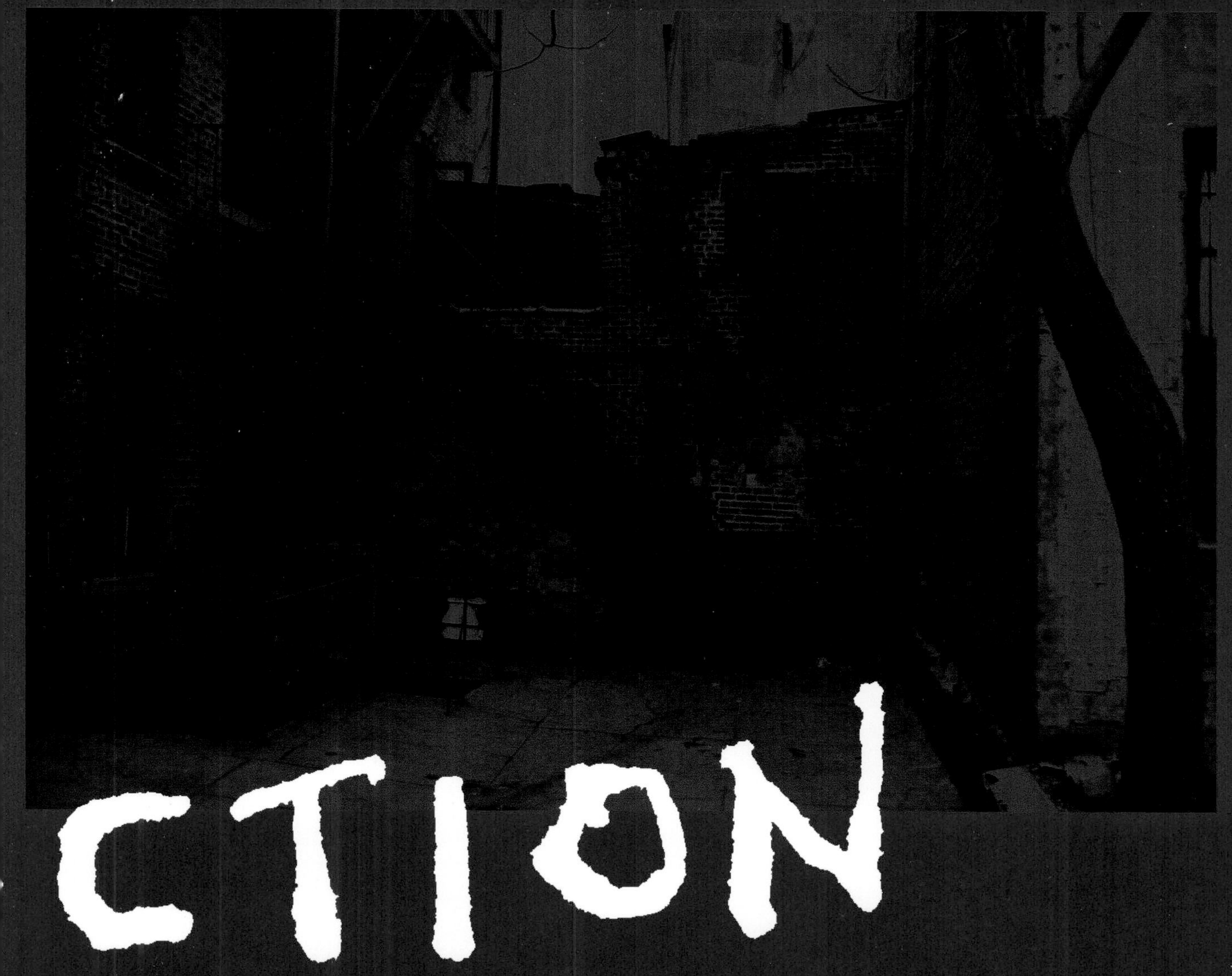
CTION

Frozen glimpses and the invisible man

"On Tenth Street, a fraction of America's art life has found a place and in doing so has also found its time," wrote the critic Harold Rosenberg in 1959, adding: "Perhaps it happened the other way around; in any case, place and time have come together." This is the subject of John Cohen's book: the coincidence of a place—the area around East 10th Street—and a time—the late 1950s and early 1960s—in shaping a portion of America's art life so vital that the appearance of these previously unpublished, very 10th Street photographs is a great occasion.

It isn't obvious, it needs saying, why this book is called *Cheap Rents ... and de Kooning.* There are plenty of places in it with cheap rents—or that had cheap rents when John Cohen photographed them—but the only de Kooning in the book is this 1956 painting by Willem de Kooning called *Backyard on Tenth Street,* reproduced here **(fig. 1)**, which John thought of including at the last minute if I wanted it in my introduction. In the book, though, is his photograph of the backyard itself **(fig. 2 and p. 39)**, which was between de Kooning's studio and Robert and Mary Frank's, above which was John's loft. John tells me that de Kooning shoveled spaghetti in his, John's, mouth at a dinner for Mary Frank, which may, I suppose, be thought a neighborly thing to do. Also that he saw de Kooning wheeling a baby carriage down Third Avenue, but he doesn't say whether de Kooning was using the baby carriage to move a painting, as Red Grooms is seen doing in two of these photographs, or whether it was a proud

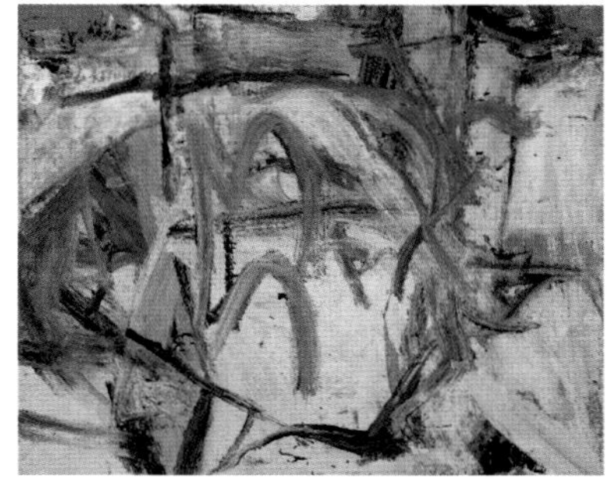
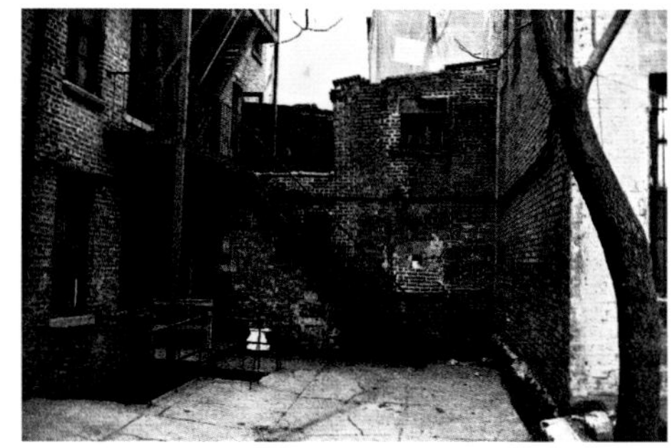

father wheeling his daughter, Lisa, who had been born in January of 1956. In any event, de Kooning was then beginning to spend more and more time outside the city, often on Long Island, so missed out being recorded by John among his colleagues and admirers, a good number of whom had come to live on 10th Street because of his presence there; hence his absence from this book with his name in the title. However, before there is any grumbling about deceptive advertising, let me say that the missing de Kooning is present in the book like an invisible asset, an invisible intangible, an invisible man.

The photographs in this book date from 1957 to 1963. How very different these two years were is evident from this simple contrast: In 1957, the year that Dwight D. Eisenhower began his second term as President, Willem de Kooning, his commercial and critical success increasing, and recently a father, applied for U.S. citizenship on April 4. The Museum of Modern Art curator Dorothy Miller wrote to the U.S. Immigration and Naturalization Service, attesting to "his good character and the high regard in which he is held, not only professionally but also personally, by those who know him." In 1963, Bob Dylan, having released *The Freewheelin' Bob Dylan,* his first album of original songs, which made him the unwilling darling of the political left, very reluctantly performed the now bitterly ironic "The Times They Are a-Changin'" at a New York State theater on November 23, the day after President John F. Kennedy's assassination.

De Kooning lived and worked in isolation from public events; Dylan didn't. And de Kooning's isolation was common to the community within which he lived and worked, a community centered very specifically on East 10th Street in Manhattan. The critic Harold Rosenberg called it a colony, because everyone had moved there from somewhere else, many of the colonists being in fact immigrants or the children of immigrants. Rosenberg lived there, too, and in 1959 wrote of it as having "entered a kind of metaphysical retirement, a dissident self-isolation from as many areas of social contact as possible. In the studios and among the sidewalk loungers, public events are noted spasmodically as occurrences 'outside'." What happened "inside" is the subject of the photographs in this book. But their changing cast of characters reflects the changes that occurred as the 1950s gave way to the 1960s, bringing the outside in.

Since the majority of Cohen's photographs here are of interiors, it is worth reinforcing what the exterior shots show: Unlike Greenwich Village, not far north and west, East 10th Street and its environs were not charming, not like a European art center, which would have been a distraction for the artists living there, Rosenberg argued—meaning a distracting reminder of an older culture they were trying to supplant, and distracting because the last thing the artists wanted was to be surrounded by merely charming things.

Looking at 10th Street, Rosenberg continued, "no one could mistake it for an esthetic creation... [it] has not even the picturesqueness of a slum."

His 1959 essay in *Art News Annual,* "Tenth Street: A Geography of Modern Art," is required reading on the subject, suggesting that he could have been a great travel writer instead of a sometimes over-philosophical critic. Chief among the essay's merits is the insight that 10th Street seemed like a realization of what de Kooning called "no environment." I will come to that later; but first we need to know what 10th Street looked like. Most of Cohen's photographs are of views inside galleries and places with low light, but there are images of the street and its surroundings. They bear out Rosenberg's description of what he called "The Block of the Artists," that is, the block of 10th Street between Third and Fourth Avenues:

Apart from two pawnshops facing each other on the eastern corners, everything on Tenth Street is one of a kind: a liquor store with a large "wino" clientele; up a flight of steps, a hotel-workers' employment agency; in a basement, a poolroom; in another, something stored; in the middle of the block, a metal-stamping factory with a "modernistic" pea-green cement and glass-brick front; on the western corner, to be sure, an excavation.

Strange though it may seem, Rosenberg has neglected to mention the art galleries. John gives us their names: Area, Brata, Camino, Green, Hansa, March, Phoenix, Tanager. They sound now like code names for secret societies, quite different to the reality of the busy, crowded spaces in the photographs.

A few words with some background: By 1957, East 10th Street, and especially the block between Third and Fourth Avenues, had become the crowded mecca for new art and all that surrounded it, impromptu poetry readings, jazz sessions, early "happenings," and lots of parties. In five years, six art galleries had opened on or near 10th Street, none at all sumptuous—in fact, to the contrary—but bustling with activity. In 1952, the Tanager Gallery, whose manager Irving Sandler became the Vasari for the artists of the period, opened at 90 East 10th (next door to de Kooning's studio). It was followed by the Hansa Gallery at nearby 70 East 12th, to be superseded there in 1954 by the James Gallery. In 1956, the Camino Gallery opened at 92 East 10th, and in 1957 there came the March Gallery at 95 East, and the Brata Gallery at 89 East.

The range of artists represented by these galleries and appearing in the photographs was ecumenical: Their names appear in the long cast of characters at the end of this book. Worth noting now, though, is that they brought together, in place and time, people whom the historical record has now put into separate groups, but who actually went to the same parties and openings, talked and drank with each other, and ran into each other on the street—as the photographs in this book show.

So, in order to indicate the extent of their immingling, let us see a selection of these people arranged in the groups to which history has allotted them: The most senior group comprises members of what is commonly understood to be the first Abstract Expressionist generation, Hans Hofmann, Franz Kline, Ad Reinhardt, and Milton Resnick. However, of this group, only the gregarious Kline and Reinhardt appear prominently. Hofmann, making only a single appearance, was not a downtown artist, as neither were the unrepresented Abstract Expressionists, Robert Motherwell, Barnett Newman, Clyfford Still, and Mark Rothko. Jackson Pollock had died in 1956, and de Kooning was now often absent. In the 1957–63 period, then, the downtown avant-garde was without its senior representatives, and not only enjoying its liberation, but also struggling with its belatedness, with the burden of coming after so innovative a generation.

Especially so were the second-generation Abstract Expressionists, who comprise a far larger group, including Norman Bluhm, James Brooks, Michael Goldberg, Philip Guston, Grace Hartigan, and Jack Tworkov. In the same generation, but pulling further away from Abstract Expressionism were the artists exploring forms of figuration, like Alex Katz, Alice Neel, Larry Rivers, and Tom Wesselmann; those developing a more severe abstraction, like Al Held and Ludwig Sander; and those moving into assemblage and more besides, like Robert Rauschenberg. It was all of these artists, and others like them, who were at the center of the 10th Street colony, because they were tethered to Abstract Expressionist sources even as they sought to expand or escape them.

Less clearly tethered, obviously, were those other than painters represented here: the Beat writers and poets, Gregory Corso, Allen Ginsberg,

Jack Kerouac, and Peter Orlovsky; in 1959, the Alfred Leslie / Robert Frank film *Pull My Daisy* that brought together the Beat poets, the painters Neel and Rivers, and the gallerist Richard Bellamy; and those who expanded painting into performance, into happenings, like Jim Dine, Red Grooms, Allan Kaprow, and Claes Oldenburg. It was owing to the activities of this group—that is to say, to the various transitions from painting to performative and poetic mediums—that the character of 10th Street changed. These were temporal transitions, of course; but, as the newer emerged, the older remained, and older and newer partied together—at the Cedar Bar in the form of Franz Kline drinking with Allen Ginsberg, for example. And different forms of post-Abstract Expressionist activity partied together: Jack Tworkov with Philip Guston; Larry Rivers with Jack Kerouac; and so on.

Aiding the alliances and the transitions were the photographers Rudy Burckhardt, Cohen, and Frank; and the composers John Cage and Morton Feldman; and the dealers and the critics Bellamy, Leo Castelli, Thomas B. Hess, and Frank O'Hara. They saw how, by the end of this period, the vitality of the downtown scene was not longer lodged in the visual arts alone. But so did most of those in the 10th Street scene: It was nonsectarian, hybrid, unpredictable in shape and form.

Moreover, the transitions from painting to performative and poetic mediums encouraged, and were encouraged by, the parallel transition from interest in what was only "inside" to what was "outside" the artistic colony

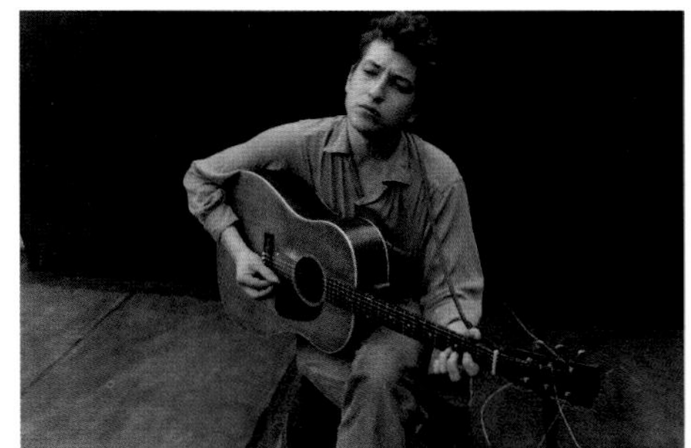

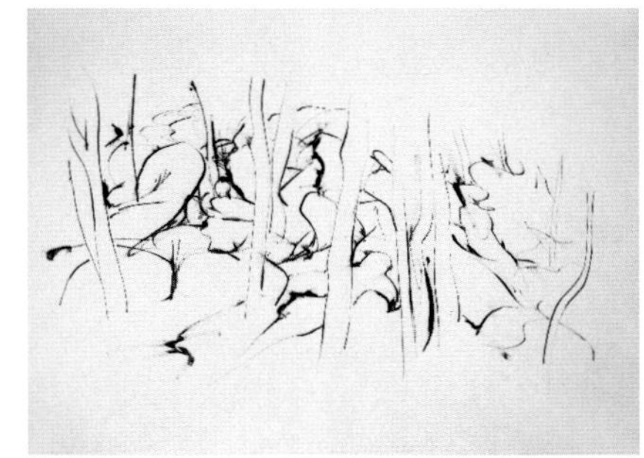

itself. Art thus came out of its "metaphysical retirement [and] dissident self-isolation from as many areas of social contact as possible"—and into the social and political world. In John's case, this is symbolized by his own turn to performance upon his founding the musical group, The New Lost City Ramblers, in 1958; and by the appearance in his life of Bob Dylan, whom he photographed on the roof of his loft building in 1962 (fig. 3).

Cohen had painted and drawn (fig. 4), but he is a prime example of someone who took from the 10th Street experience the lesson that it was possible to be multifarious in his own practice, and to focus on both "inside" and "outside" for his inspiration. This would take him, as a photographer, a long way geographically, stylistically, and philosophically from 10th Street. But more than a little of 10th Street remained in his bones.

What of his photographs of 10th Street themselves? My answer is that they not only provide a vivid portrait of what 10th Street looked like, on the street itself and in the studios and galleries, and would be more than welcome for that alone. They also do that in a very 10th Street way: They show us what the invisible man in this book called a "no environment," a place so ordinary that it could be anywhere, but which gained its character—a very distinctive character—by what happened there; and a place so various that it comprised many non-specific places, disparate things and details of things colliding together. And they show it in a very particular 10th Street way, which the invisible man also used.

De Kooning said he wanted to paint the effect of suddenly catching sight of something—while coming into a room, or glancing out of a window, or crossing the street quickly. What you see suddenly, and attempt to capture— in paint or on film—is, he said, "an occurrence" or "an encounter." When "you meet something," that something literally flashes by you, or seems to do so because you yourself flash by it: In either case, what you see are, he said, "like frozen glimpses." In fact, what we call "content," he said, "is a glimpse of something, an encounter, like a flash"—so vivid it didn't need to be photographed with the aid of a flash. Using the available light, John said, "had its limitations and its challenges. But at least I could see what I was photographing."

John Elderfield, April 2015
John Elderfield is Chief Curator Emeritus of Painting and Sculpture at The Museum of Modern Art, where he curated the 2011 exhibition "De Kooning: A Retrospective."

THE SP...

OF GOIN...

ACE
BACK

In the late 1950s a one-block neighborhood of artists' lofts and cooperative galleries on 10th Street in New York City became the center for anything new and avant-garde in downtown Manhattan. It is a nearly forgotten moment in the history of American art. Fifty years later I found myself revisiting that scene through the photographs I took as a young artist. It was my home … I lived there from 1957 to 1963.

Artists talk of pictorial space, of perspective and Renaissance space and the picture plane space. This book is set in the space of going back. Old photographs exist in this space. Making a new book from them creates new stories and rewrites history.

As I went back to the darkroom to re-print old negatives, unexpected images appeared, unleashed by the photographic process. A test strip floated in the chemicals and settled on an image of Robert Rauschenberg. It began to resemble one of his paintings.

There is an assumption that a photograph documents what is in front of the camera: the informational aspect of image taking. But time has a way of changing the information. My 10th Street neighbor Robert Frank reflected about his own work: "It is difficult for me to have a positive, constructive etc. opinion about these pictures … In other words, I am no longer capable to respond like I wished I could. I am glad I did these pictures. The distance between me and these photos is the past multiplied by everything that has happened."

The explorations made by individual artists have since become the name of art movements; the Abstract Expressionists and Pop artists have become the avant-garde of the past. "The ground itself is shifting under you," wrote my friend Bob Dylan. These pictures of 10th Street have been sitting in boxes in my barn, sleeping for fifty years. Making them into a book now tells me that the ground has shifted, the past has multiplied; new stories emerge in the space of going back.

TEST STRIP: "a strip of sensitized material, sections of which are exposed for varying lengths of time to assess its response"

ACCIDENT: "an event that happens by chance or that is without apparent or deliberate cause"

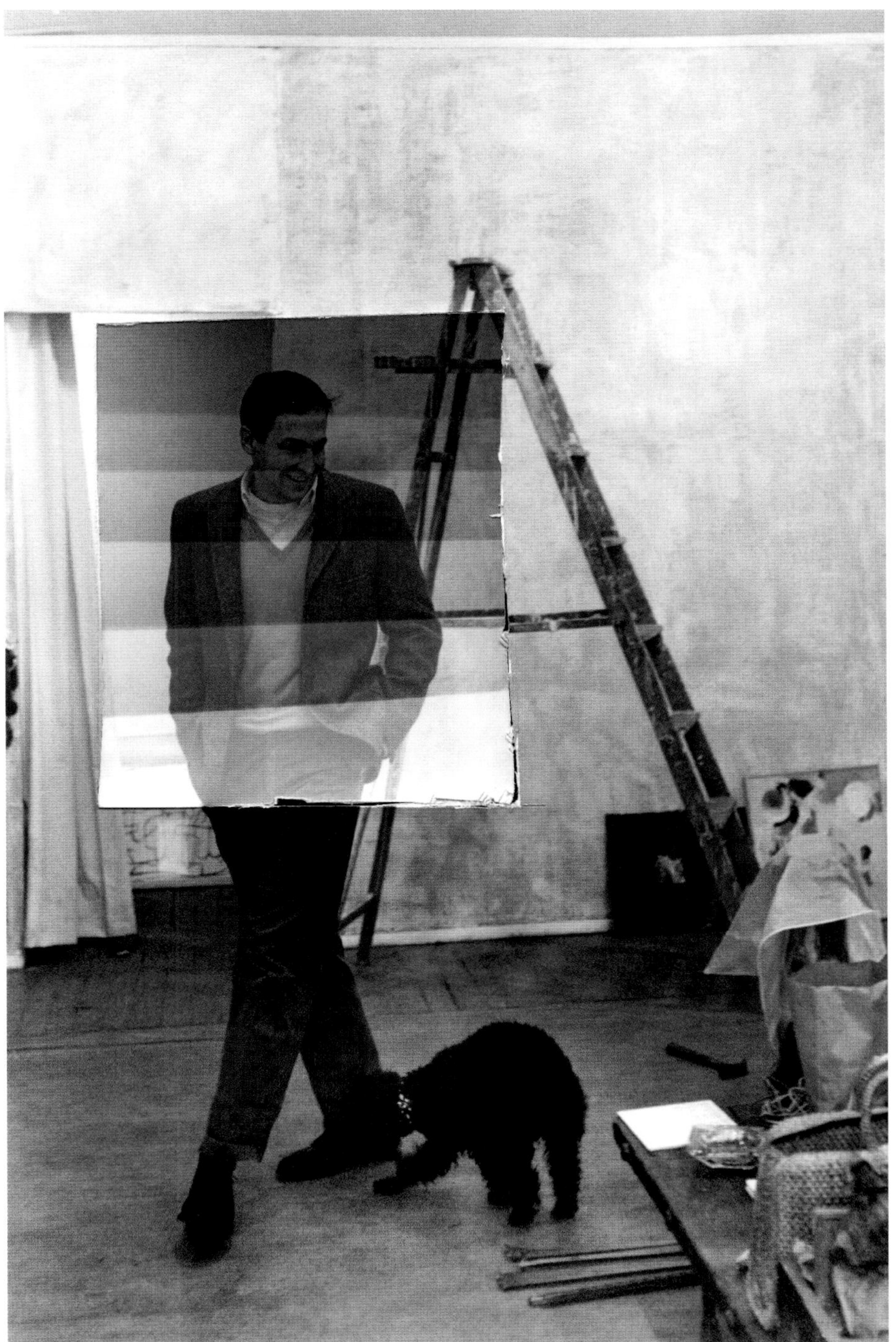

Robert Rauschenberg

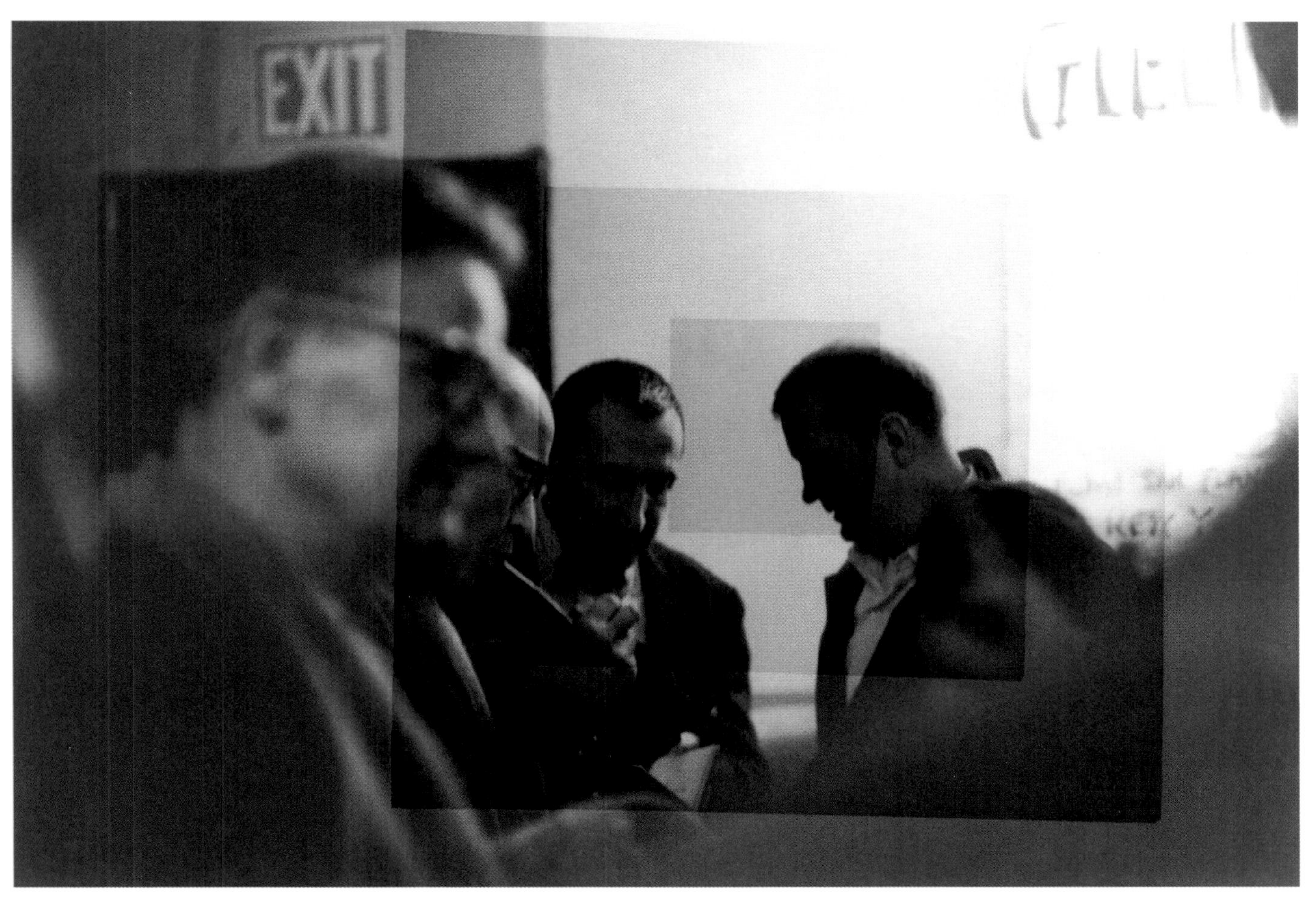

Phillip Pavia and Ad Reinhardt at the Artists' Club

Lois Dodd, Milton Resnick, Irving Sandler

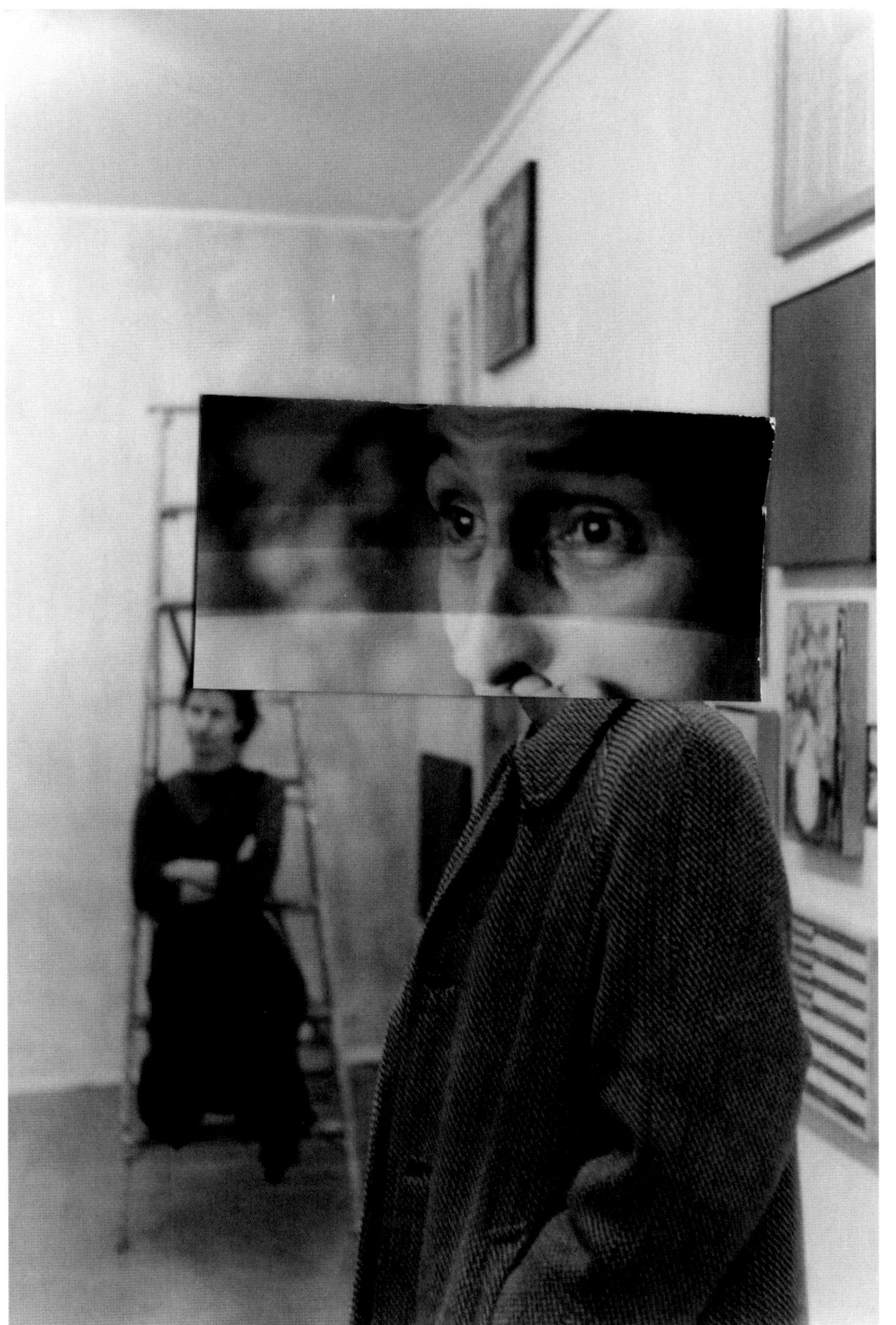

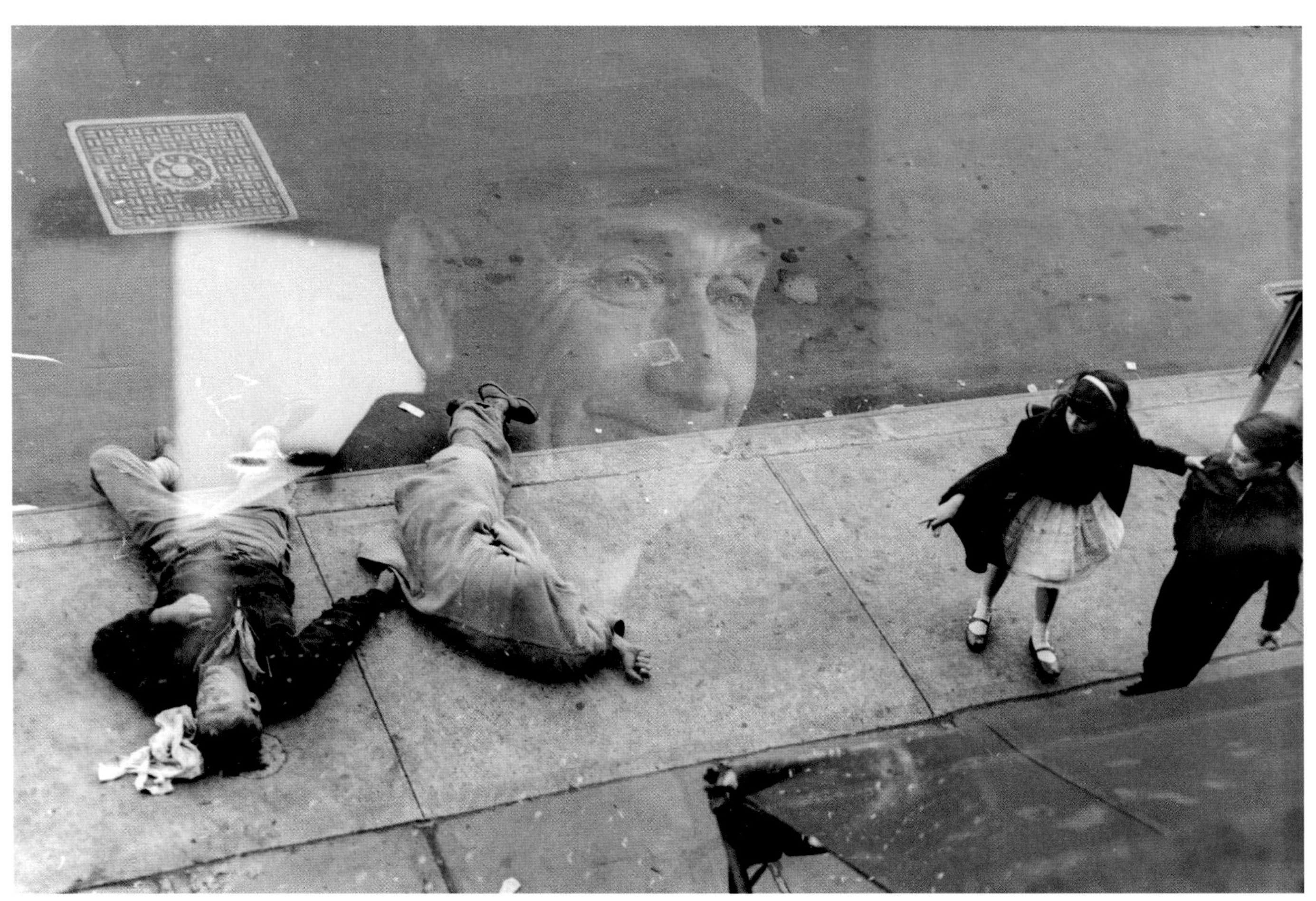

Andrea and Pablo Frank on Third Avenue

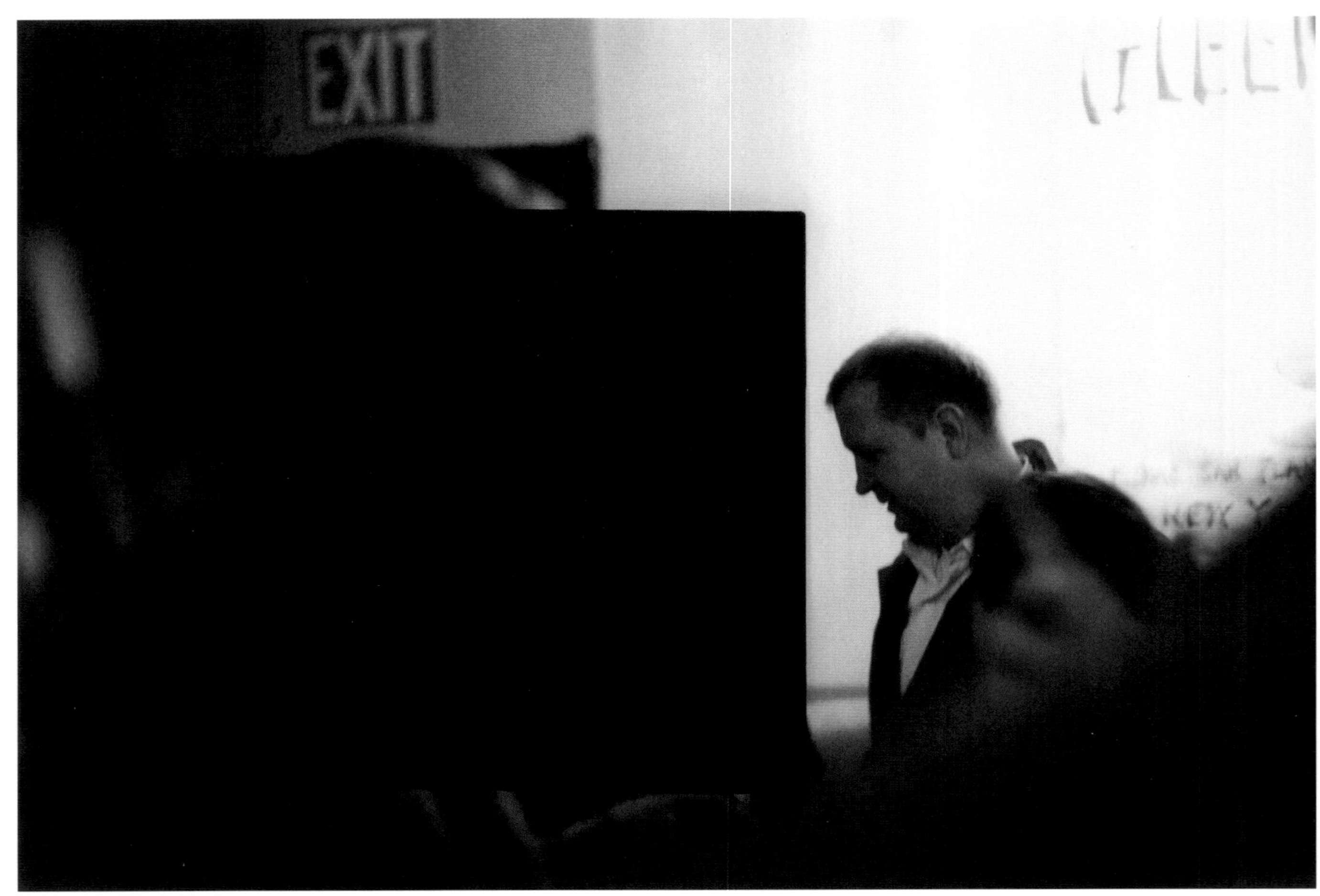

Ad Reinhardt

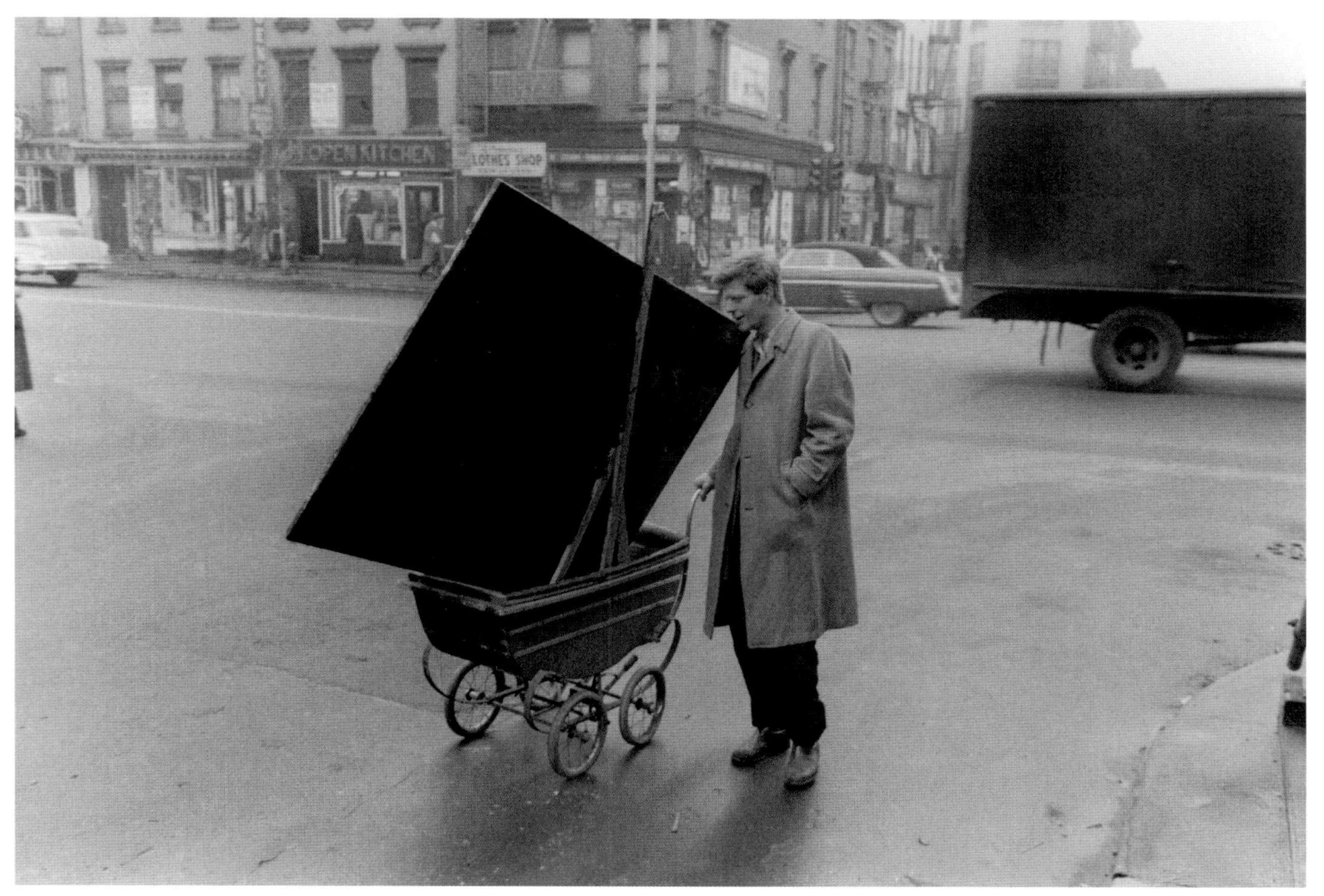

Red Grooms

10th Street between Third and Fourth Avenues

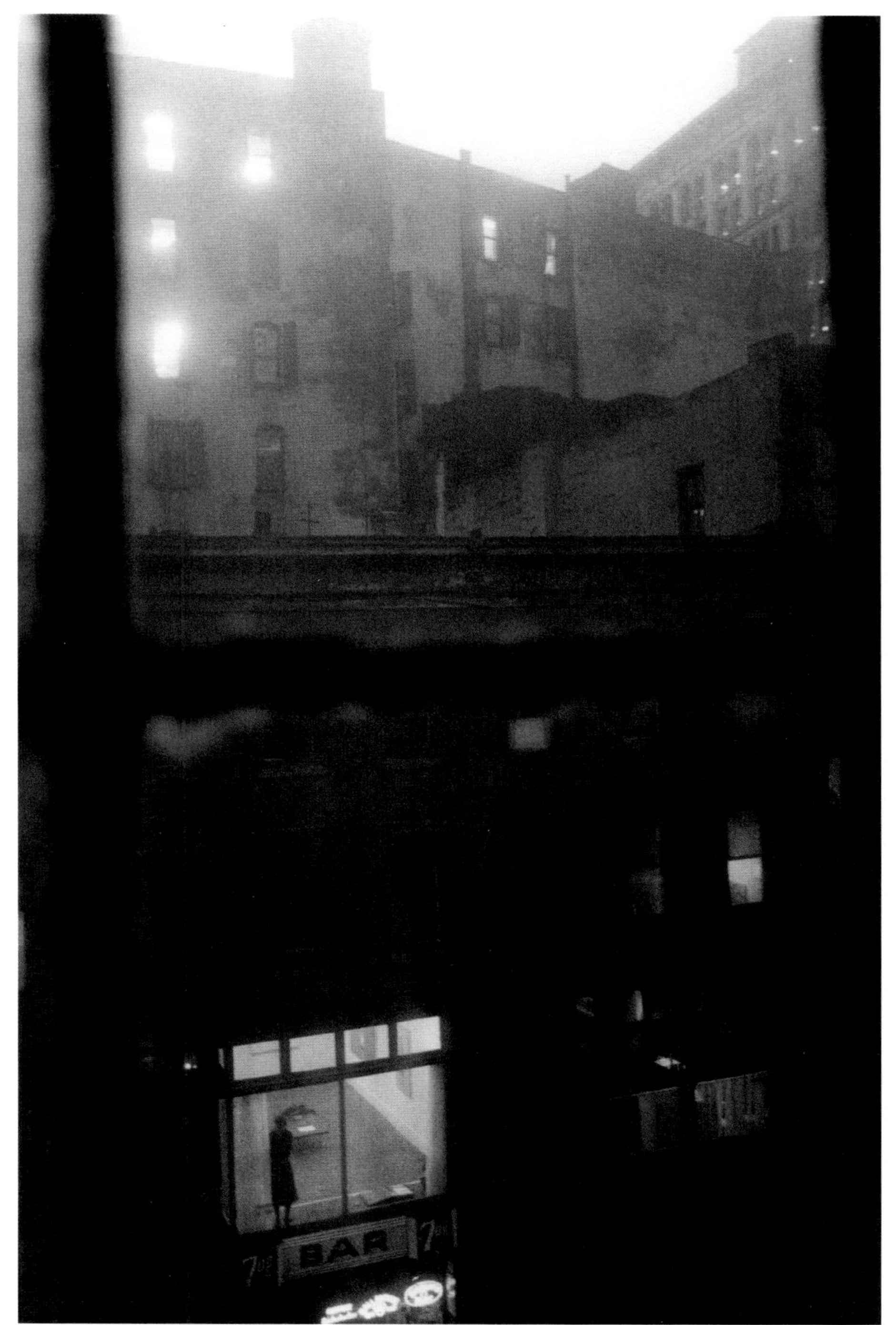
BAR

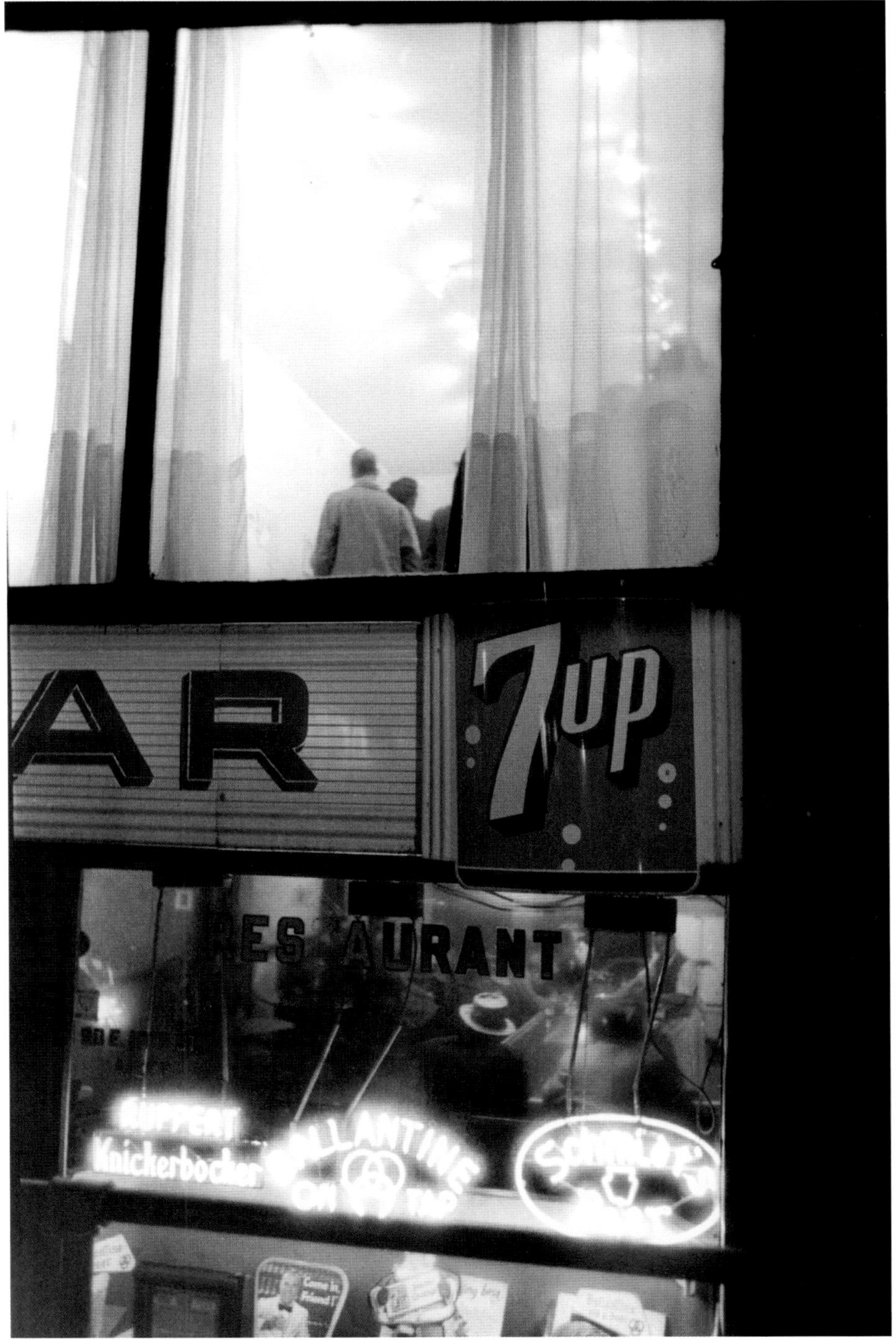
AR
7UP
RESTAURANT
Knickerbocker BALLANTINE
on tap

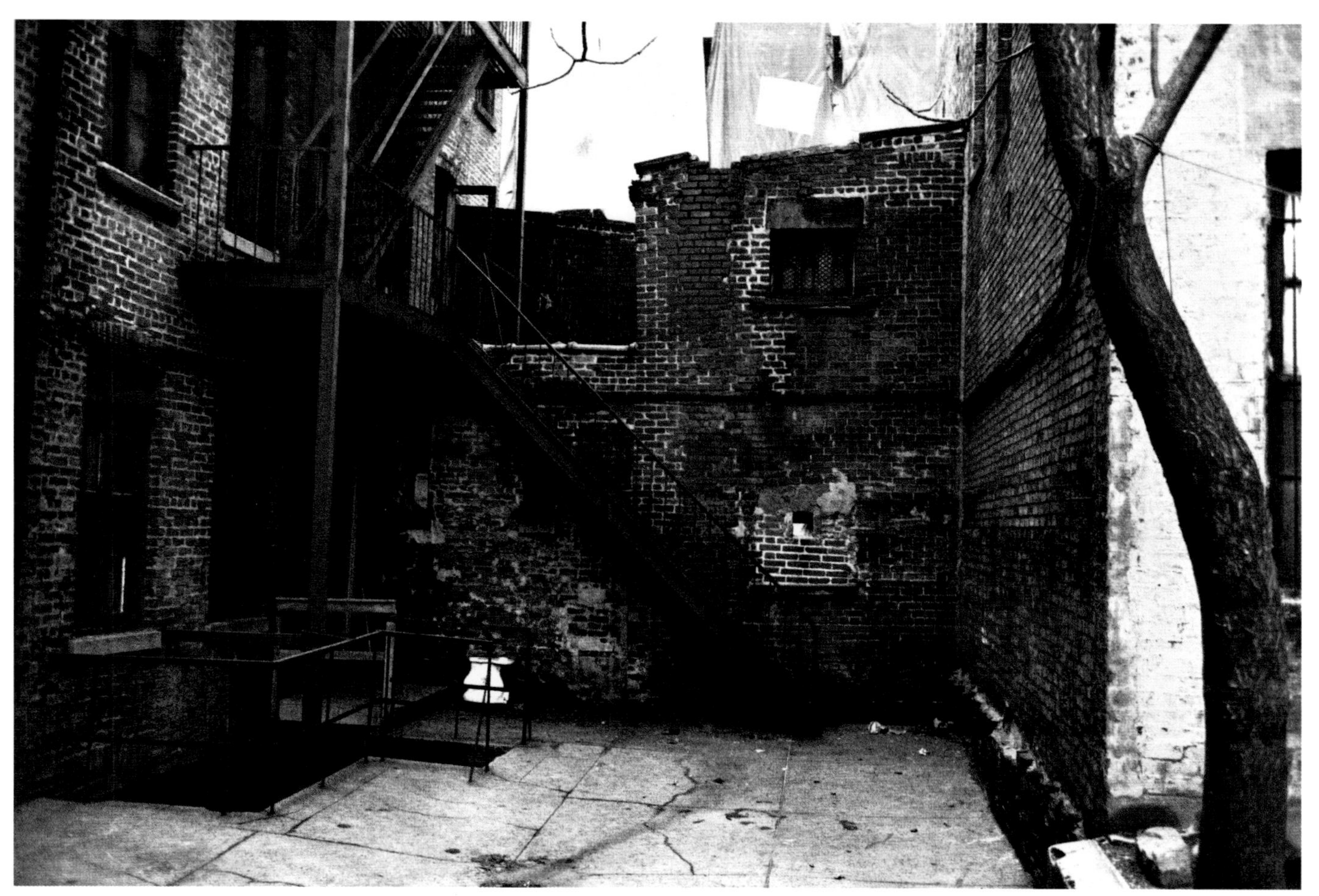

Backyard on 10th Street

**Red Grooms crossing Third Avenue

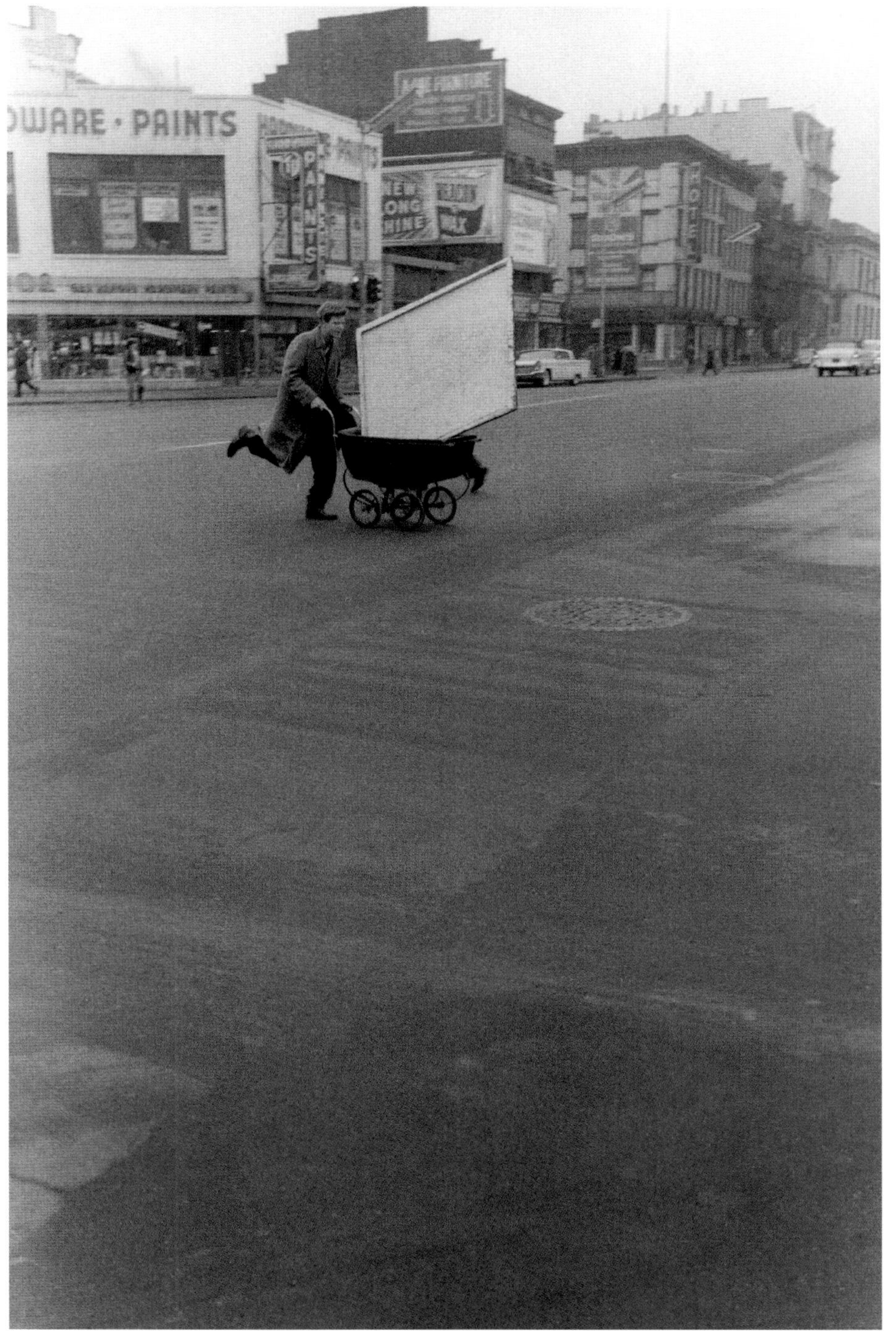

DWARE · PAINTS
PAINTS
PAINTS
NEW
LONG
SHINE

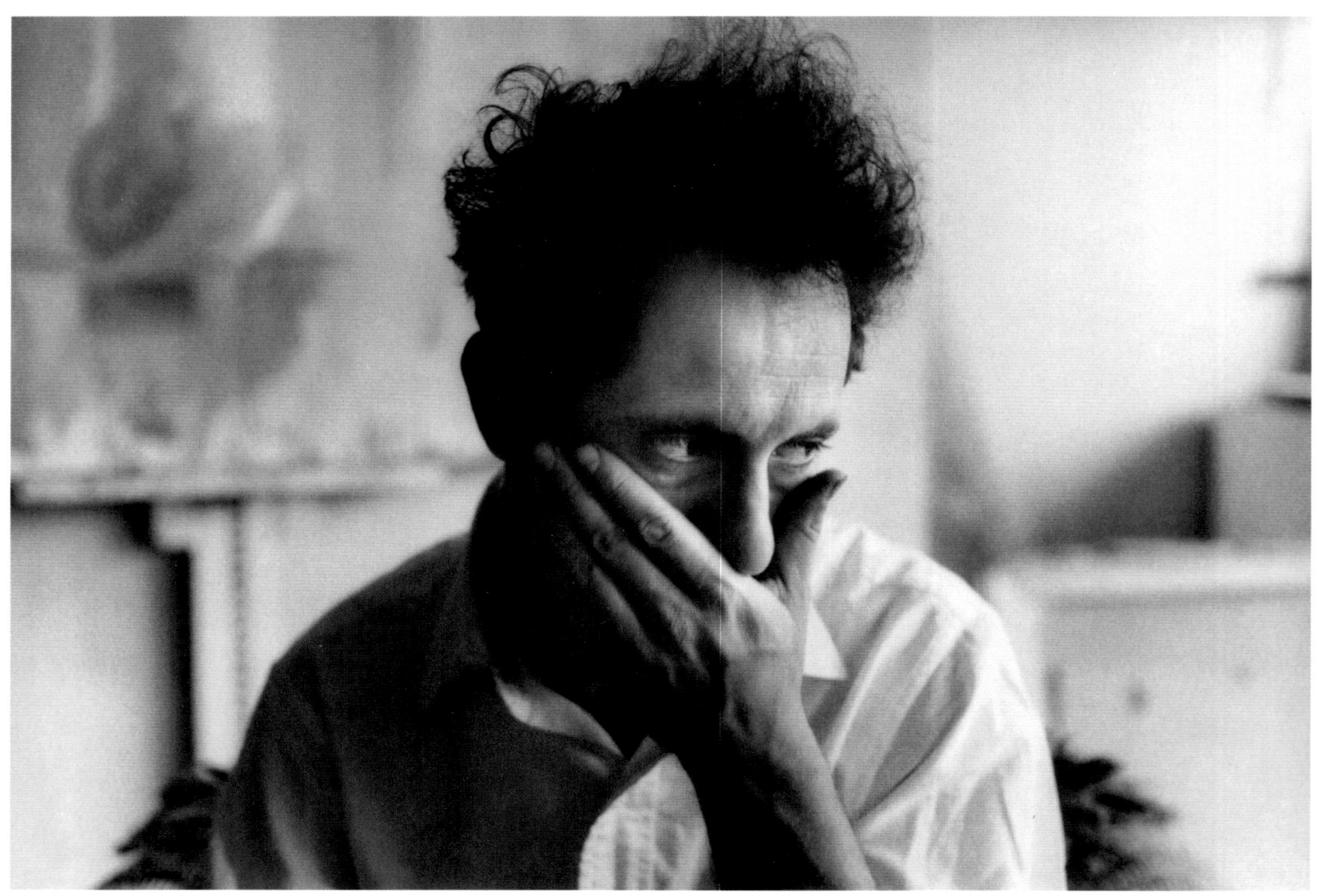

Robert Frank

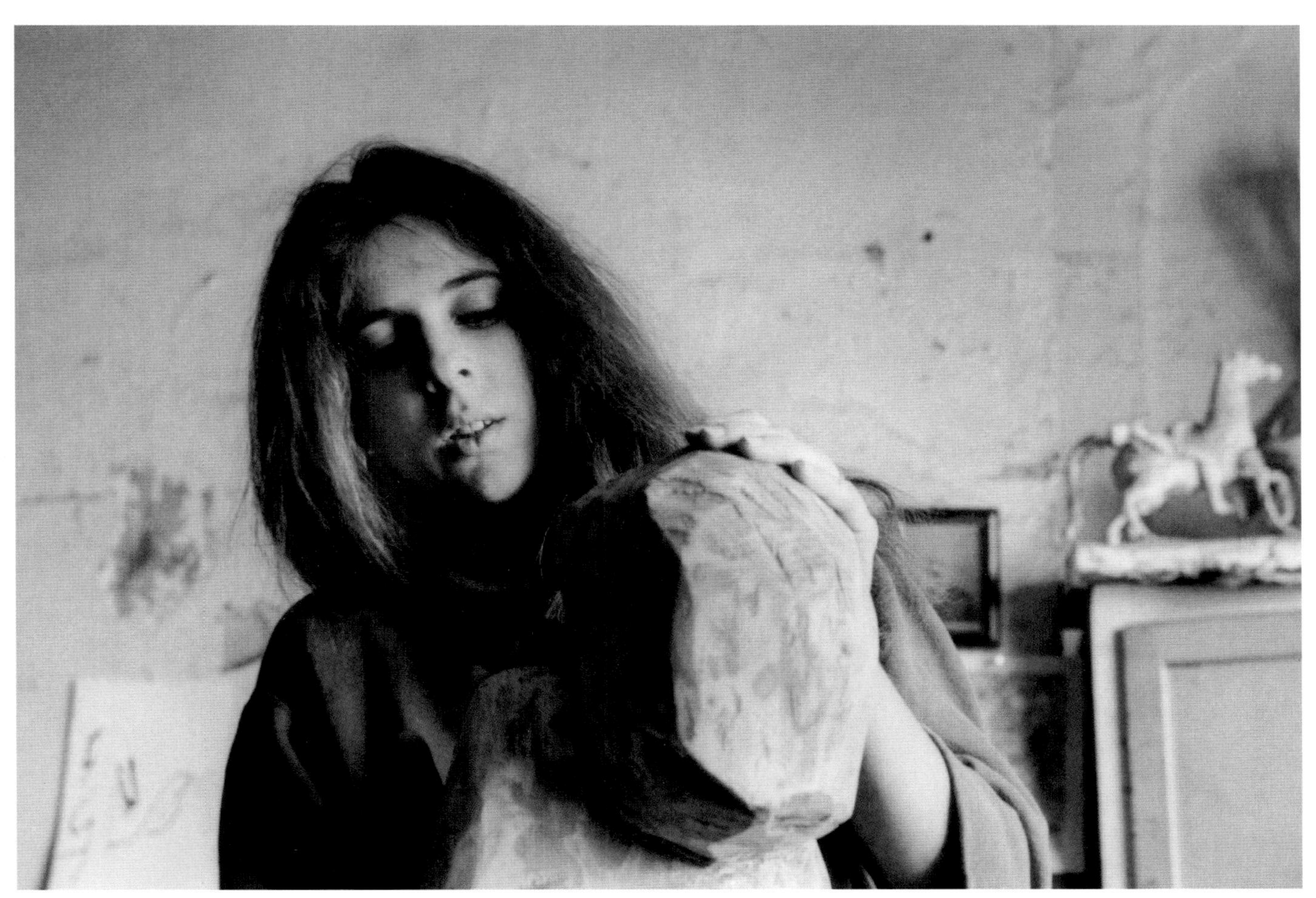

Mary Frank

Milton Resnick

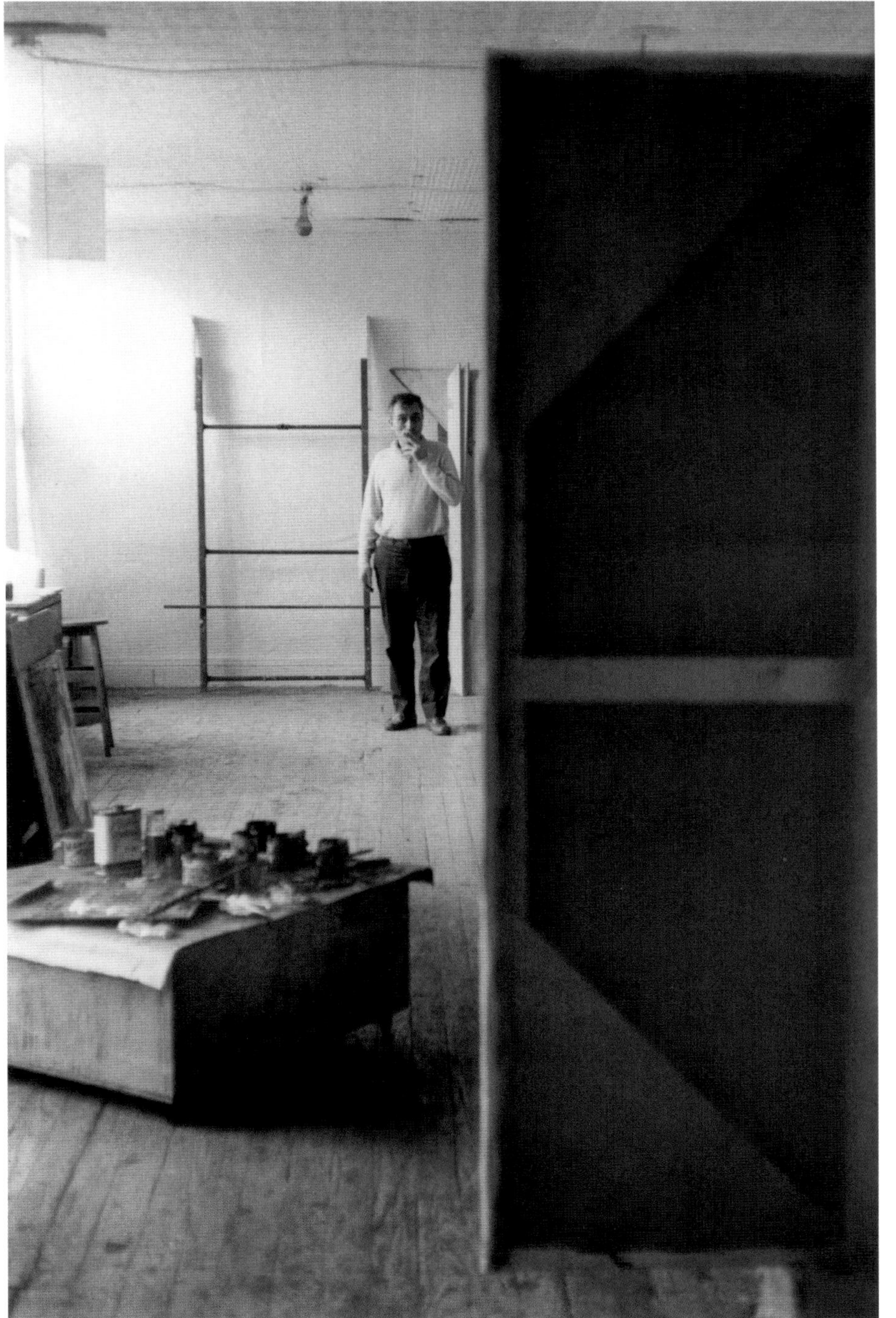

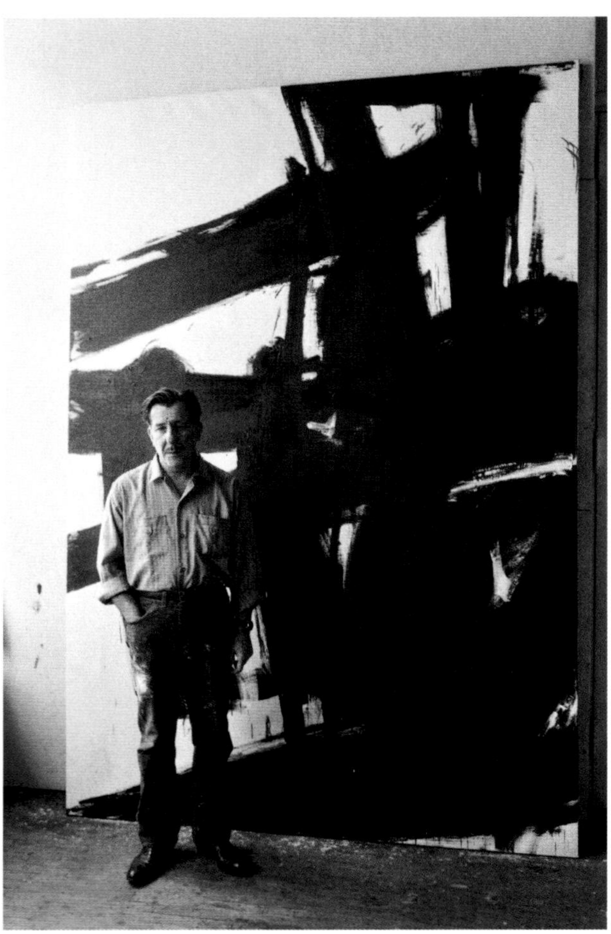

Franz Kline

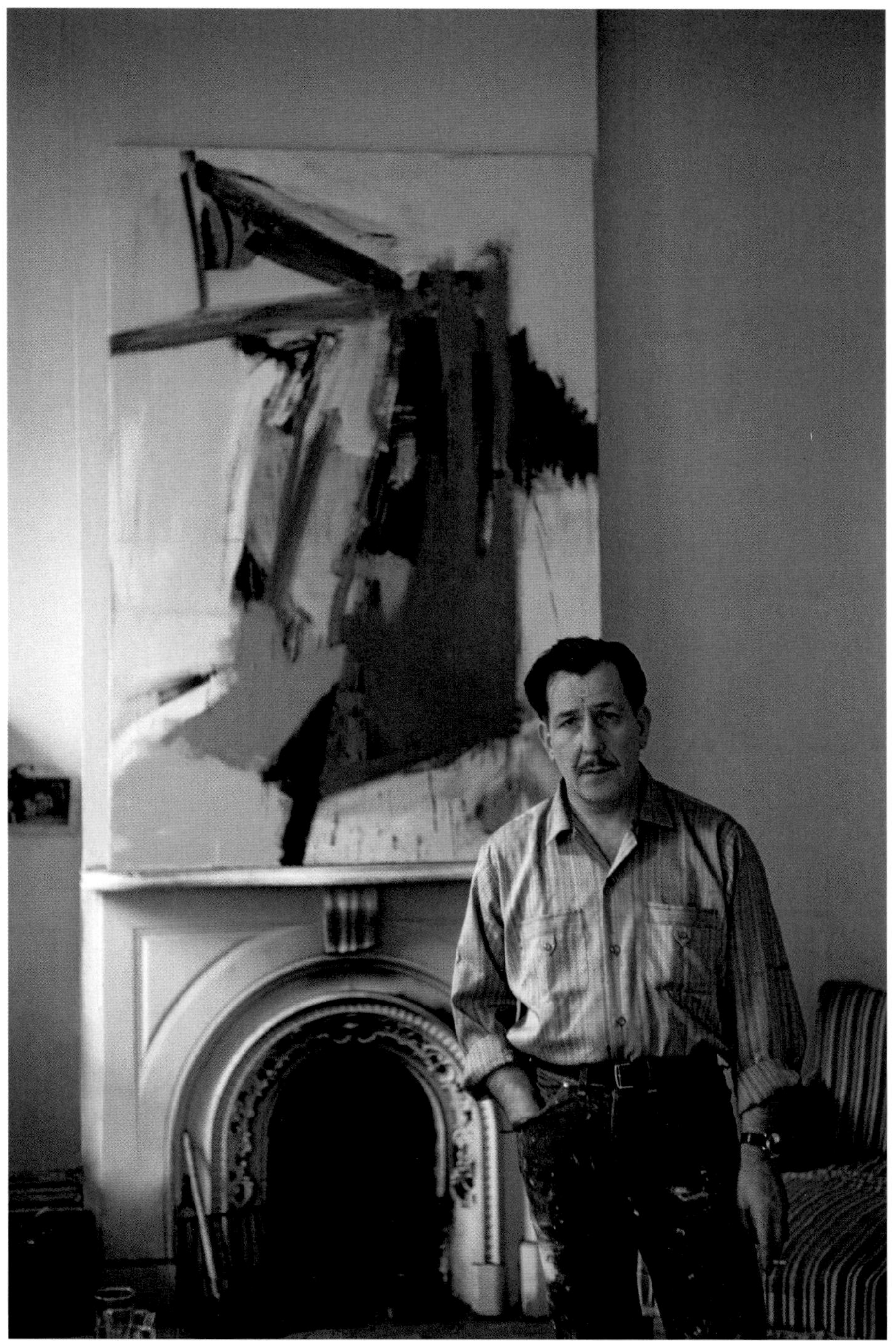

IN THE N

OF THE B

MIDDLE
LOCK

"cheap rents ... and de Kooning"

There were two art galleries on 10th Street when I arrived in 1957.
Then, more emerged between Third and Fourth Avenues. The earliest were
the Tanager, Brata, March, Area, Camino, and Phoenix. Rents were cheap
and de Kooning's studio was in the middle of the block. His artistic energy
and charisma attracted artists, and they moved here to share the creative
environment. These were the best of circumstances to do work: available
spaces, low rents and an emerging art community. It was probably like this
around Picasso years ago in Paris.

The first wave of Abstract Expressionists had made their mark on the
art world: Pollack, de Kooning, Rothko and Kline had left painting ideas
scattered all over. On 10th Street their legacy was thrashed out in artworks
and galleries, taken up by second-wave Abstract Expressionists, as well as by
former students of Hans Hofmann, graduates from Black Mountain College
and Cooper Union (which was nearby). Downtown 10th Street became the
main street of the art world in the late 1950s: a New York City block in the
nowhere land between Greenwich Village and the Lower East Side. It was a
street full of cooperative galleries run and owned by the artists themselves.

I liked the inventive atmosphere, and photographed whatever was
around me. I didn't set out to make a documentary. The painters had devised
a way to get their work shown by banding together and running their own

galleries. In an indifferent Manhattan, business and uptown seemed far away.
There were few prospects of a wider audience, of selling work, or having
patrons or getting reviews.

ROBERT FRANK
LIVES HERE
↓

CAROLYN BROW
↳→

SAUL LEITER
←

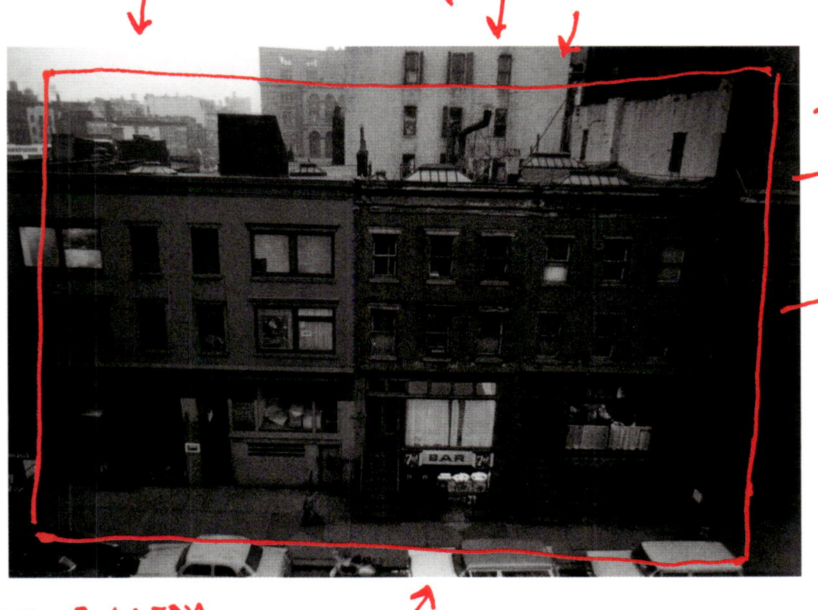

PHOTOGRAPH
BOB DYLAN - HERE
DE KOONING'S STUDIO
MILTON RESNICK'S STUDIO
ESTABAN VINCENTE'S STUDIO
RUBEN GALLERY "HAPPENINGS"
ARTIST'S CLUB
TO THE CEDAR BAR
BRATA GALLERY
TANAGER GALLERY
MARCH GALLERY
TENTH STREET

AT THE
GALLER

LIES

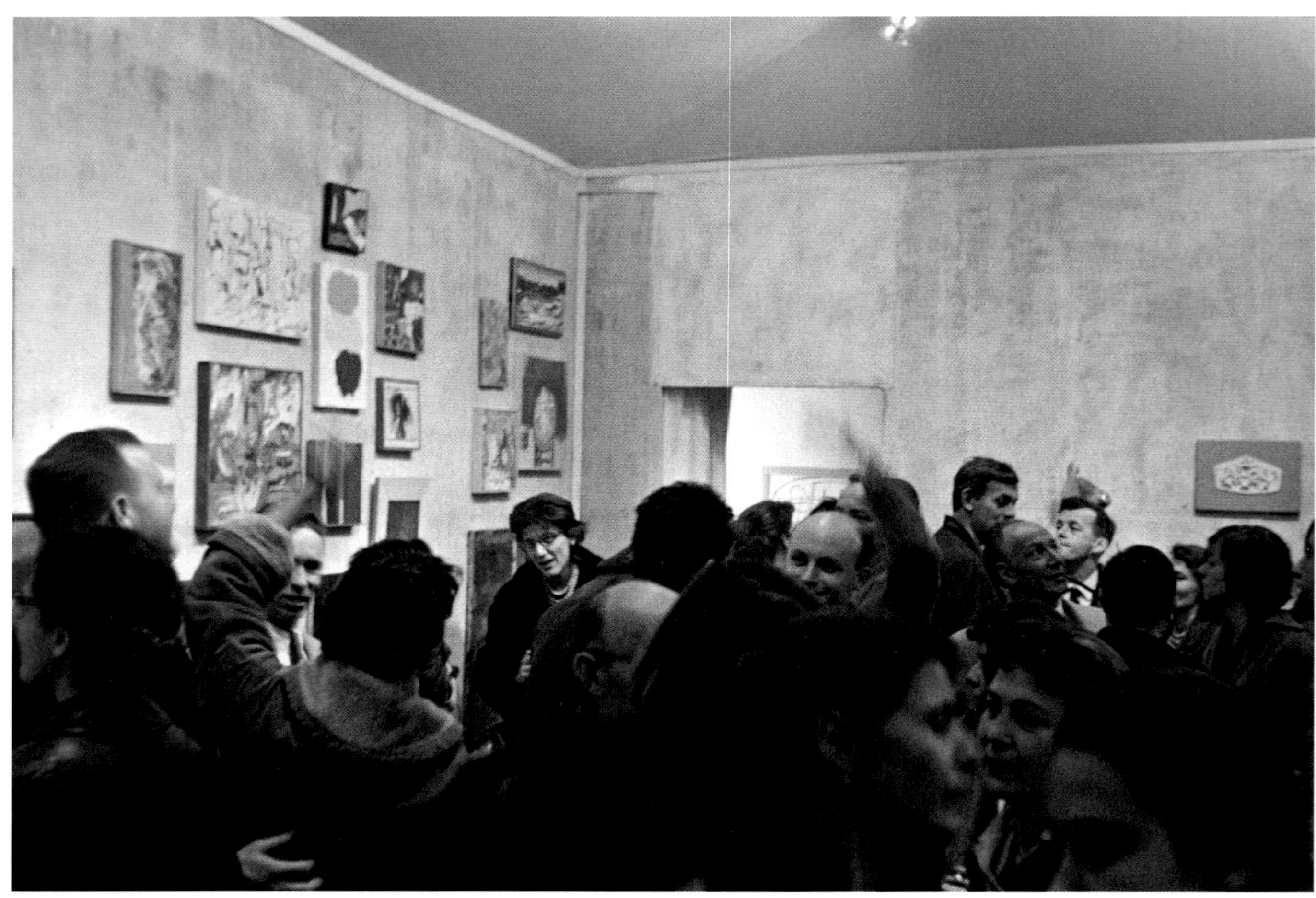

Opening at the Tanager Gallery

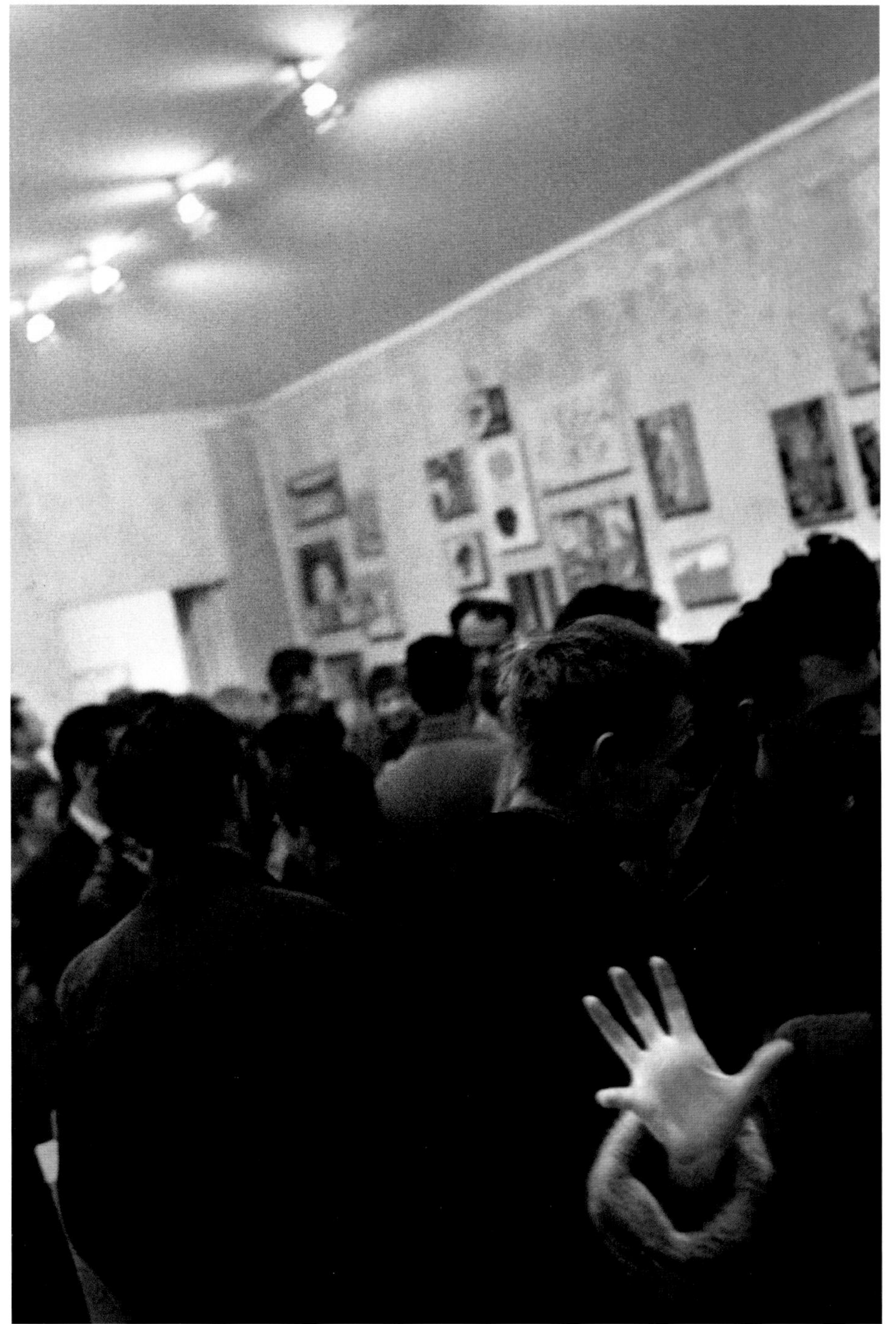

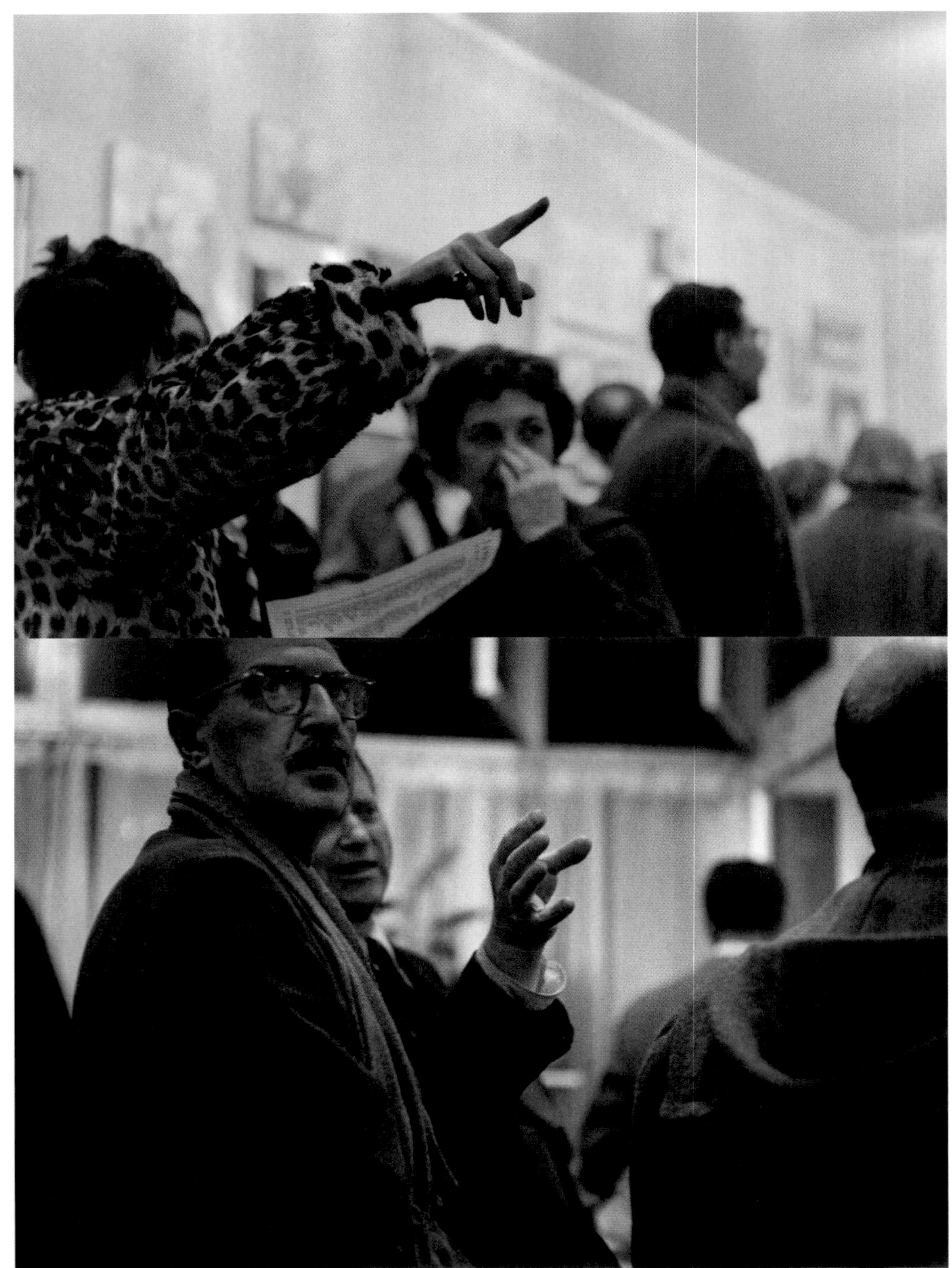

Al Kotin, Landis Lewitin

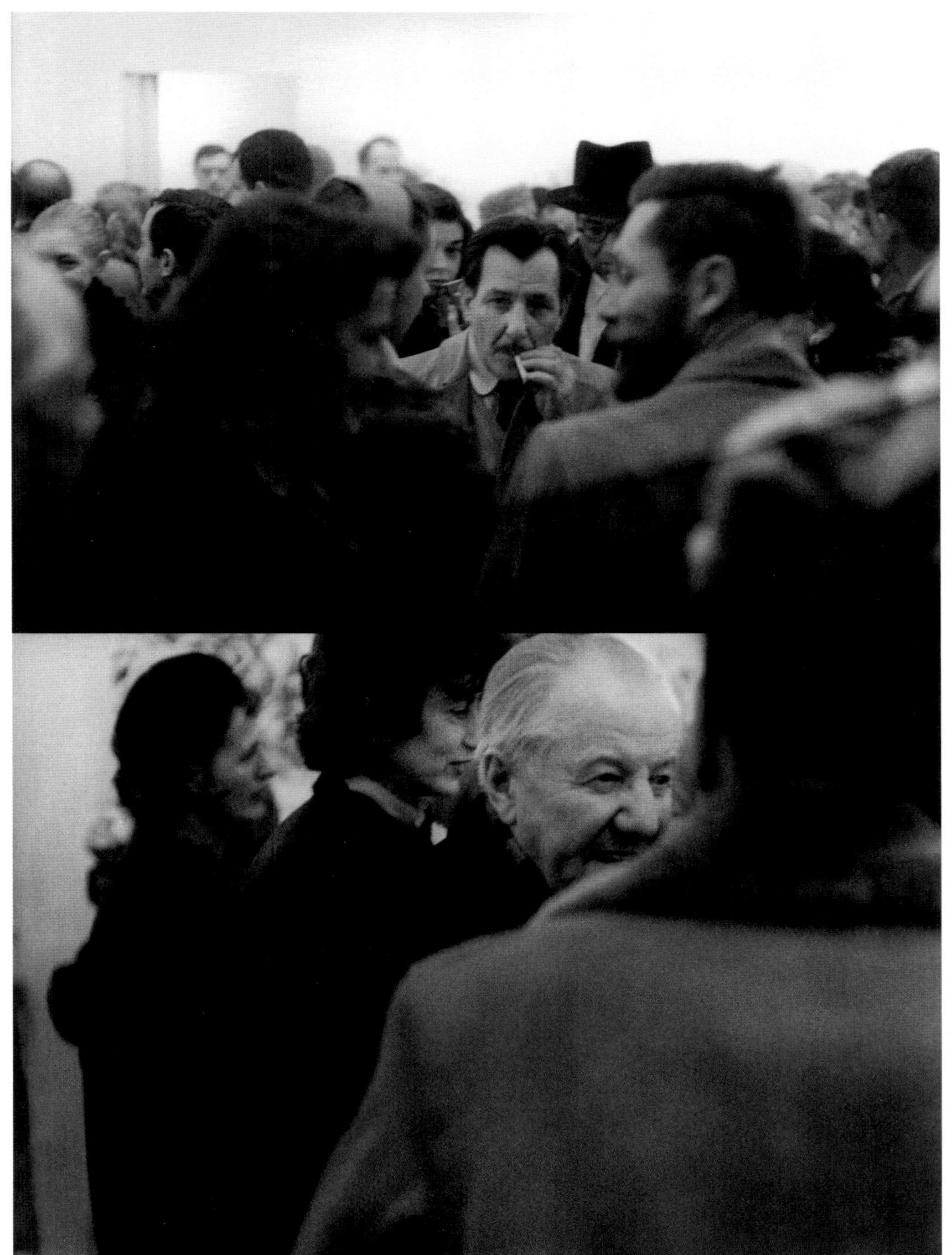

Franz Kline
Mercedes Matter, Hans Hofmann

Leo Castelli

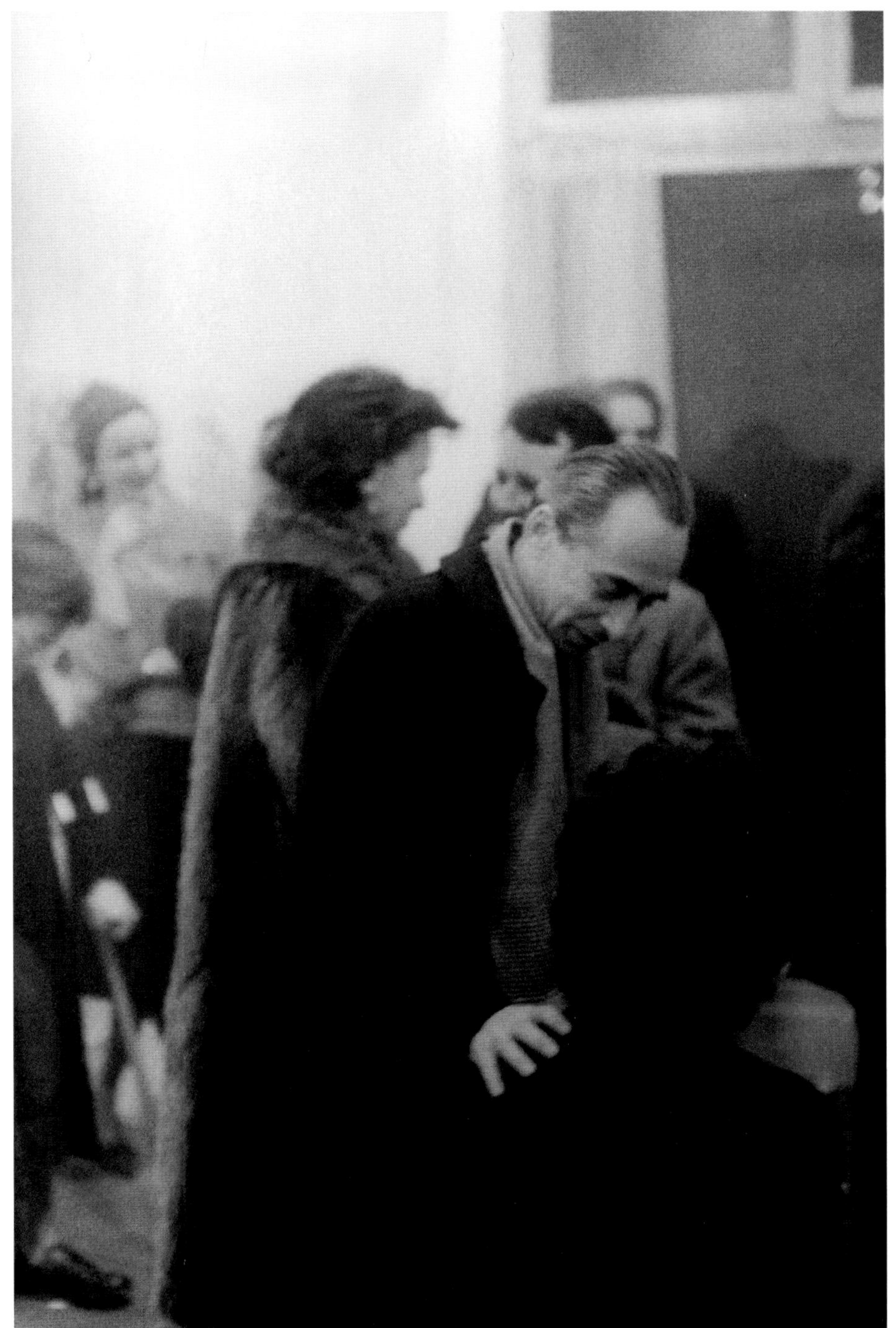

Jackie Ferrara, Bob Beauchamp, Milton Resnick

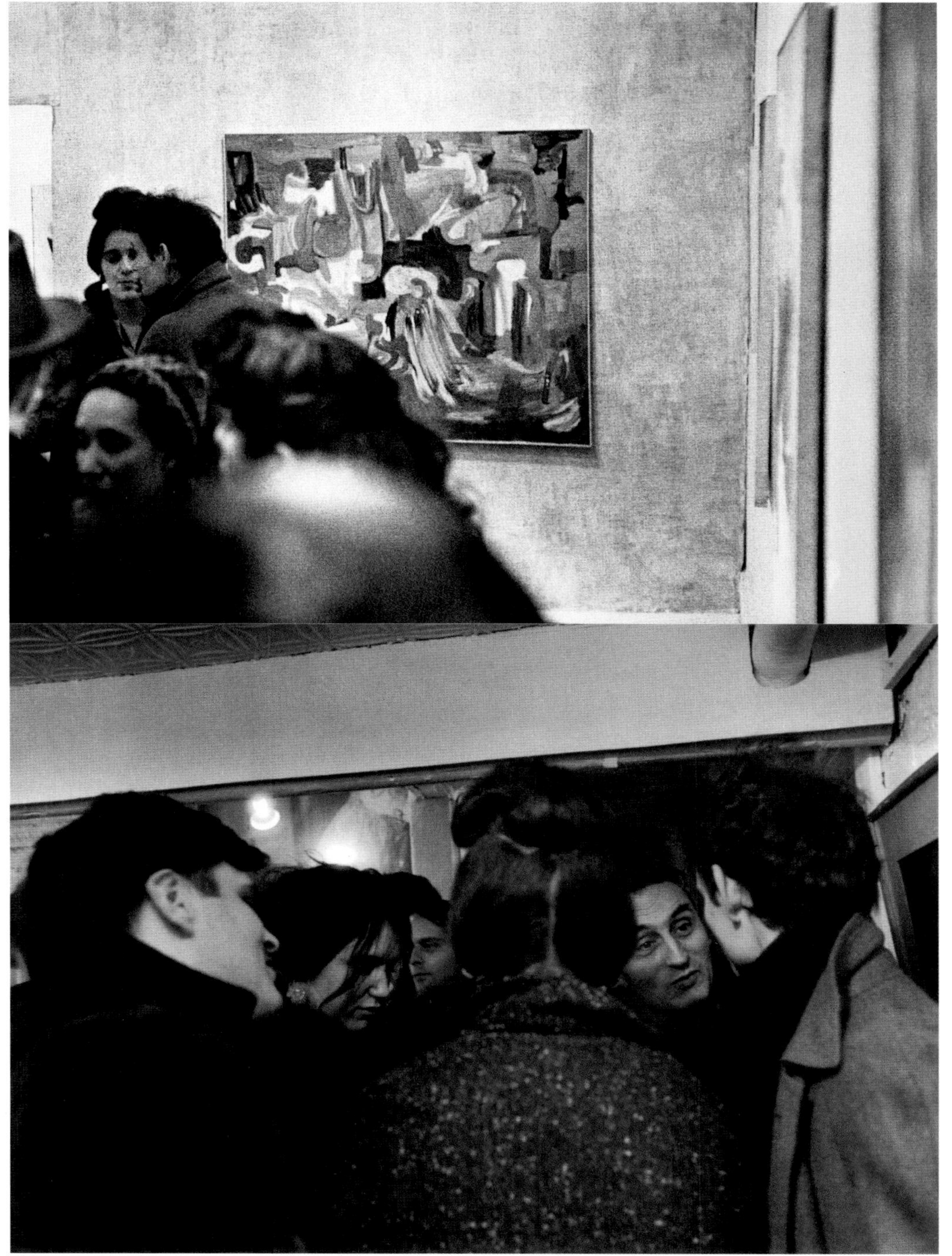

There were poetry readings in the galleries as well as jazz. Musician David Amram and Jack Kerouac performed and recited together at the Brata Gallery. Beat poets and folksingers were heard on MacDougal Street, while the painters gravitated to the Five Spot for jazz.

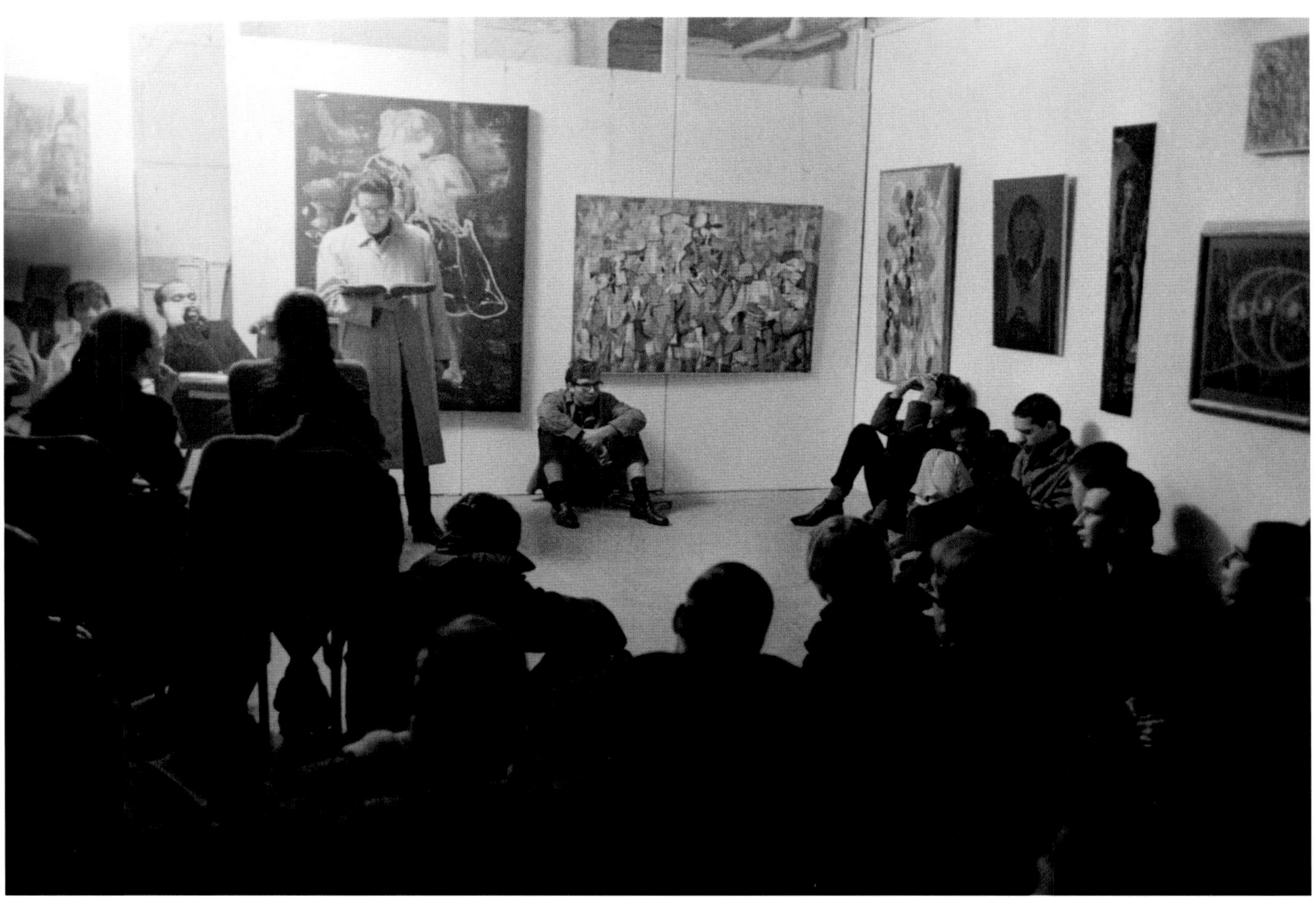

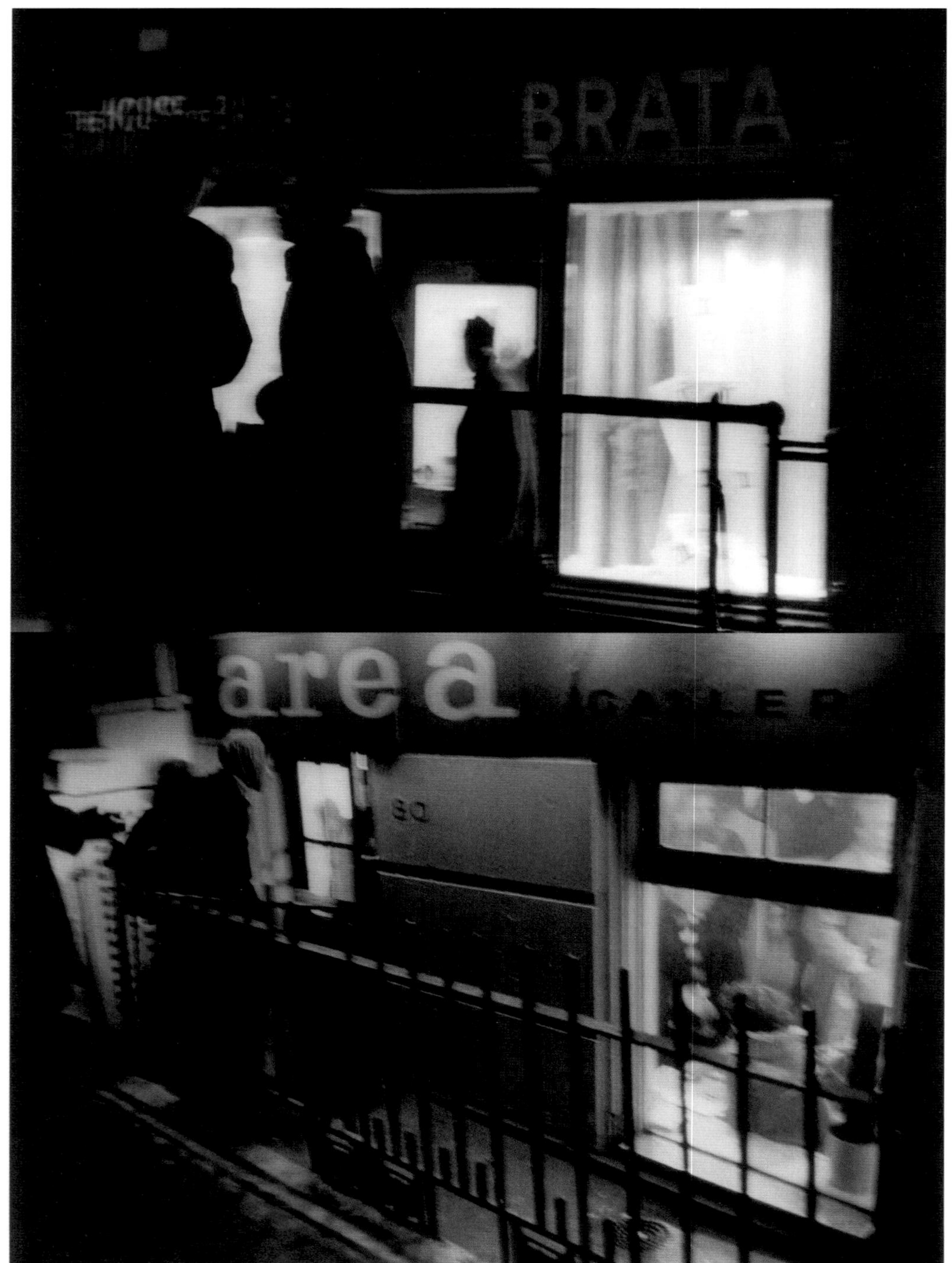

BRATA
area

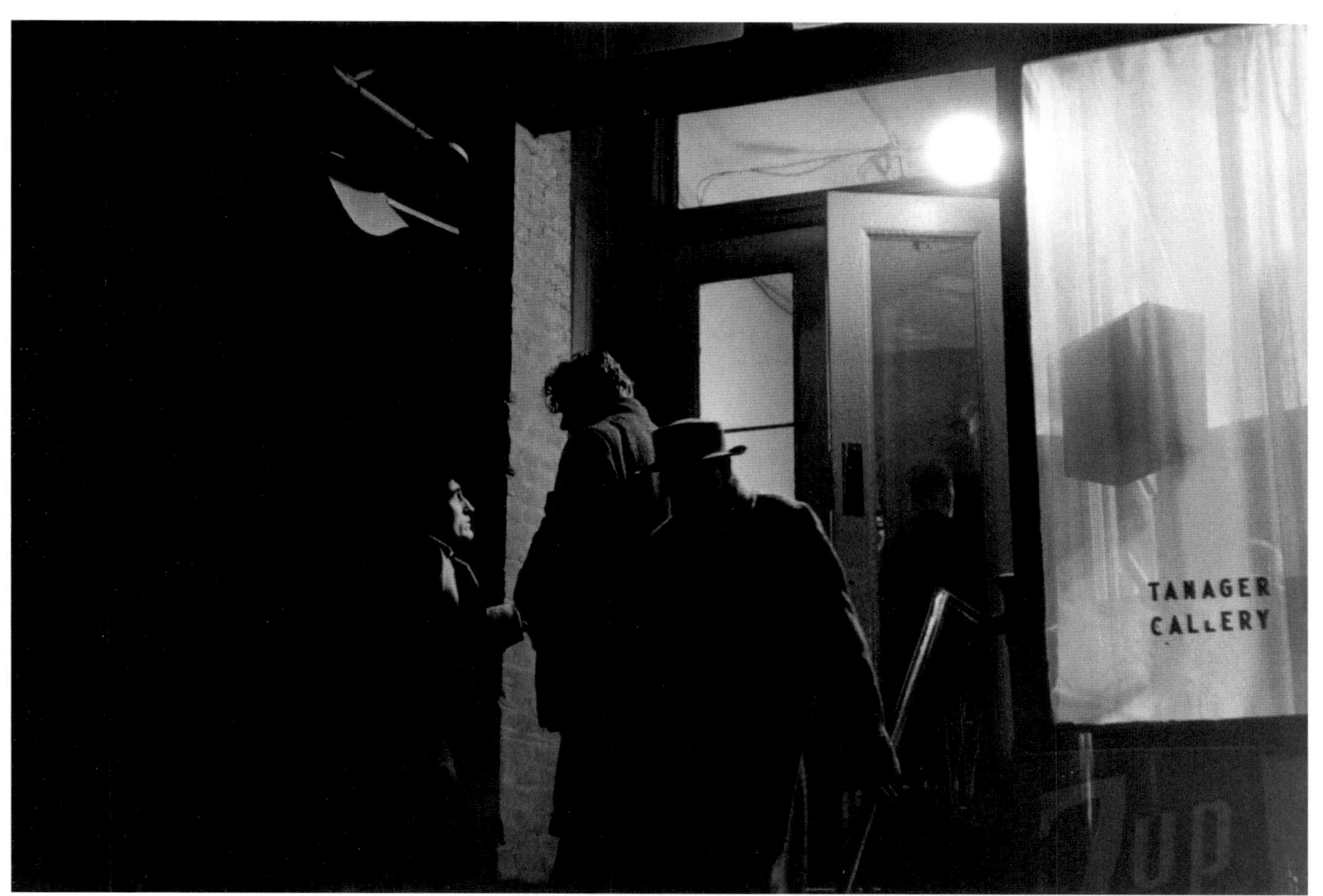

TANAGER
CALLERY
7up

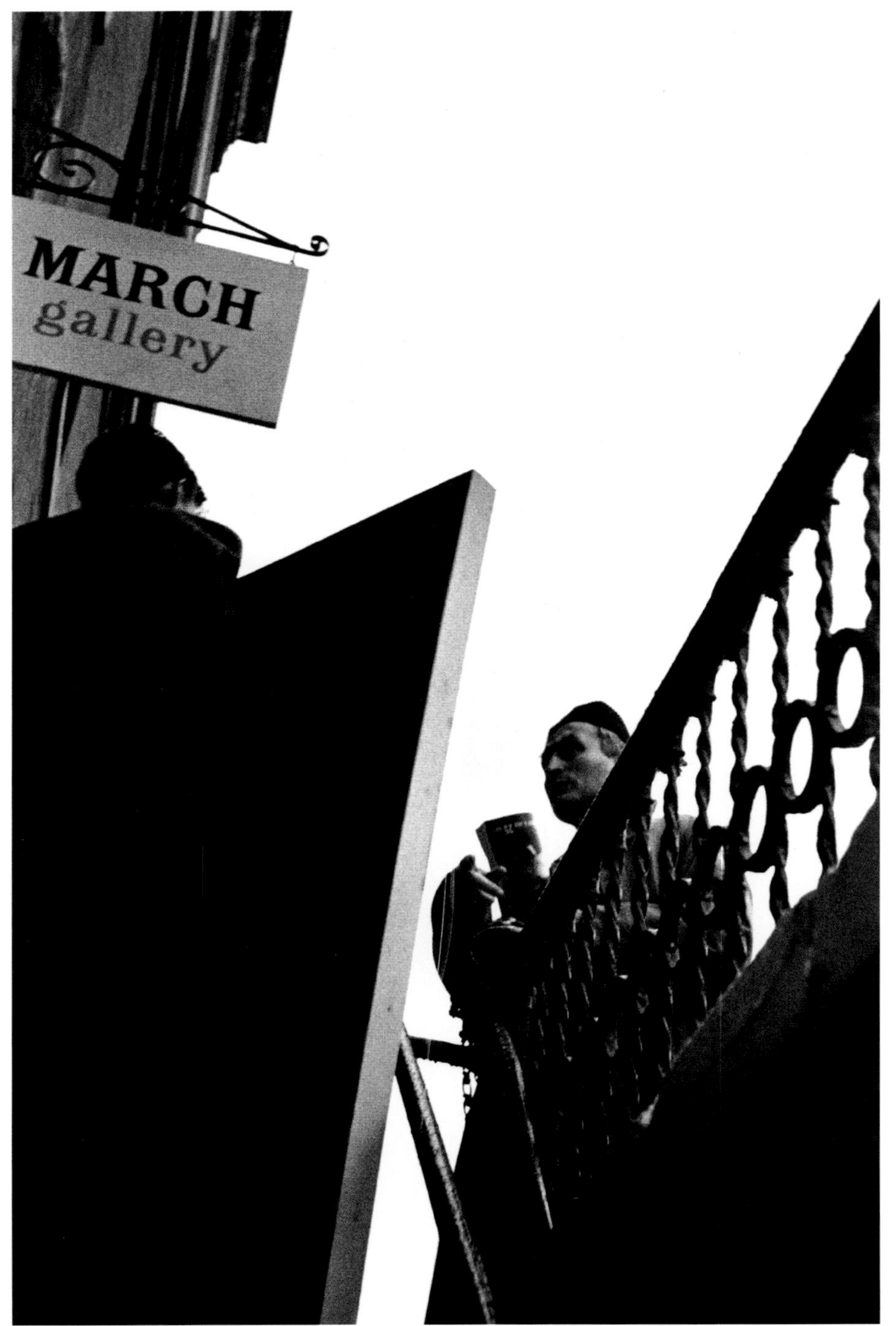
MARCH
gallery

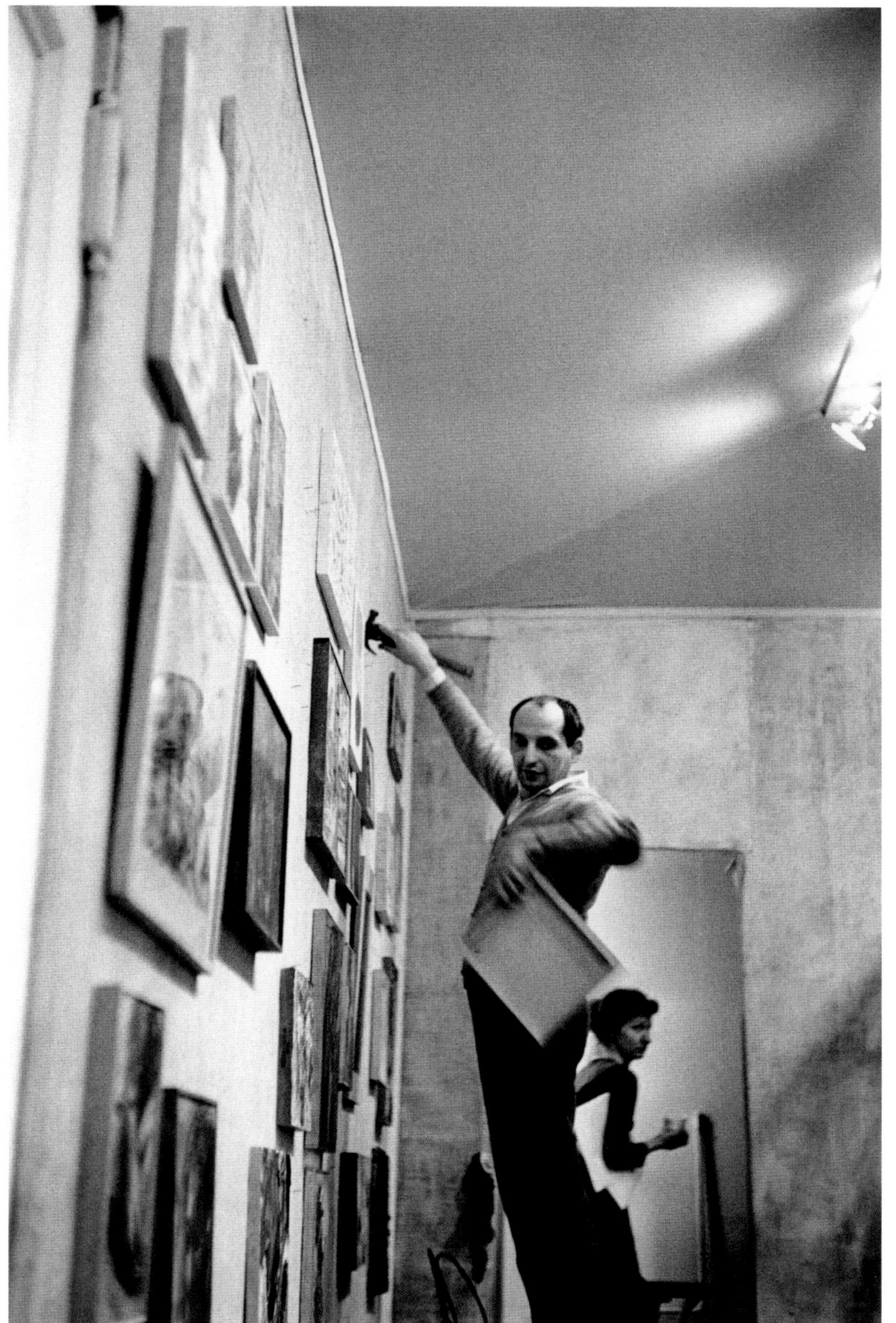

Angelo Ippolito, Lois Dodd

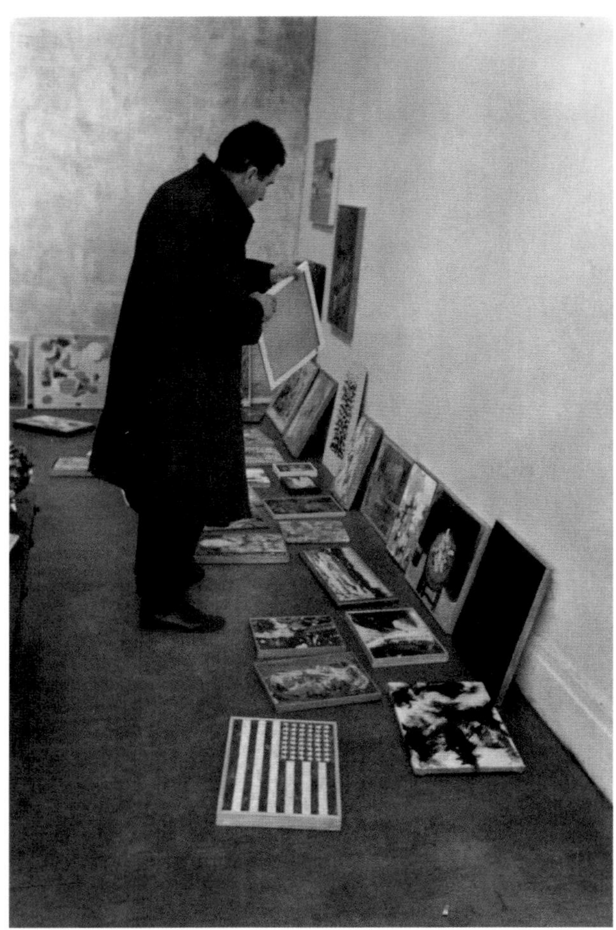

Michael Goldberg

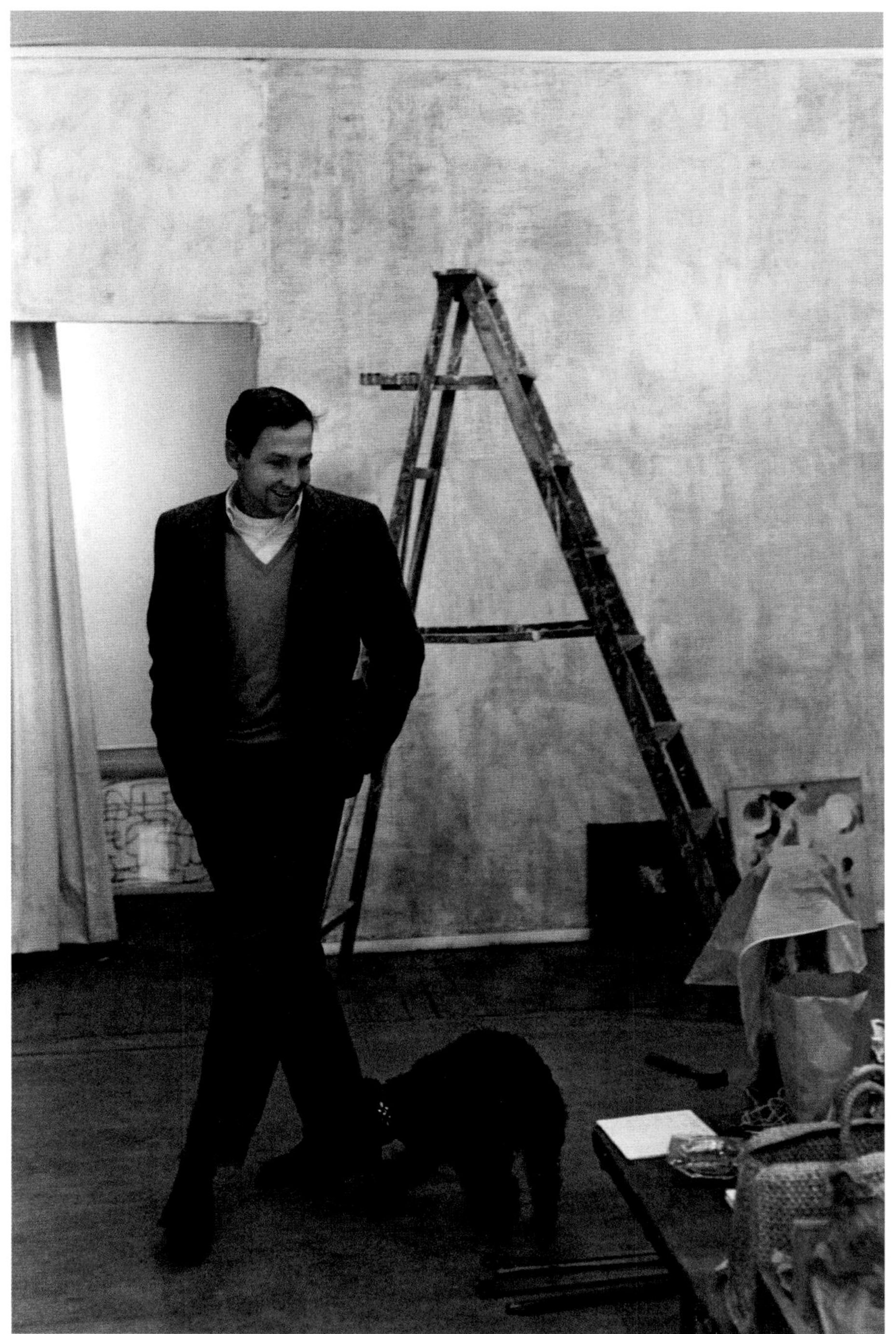

Robert Rauschenberg

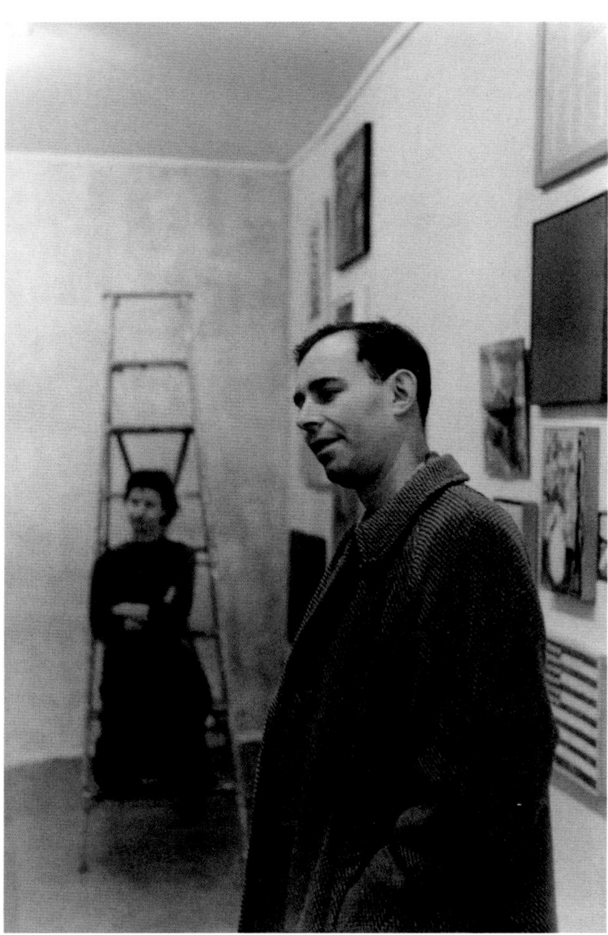

Irving Sandler

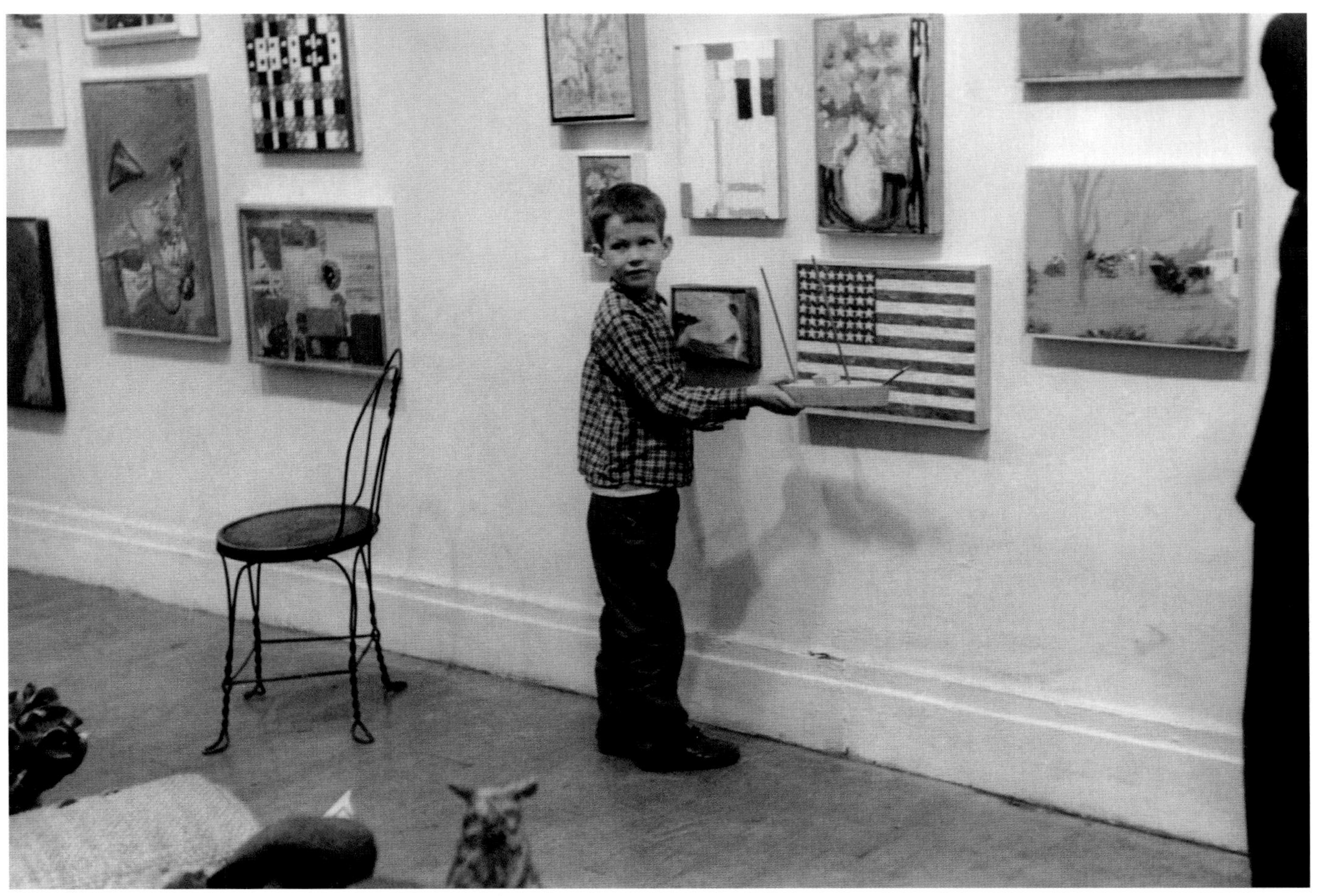

Eli King

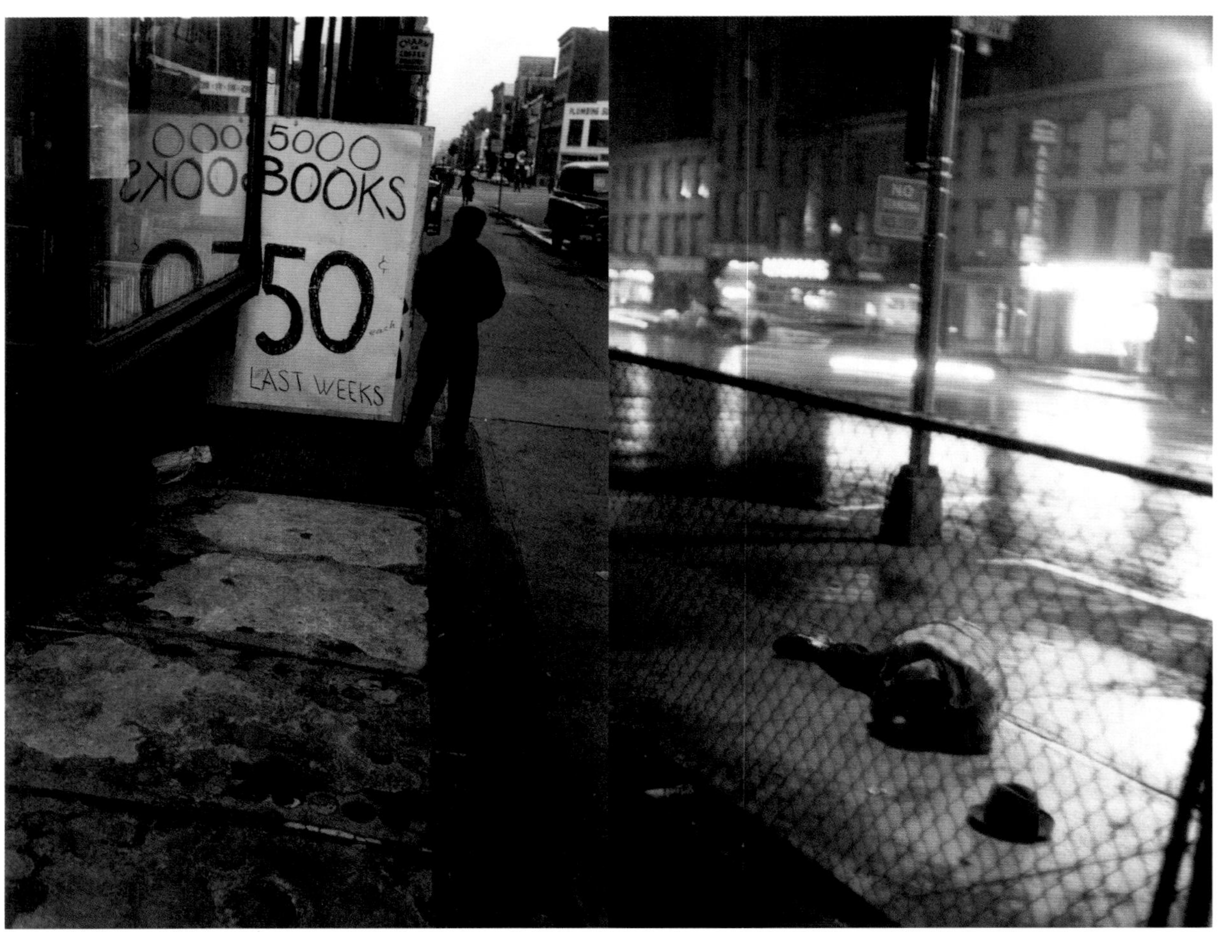

5OOO
5000
BOOKS
OOKS
50
each
LAST WEEKS
NO
STANDING

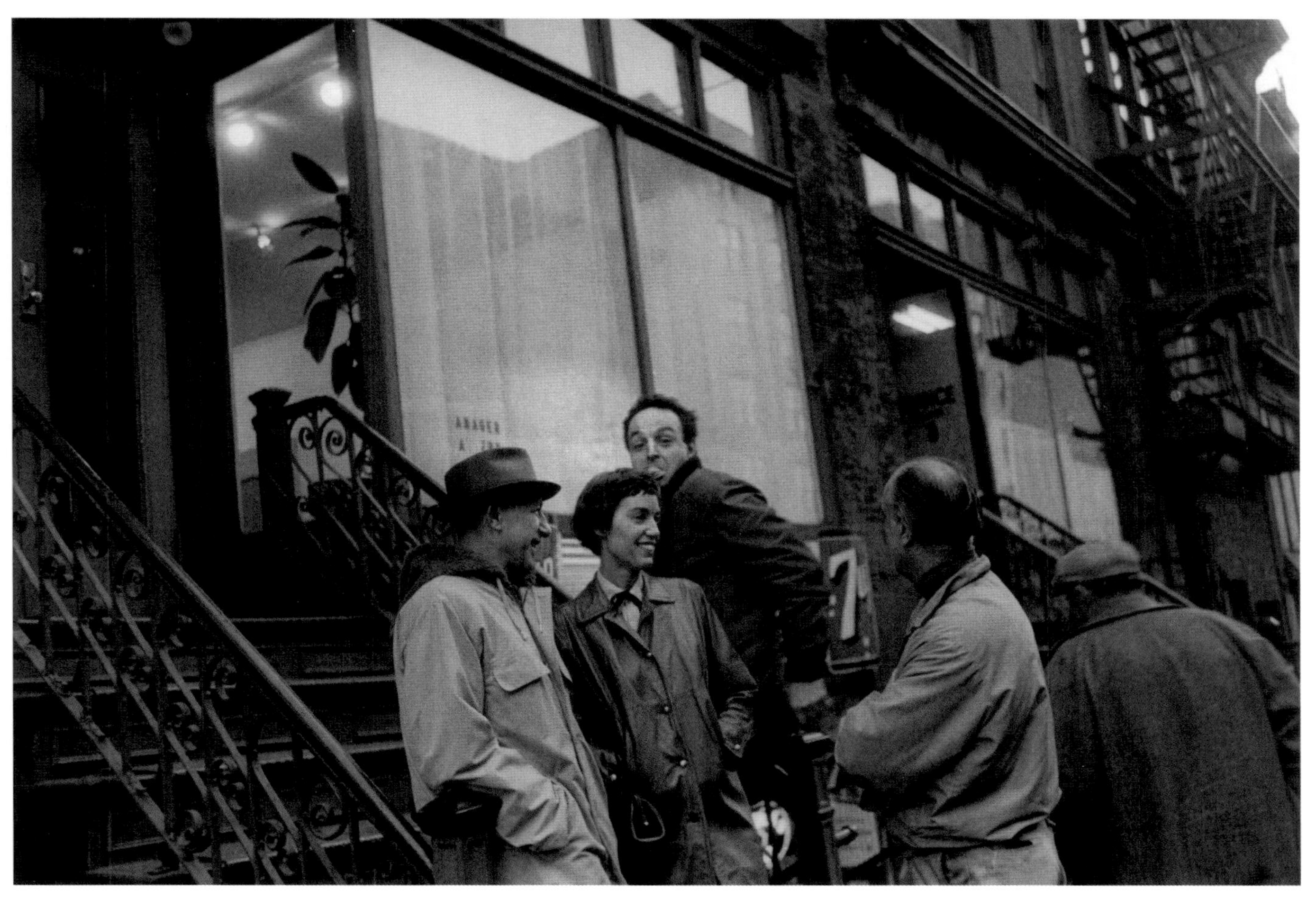

Jack Tworkov, Al Held, Esteban Vicente

WHERE P
TALKED A

INTERS

BOUT ART

The Artists' Club was on Fourth Avenue around the corner from the galleries
... a non-academic gathering where forward-looking artists could discuss
their own issues. The founding members included de Kooning, Joop Sanders
and Phillip Pavia, and many of the original members of the club were still
there in 1960.

In 1951 my friend, the painter Emily Mason took me to the club, which
was then in a second floor loft on 8th Street. It was informal, dark and serious.
People hung around the coffee pot while ideas were in the air. Paul Brach gave
a talk about images of "Heaven and Hell in Art." Maybe that was what painters
thought about. It didn't resemble any art history class I knew.

The club's continued existence was reassuring. It connected 10th Street
to its past and me to its history. It was good to be there again in 1960. There
was Franz Kline, Philip Guston, Ad Reinhardt and James Brooks listening to
Tom Hess, editor of *Art News* who was part of a panel with Harry Holtzman.
Holtzman had brought Mondrian to America in 1940, and Hess had published
De Kooning paints Woman 1 in 1953. They all had been part of the club since
it started. They were discussing the present. It was still their place, attended
by younger 10th Street artists as well.

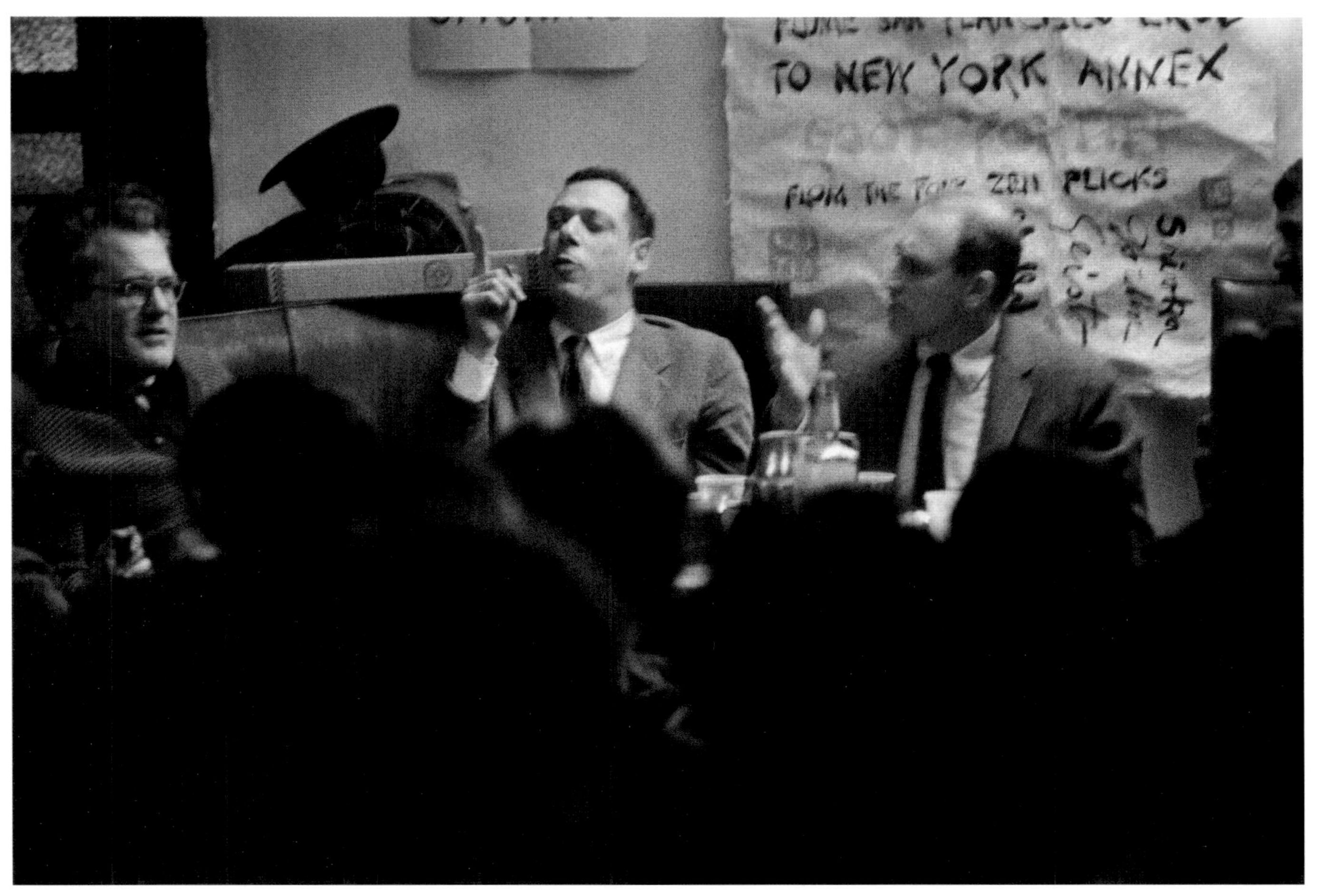

Herbert Crehan, Tom Hess, Harry Holtzman

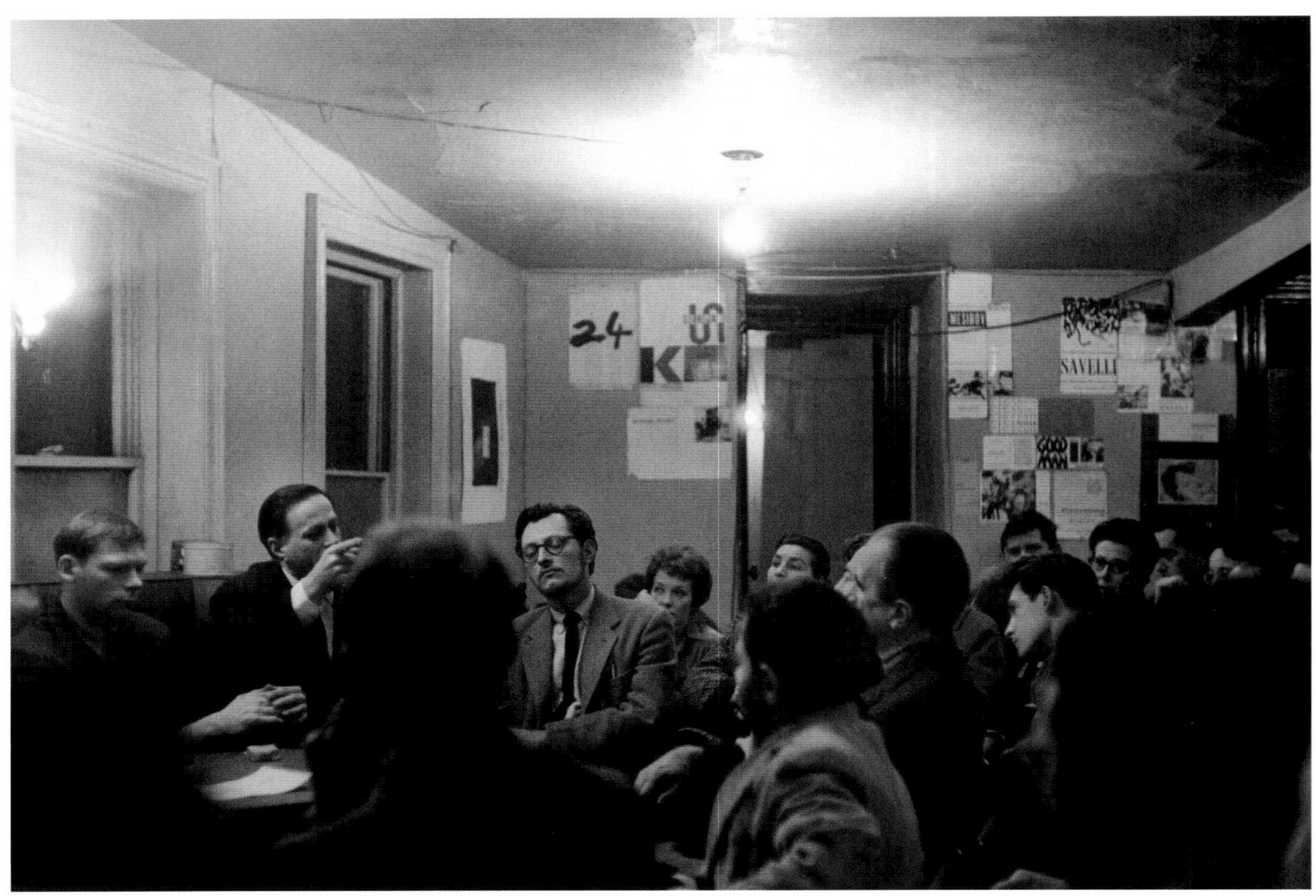

Nick Marsicano, John Krushenick

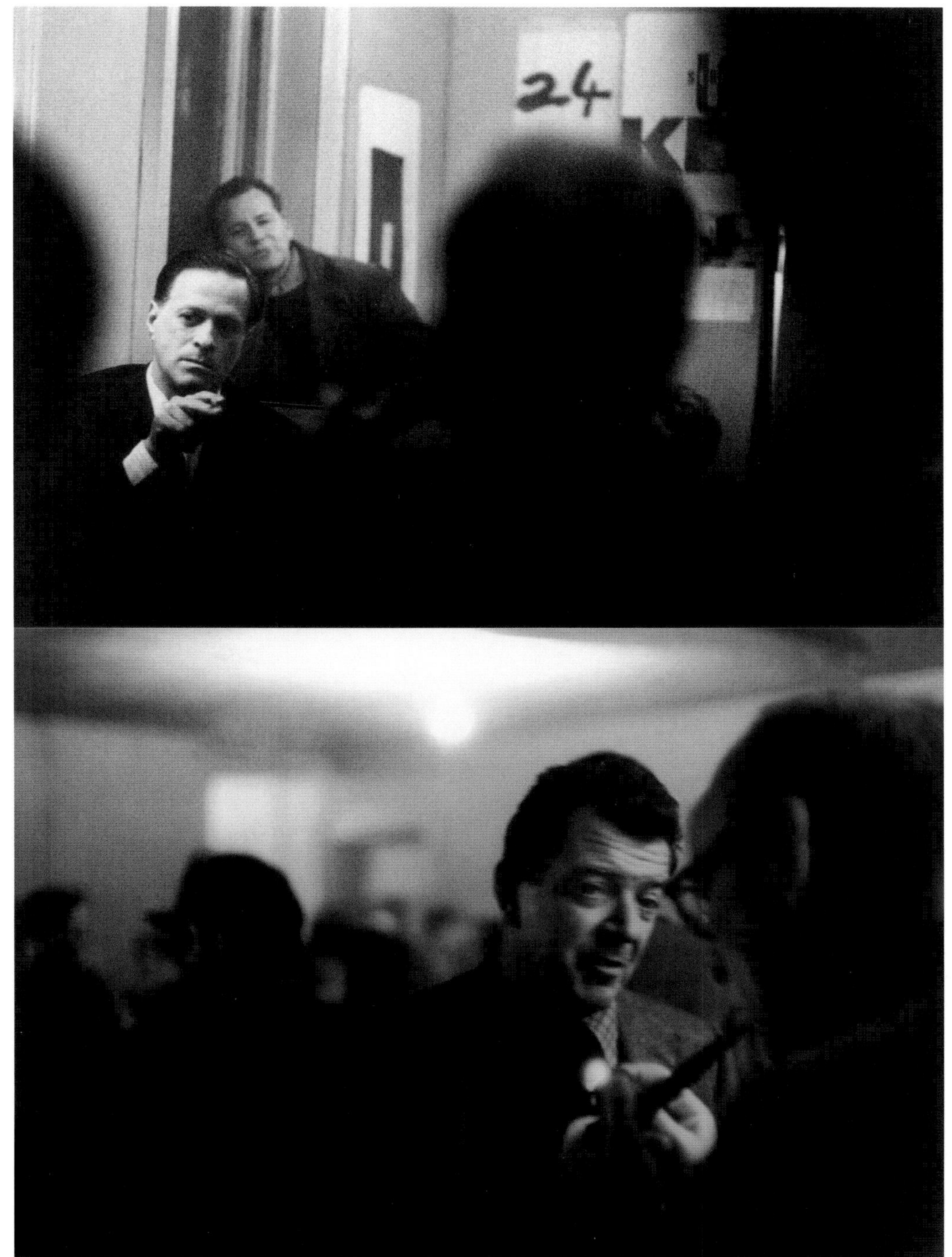

Nick Marsicano
James Brooks

THE CEO

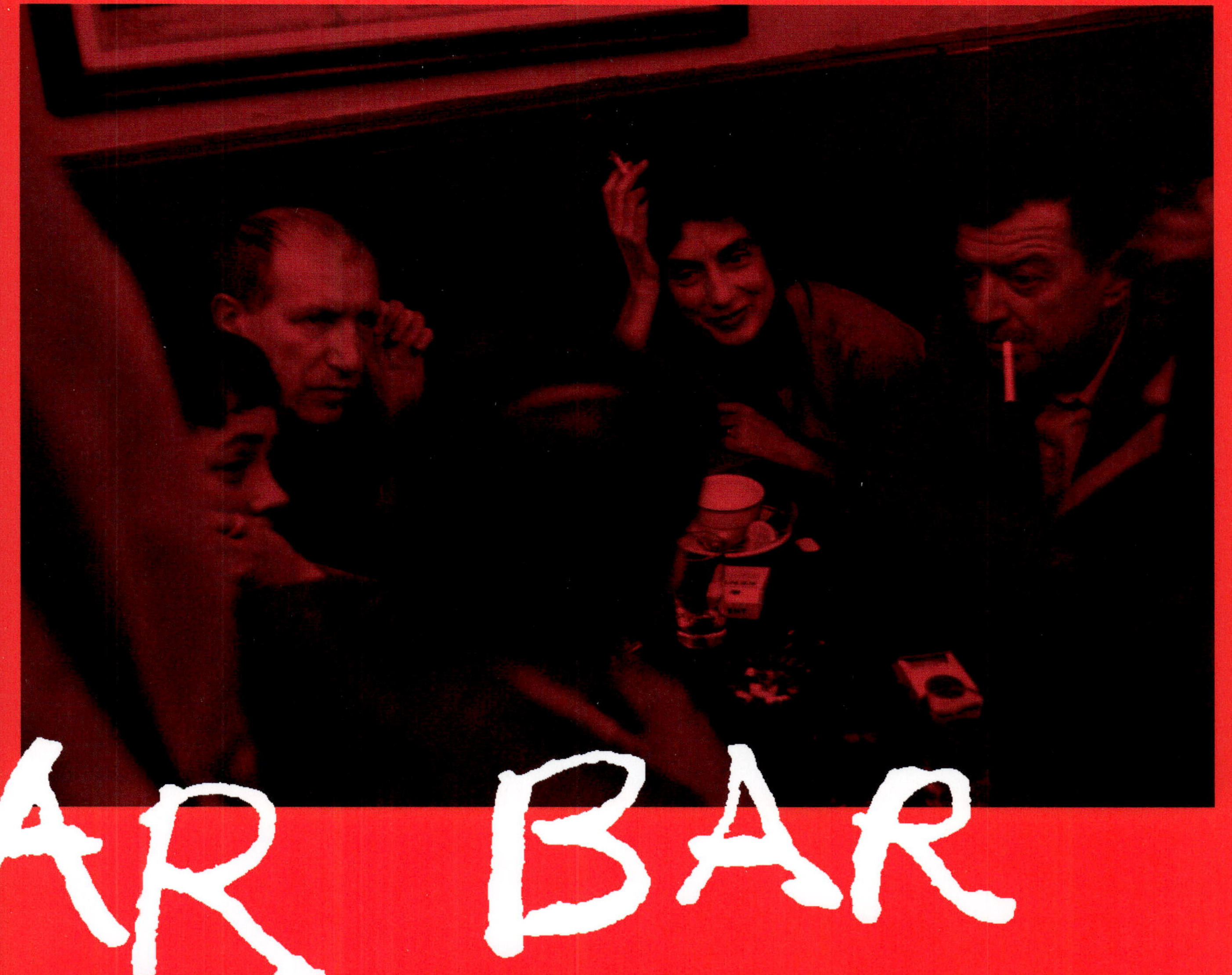
AR BAR

It was an ordinary tavern just a few blocks west on University Place: smoky, uninspiring, never exciting, never boring, filled with artists getting away from their studios, but staying inside the art world. There were no indications of avant-garde activity or abstract painting. Instead you got low lighting and English hunting scenes on the walls in a nondescript setting.

Although the total art community was small, the concentration of good painters in the Cedar Bar was intense. It was legendary within the art world, and it had its own atmosphere. I saw Philip Guston engaged with deep ideas at all hours; Aaron Siskind and Norman Bluhm doing the same nearby. Aristodimos Kaldis was loud and pushing his place in history. Around one table filled with serious talk were Charlotte Brooks, Jack Tworkov, Mercedes Matter, James Brooks; plus Giorgio Cavallon and avant-garde musician Mortimer Feldman listening to Guston. Larry Rivers was always charming; an English girl named Michaela hung out with younger artists. Lester Johnson was in one booth, Grace Hartigan's laughter lit up the darkness. Allan Kaprow talked "happenings" theory, Franz Kline was easygoing and friendly. New York School poets Frank O'Hara and Kenneth Koch were there while Beat poets including Allen Ginsberg added to the crowd.

This was the tavern where Jackson Pollack had thrown notorious fits (and was thrown out of the bar). William de Kooning hung out with the painters in the years when nobody could sell paintings.

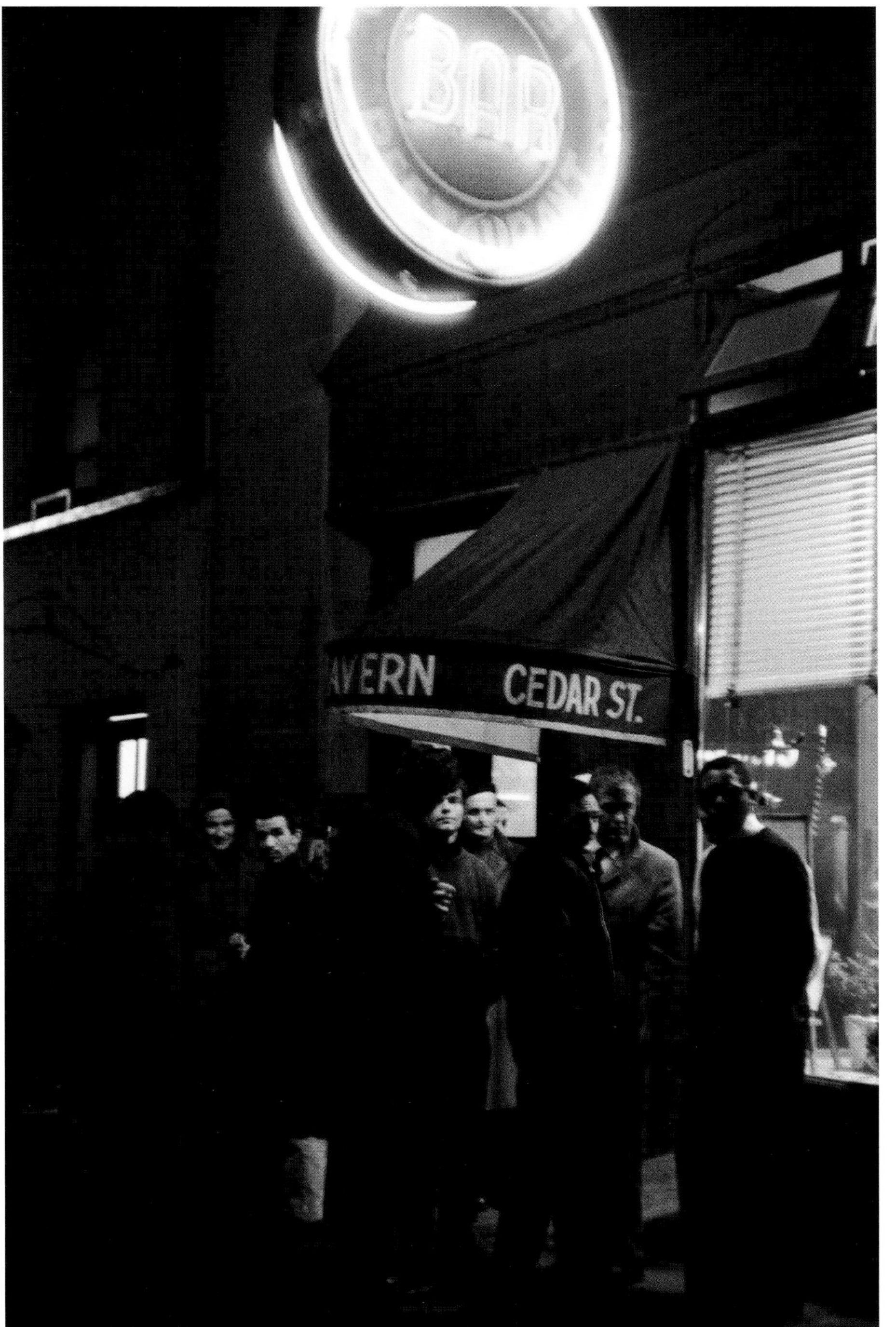

BAR
TAVERN
CEDAR ST.

Grace Hartigan

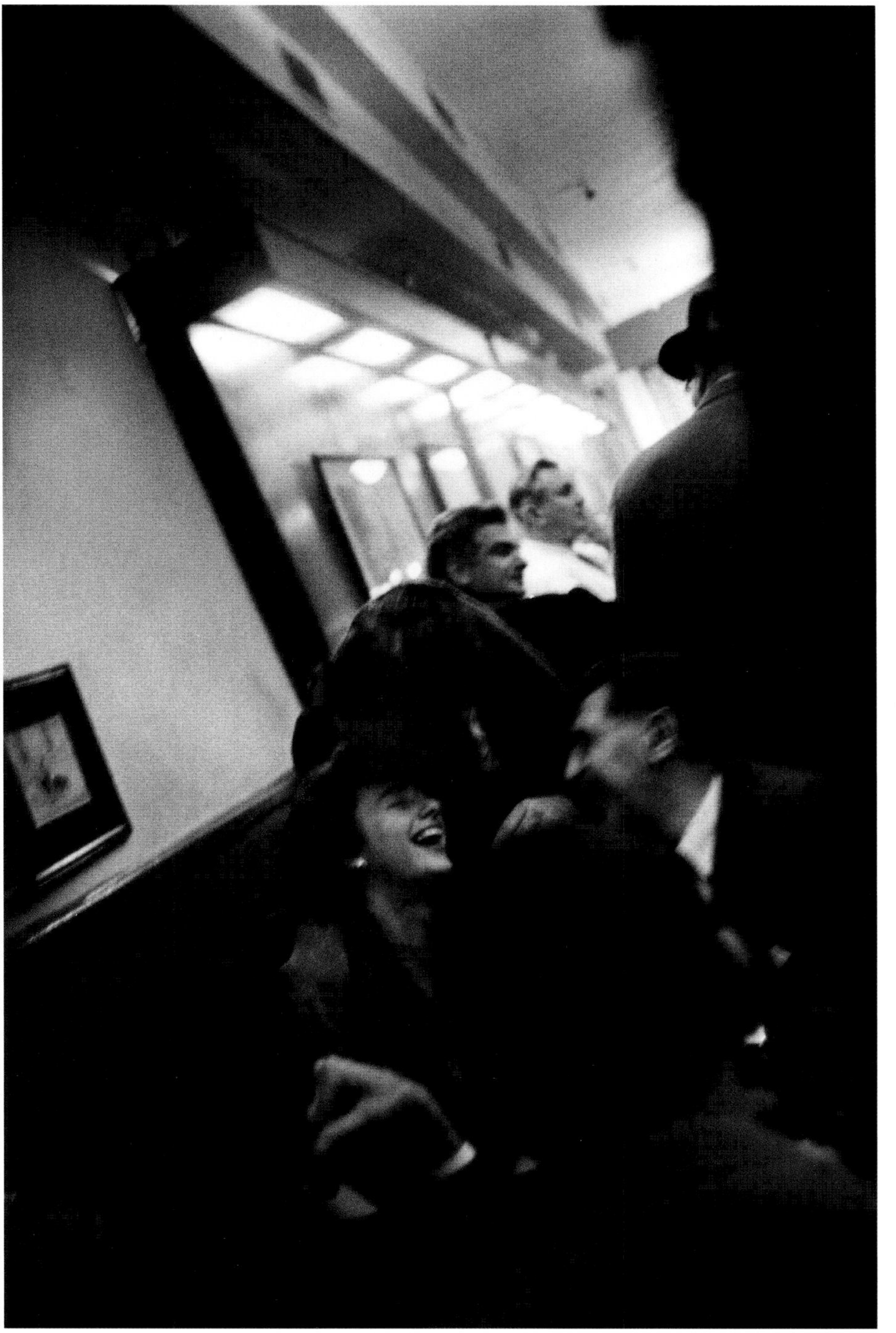

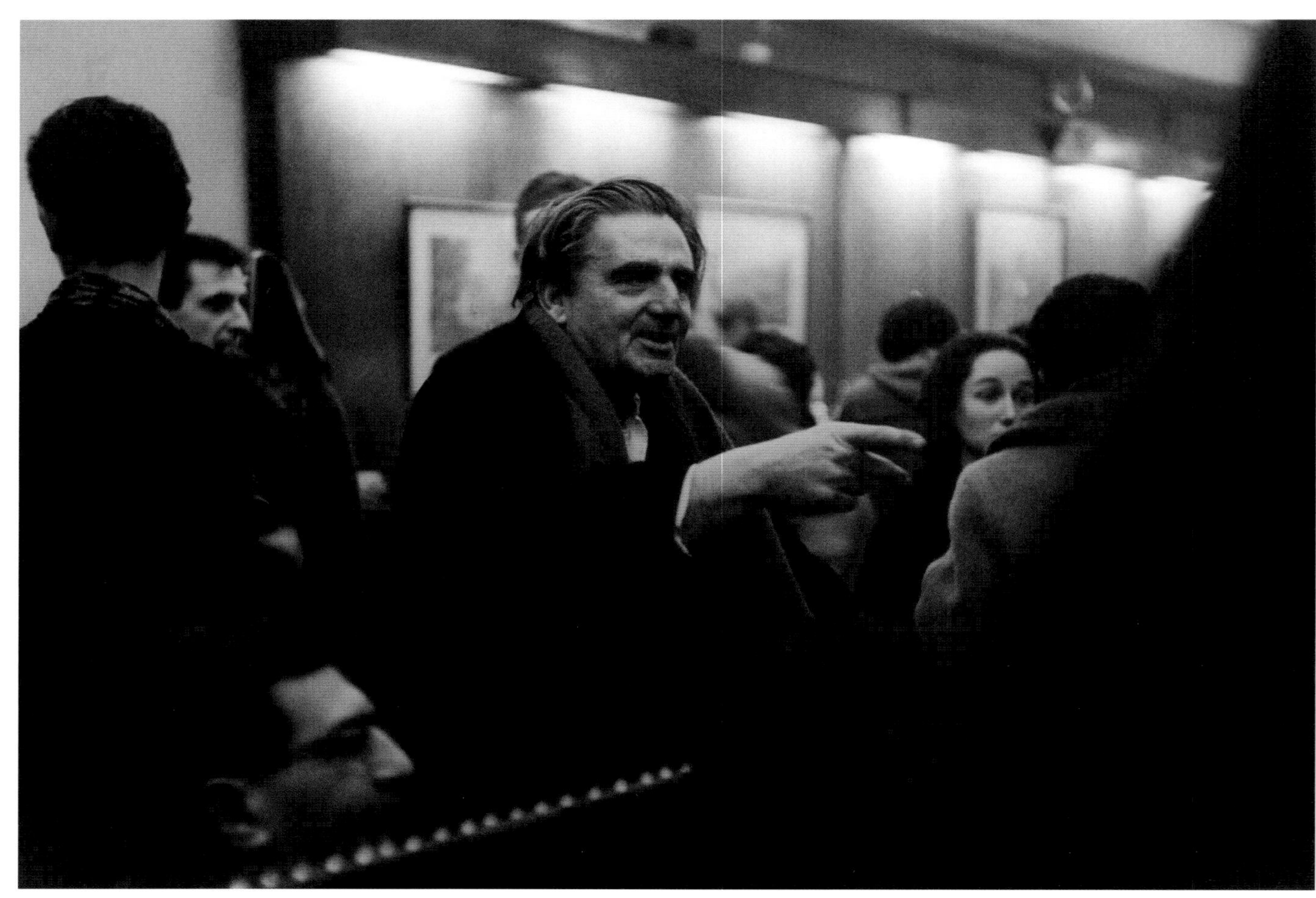

Aristodimos Kaldis

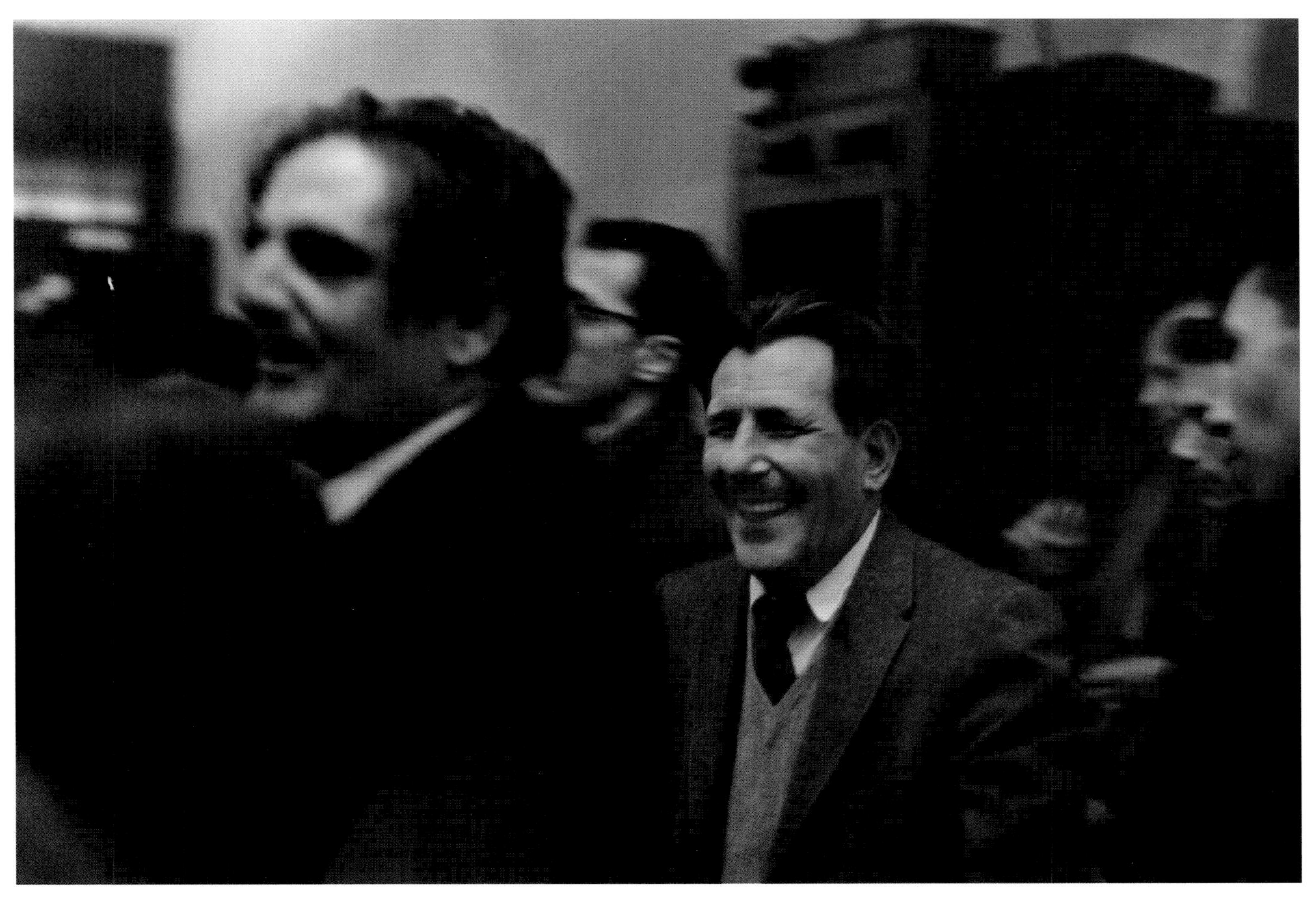

Franz Kline

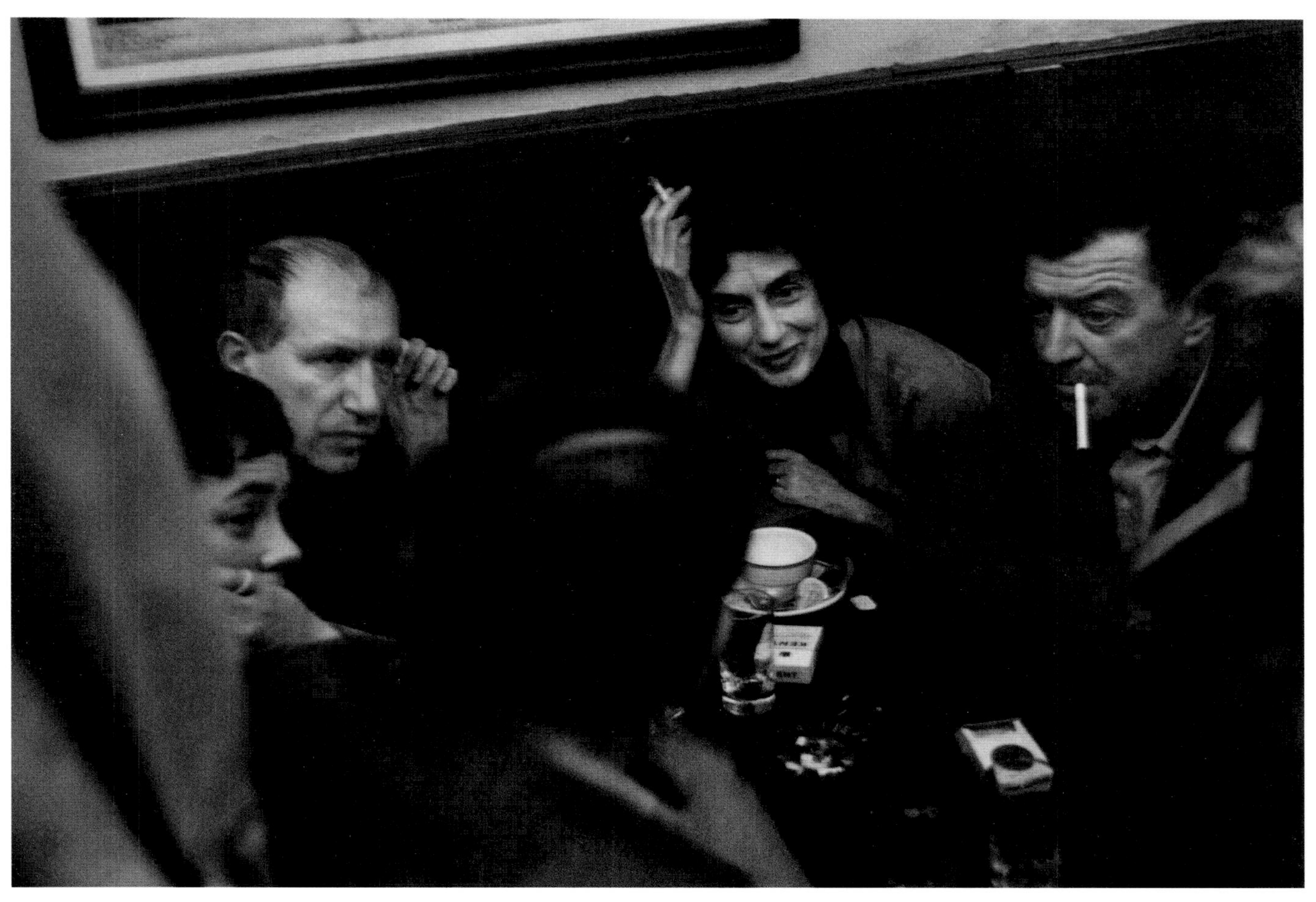

Philip Guston (from behind), Charlotte Brooks, Jack Tworkov, Mercedes Matter, James Brooks, Giorgio Cavallon (from behind)

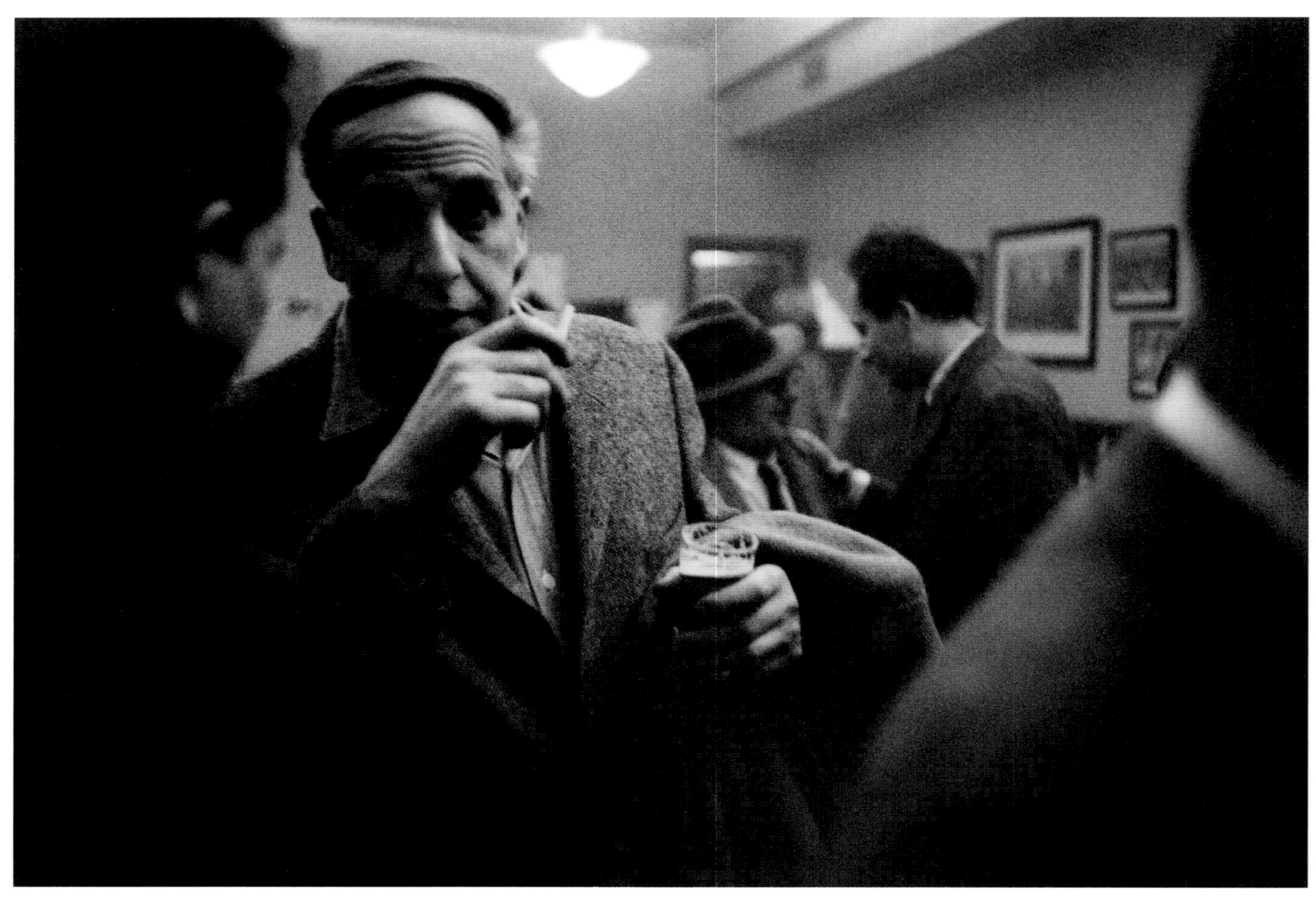

Philip Guston

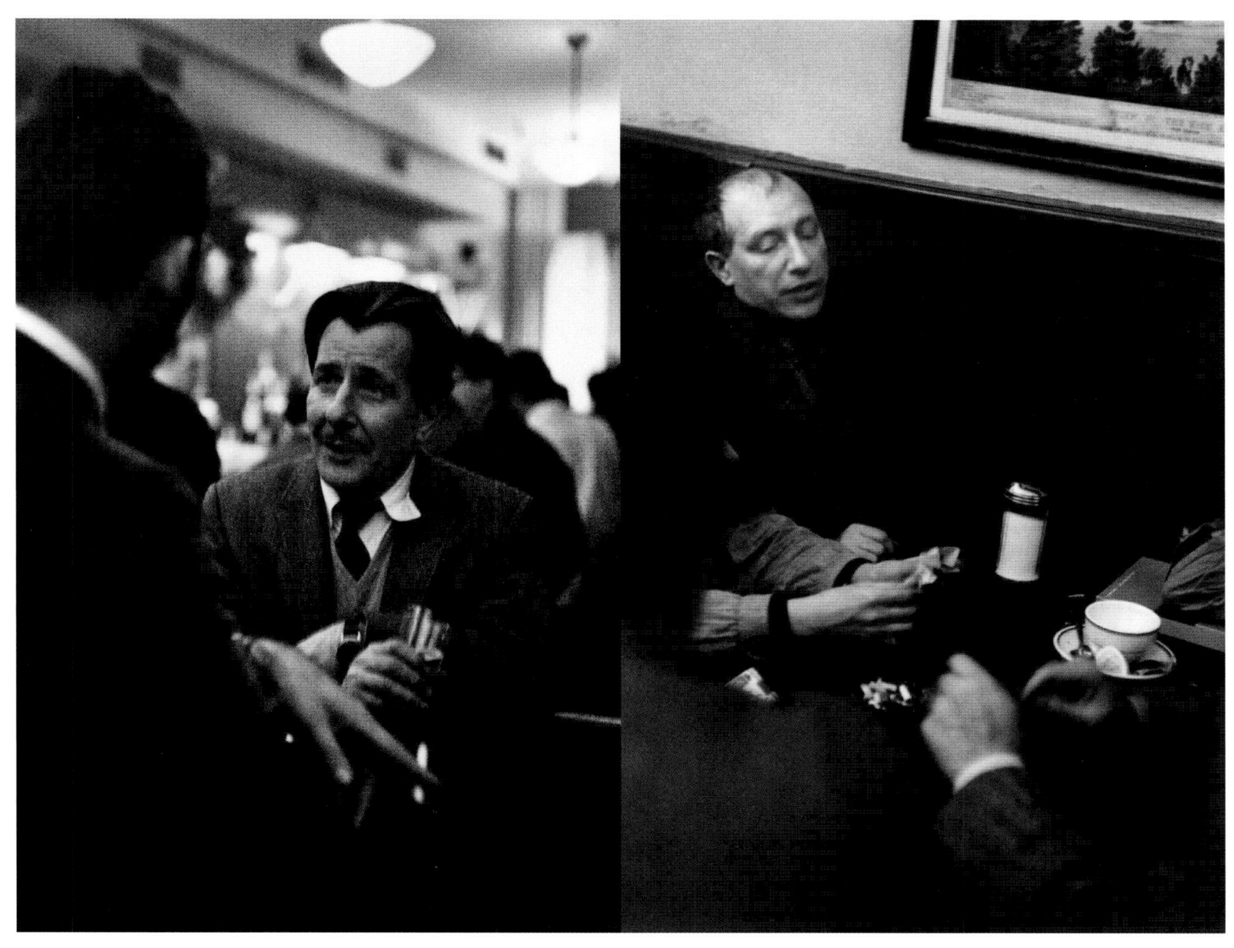

Franz Kline, Jack Tworkov

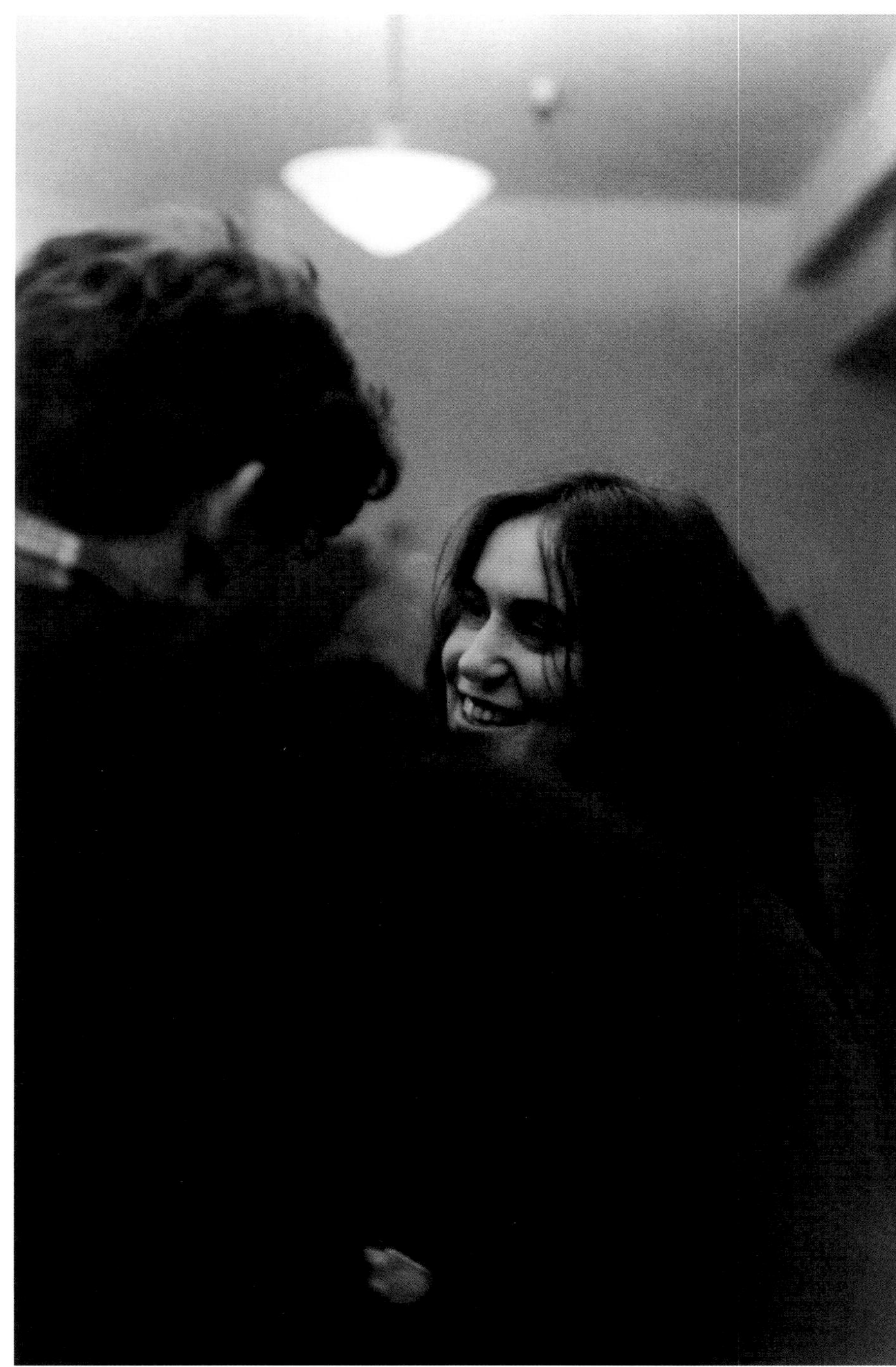

Michaela

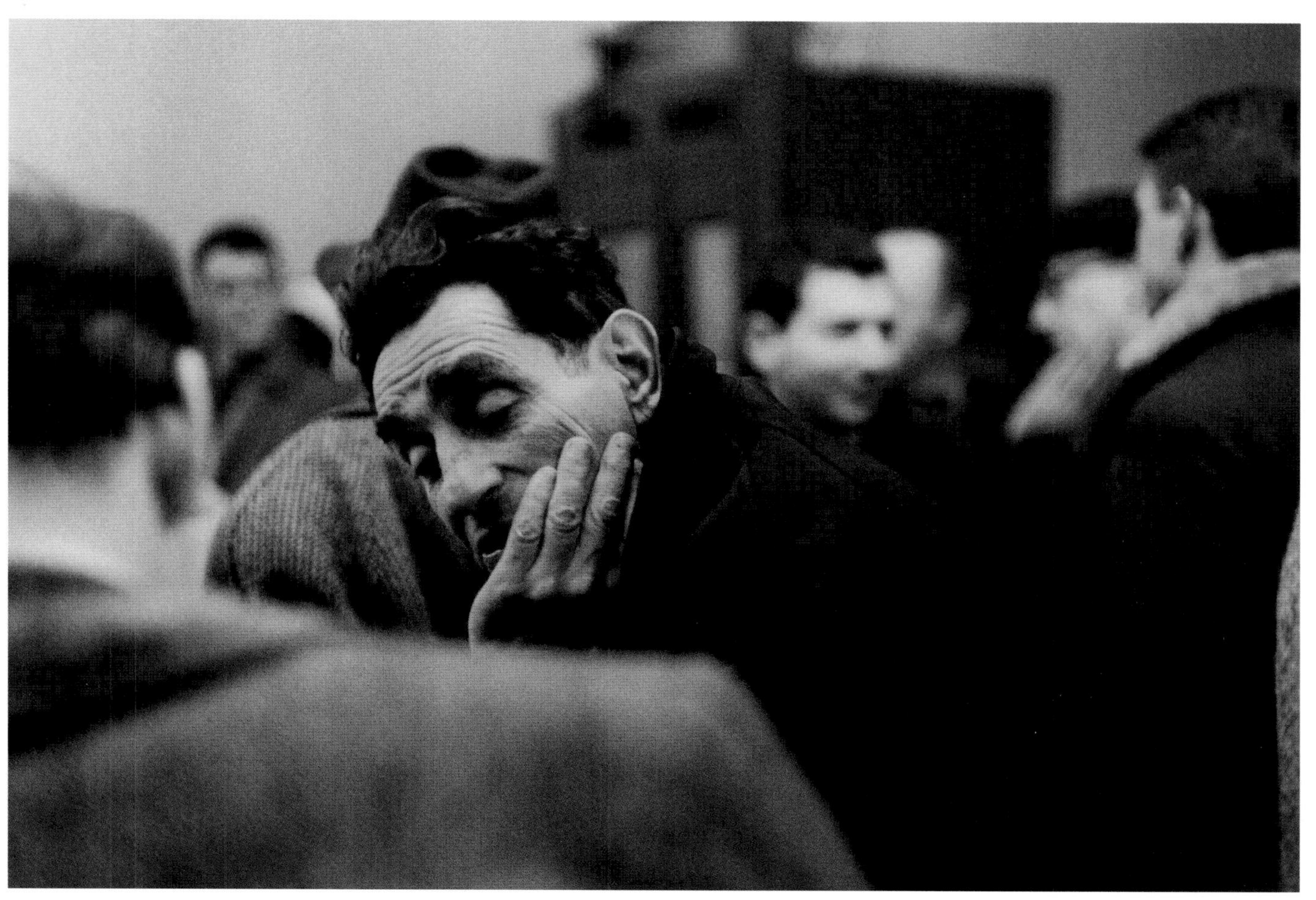

Lionel Abel

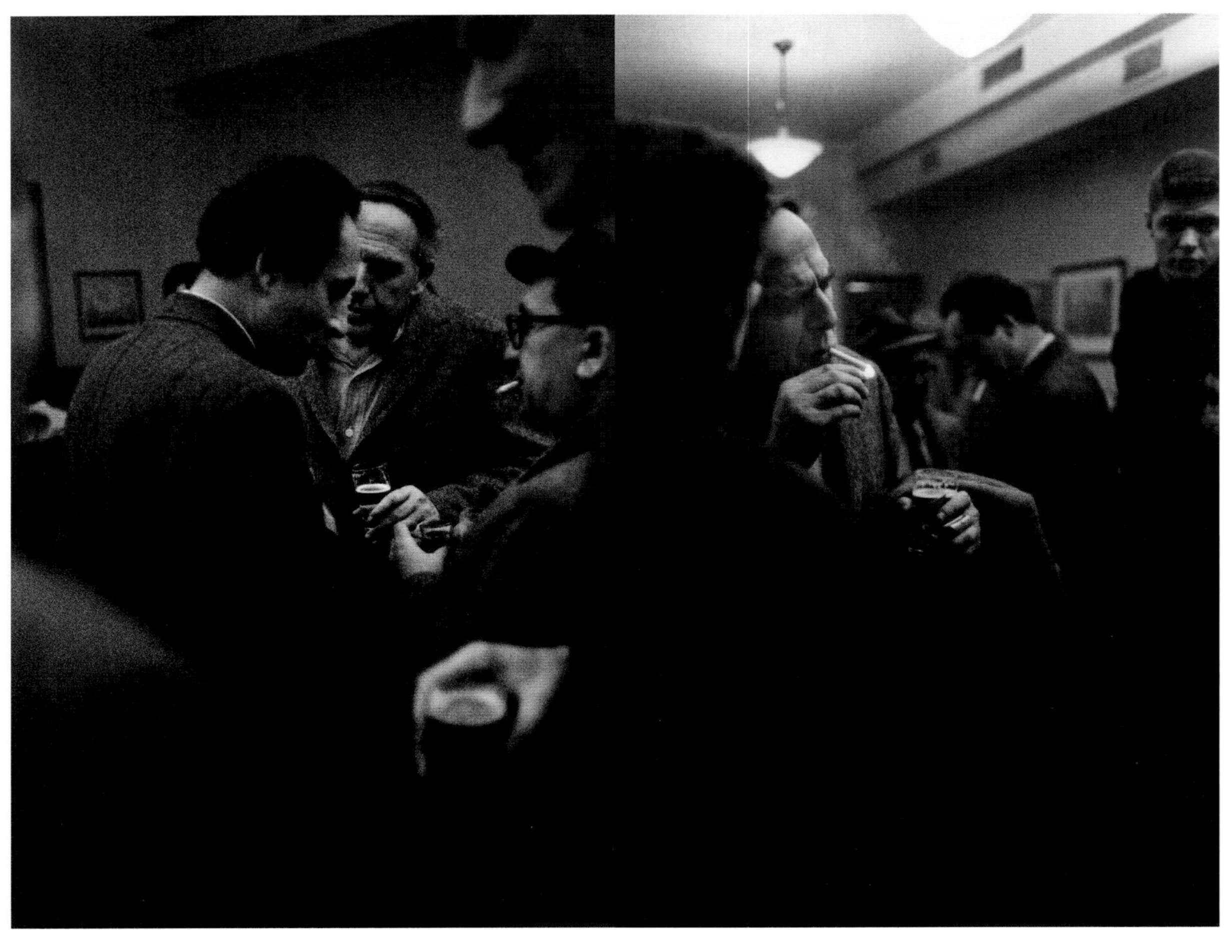

Norman Bluhm, Philip Guston, Aaron Siskind

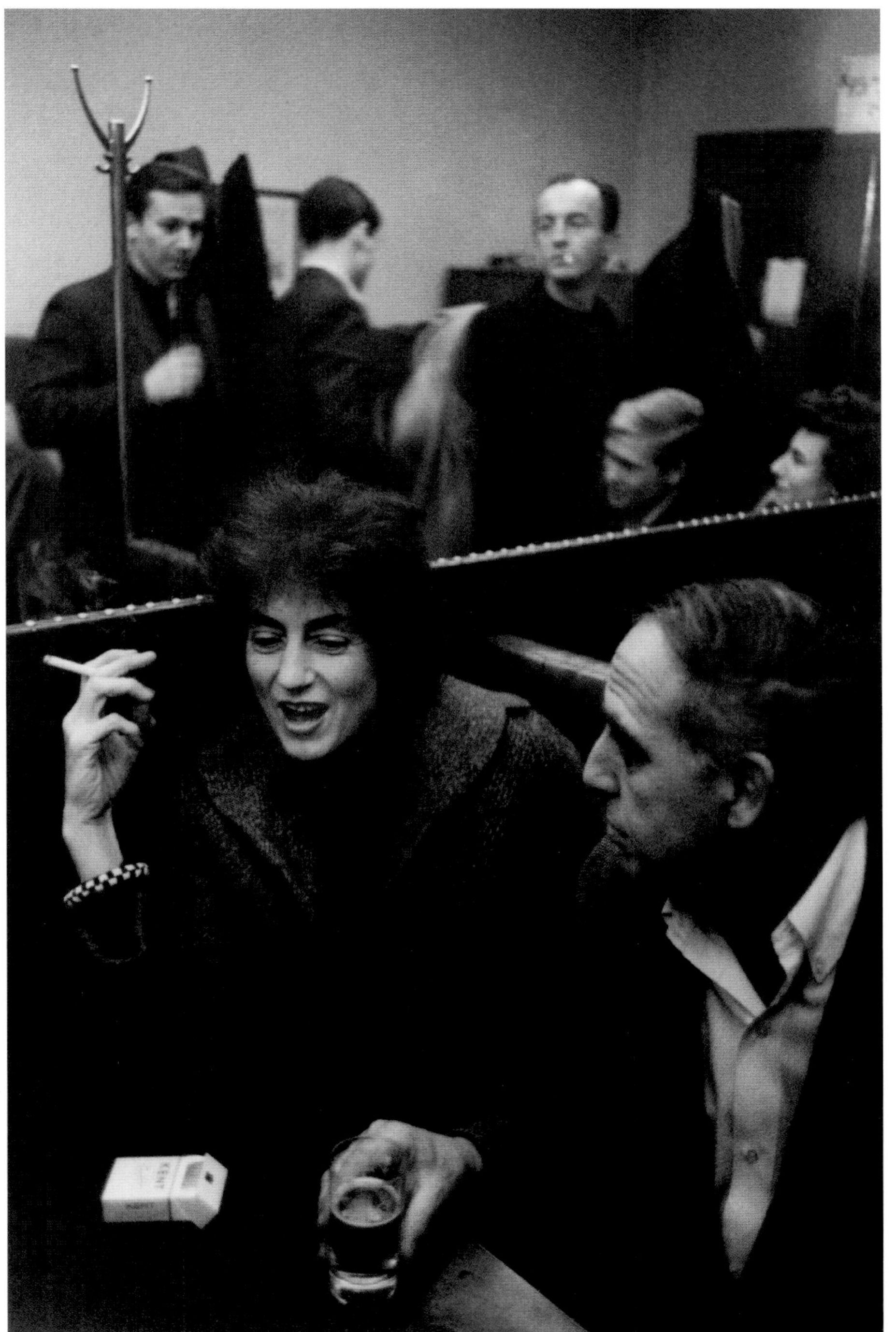

Mercedes Matter, Frank O'Hara (behind with cigarette), Philip Guston

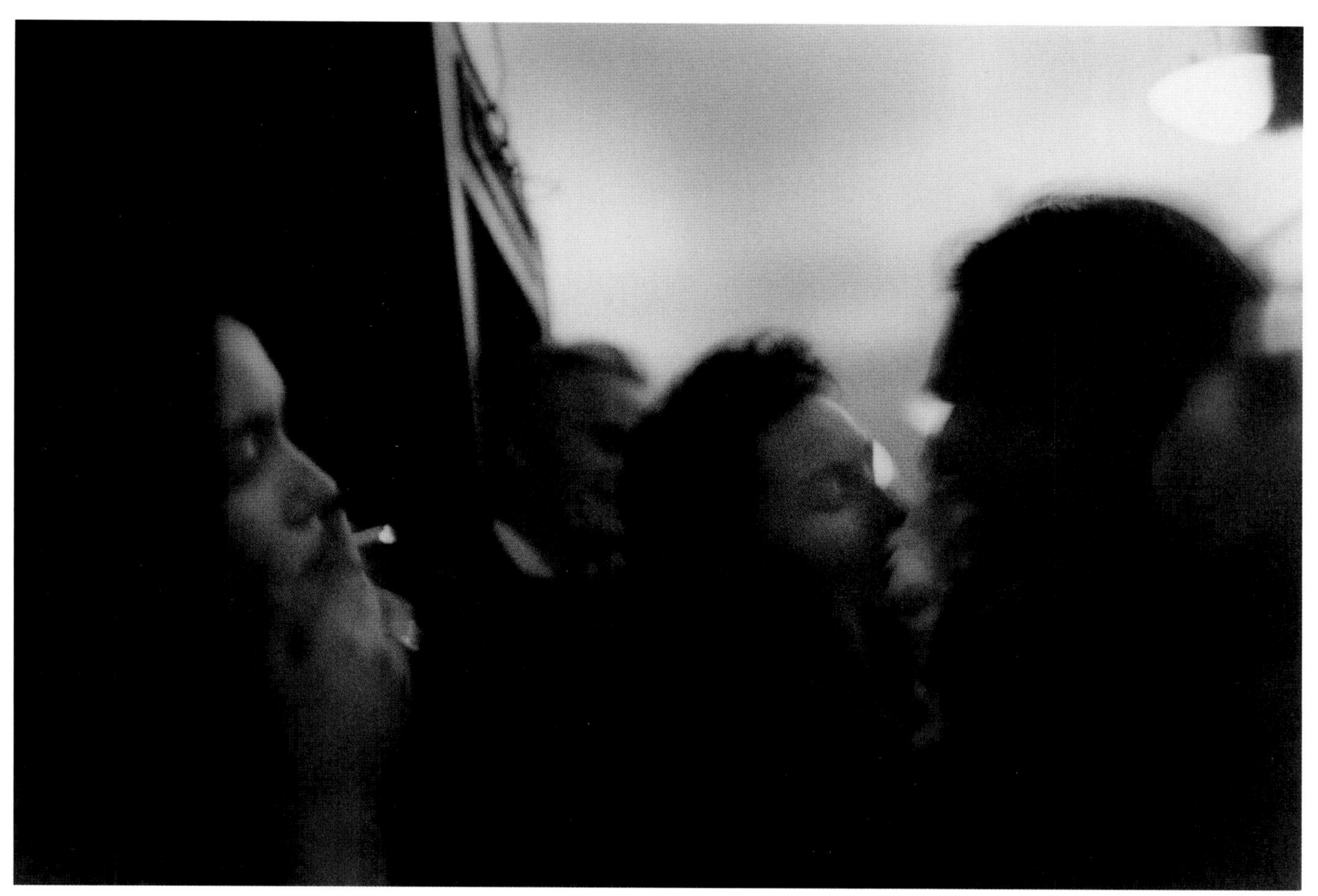

Michaela, Barbara Forst

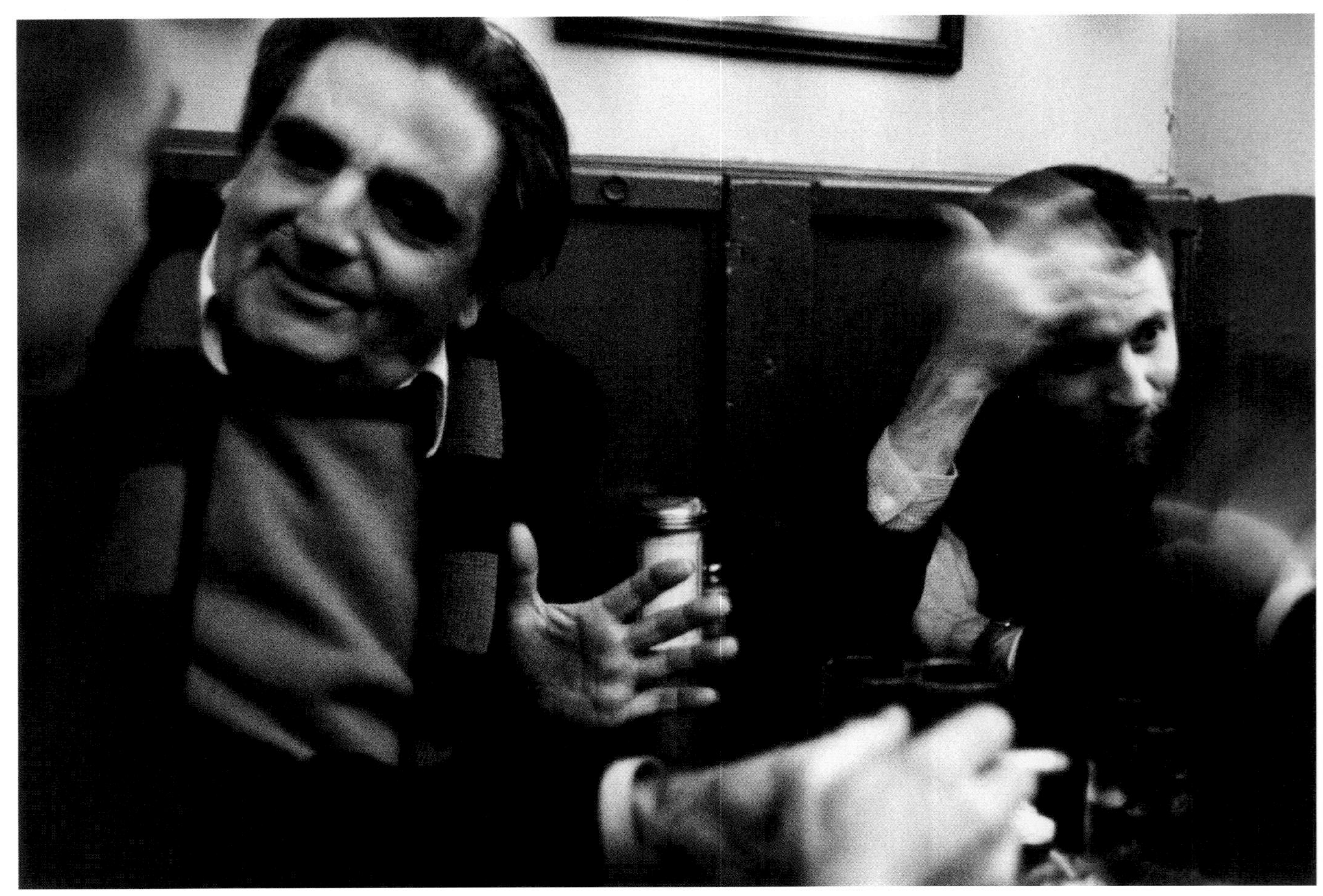

Aristodimos Kaldis, Allan Kaprow

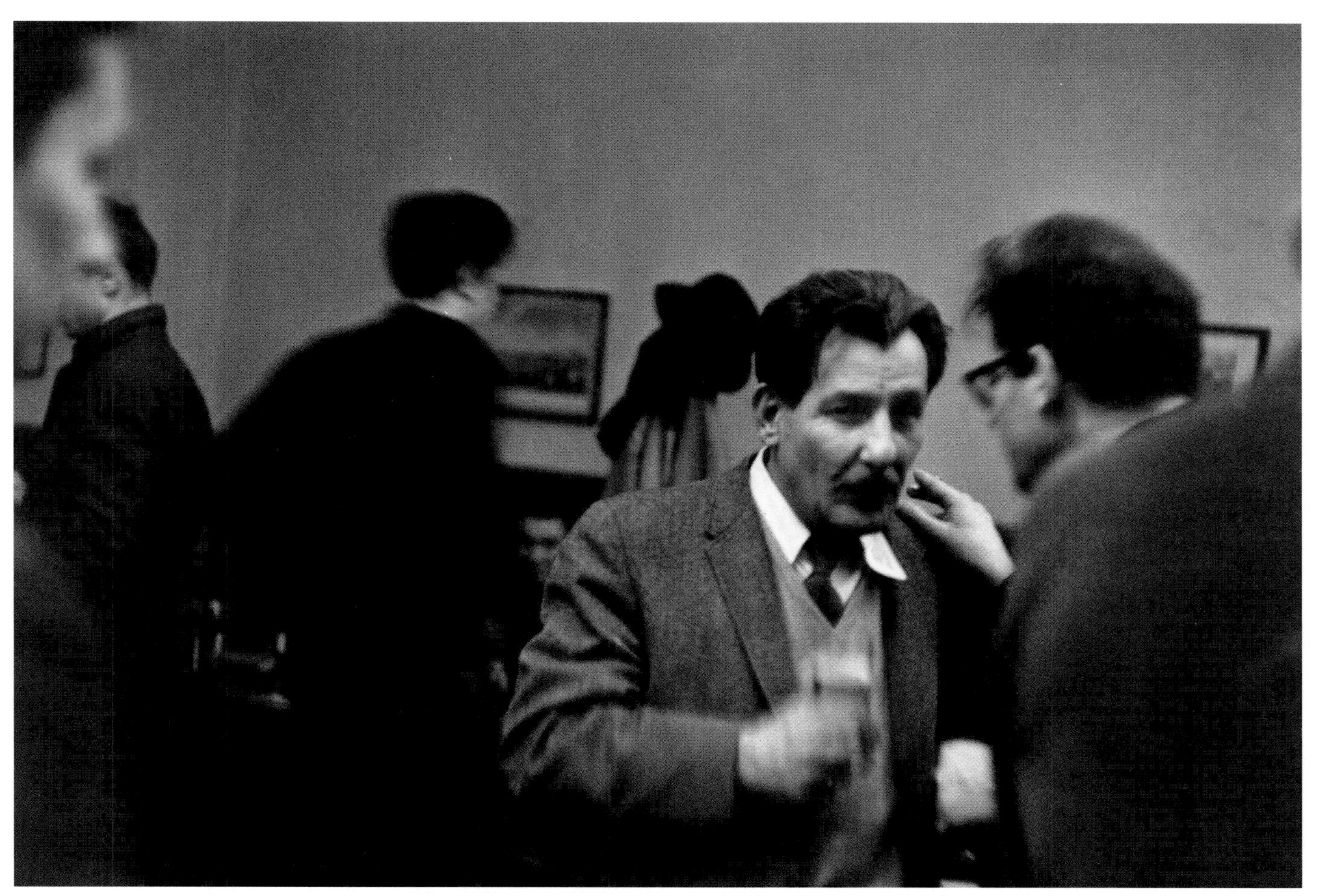

Franz Kline, Allen Ginsberg

MAKING

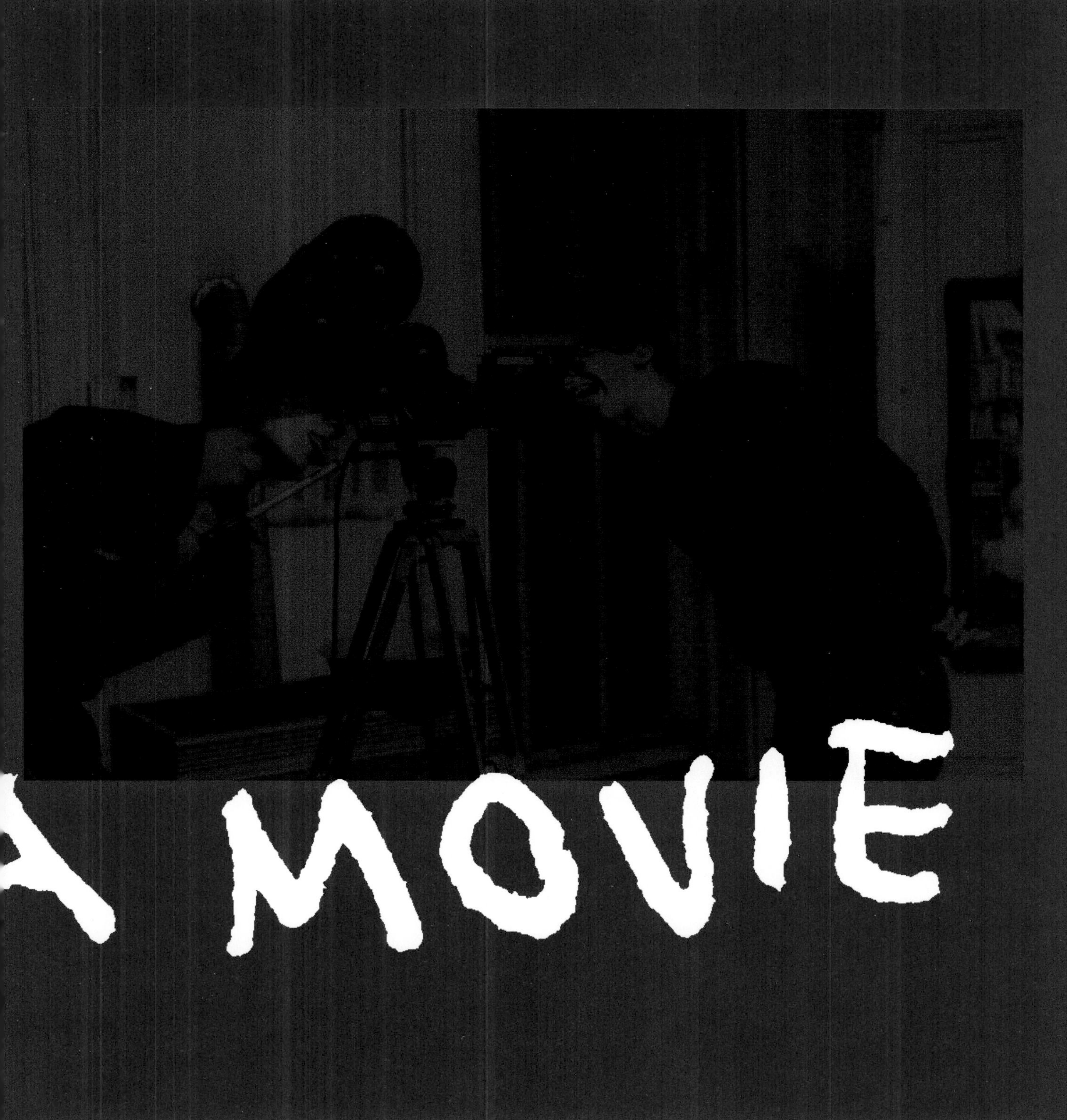

A MOVIE

A few blocks away in 1959, the painter Alfred Leslie and Robert Frank were making their film *Pull My Daisy*. Based on a chapter in a play by Jack Kerouac, the actors included Beat poets Allen Ginsberg, Gregory Corso and Peter Orlovsky, as well as NY downtown artists Alice Neel and Larry Rivers, and the gallerist Dick Bellamy. As Robert went about setting up shots for the camera, the "actors" improvised and clowned around. Musician David Amram says they had fun disrupting things. There was a script held in the hands of Leslie, and Kerouac came later to improvise a spoken narration over scenes filmed without sound.

The story depicted a household disrupted by poets. The film was acclaimed as a spontaneous achievement of independent filmmaking: an authentic improvisation where the Art world combined with the Beat Generation. *Life* magazine wanted *in* but were kept *out,* until the final celebration. They hoped to present it to the American public as "*Life* goes to a Beat party."

Eventually, *Life* didn't get its story, while the film remains today as the bedrock Beat generation film.

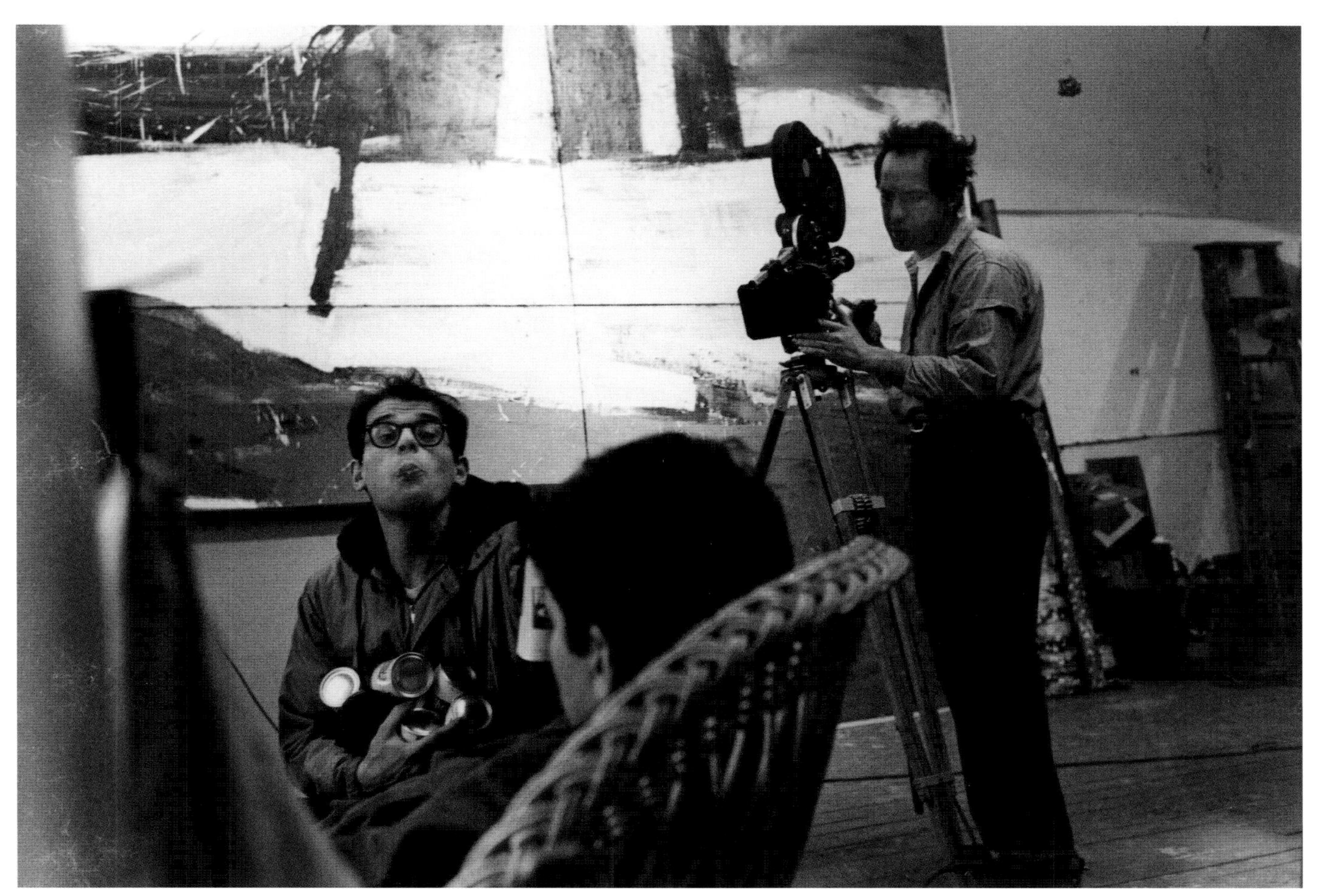

Allen Ginsberg, Robert Frank

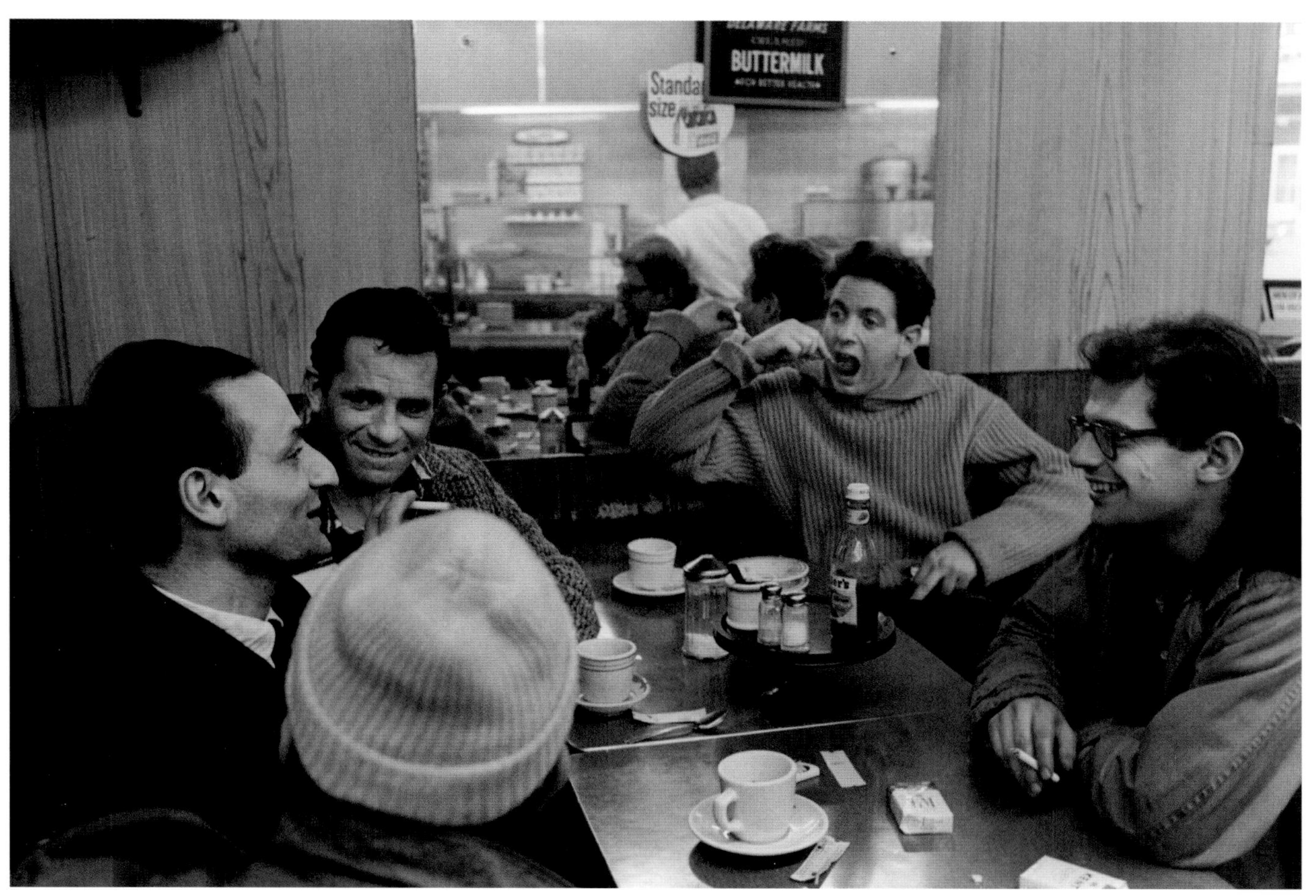

Gregory Corso (from behind), Larry Rivers, Jack Kerouac, David Amram, Allen Ginsberg

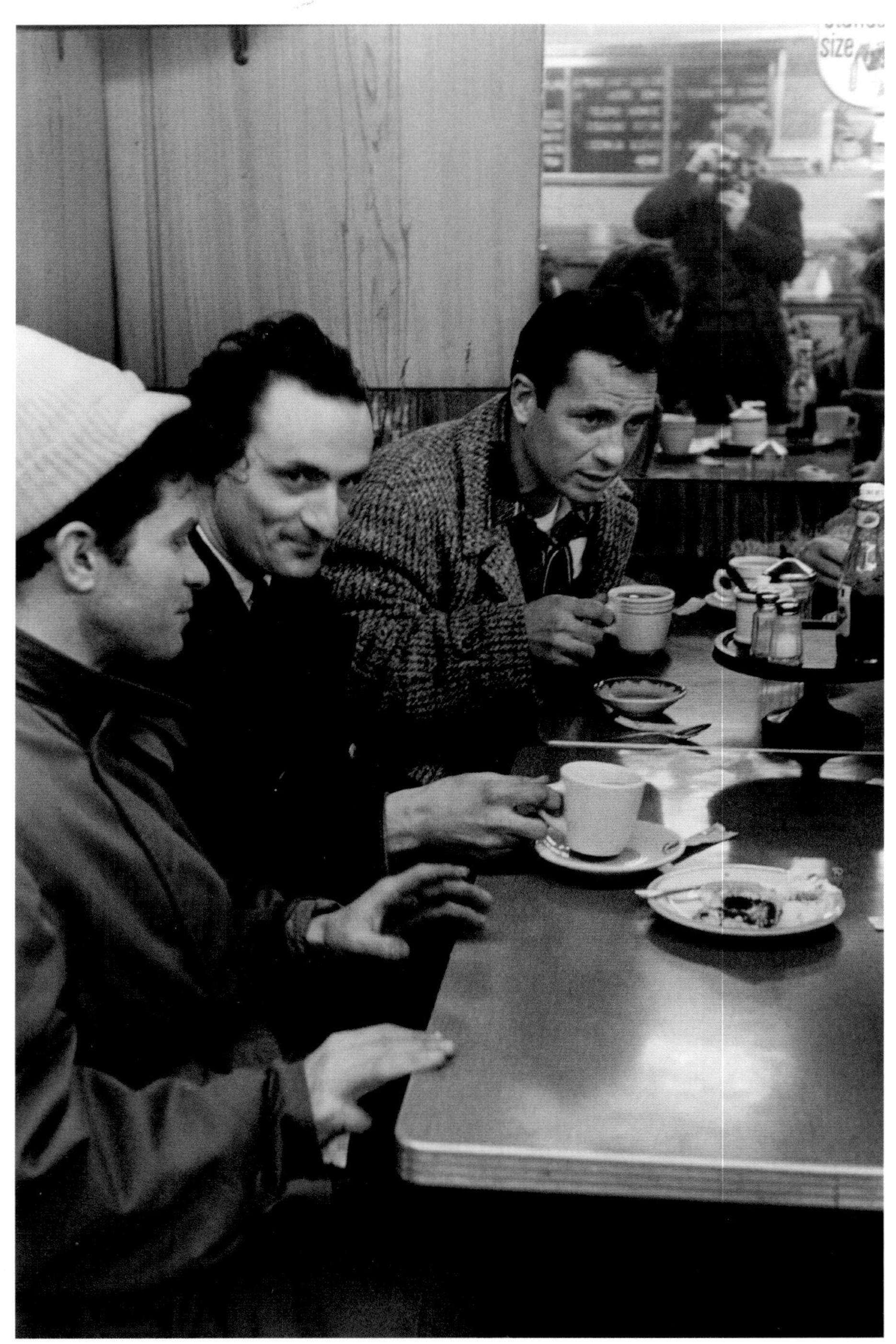

Gregory Corso, Larry Rivers, Jack Kerouac,
John Cohen (in mirror)

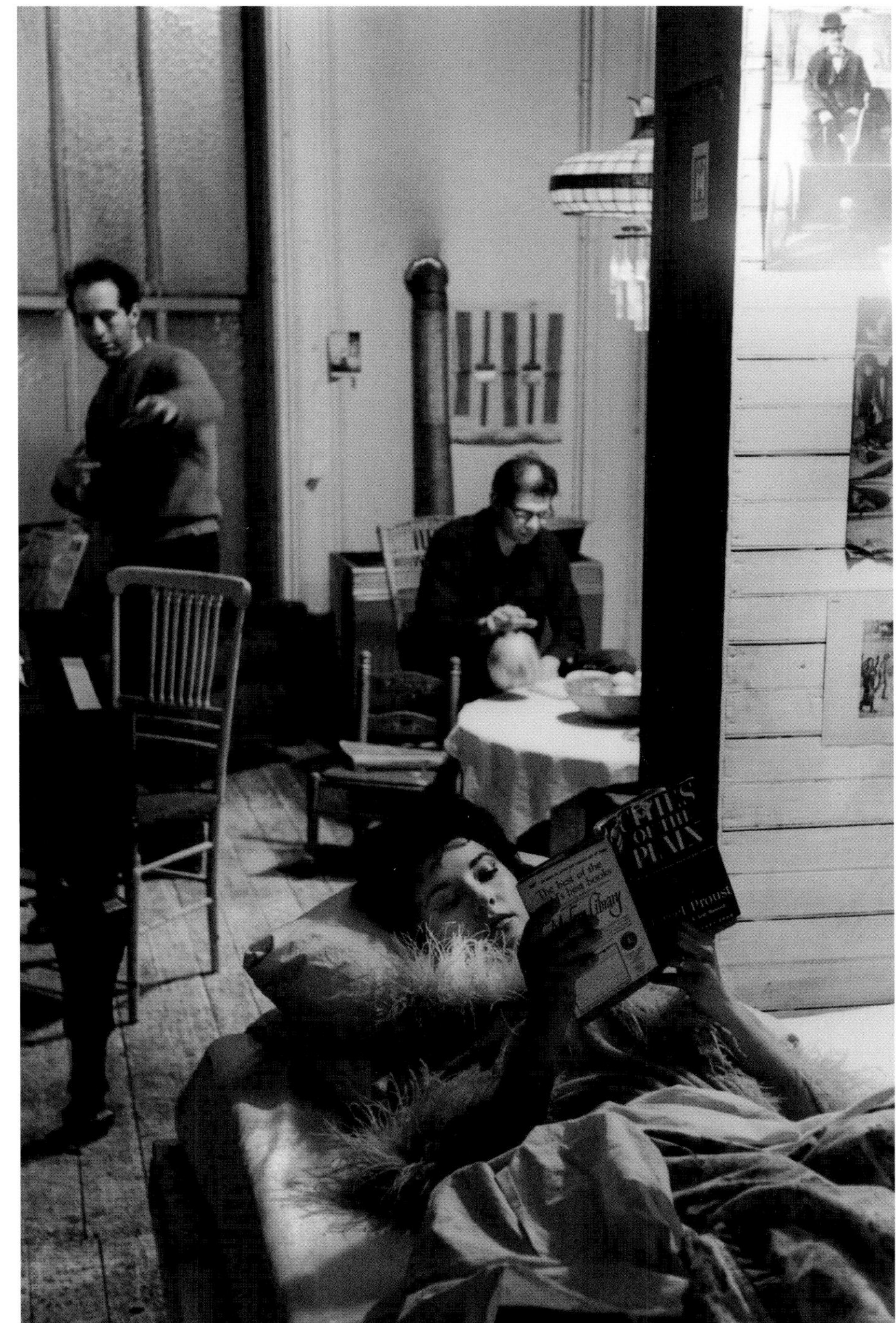

Robert Frank, Allen Ginsberg, Denise Parker

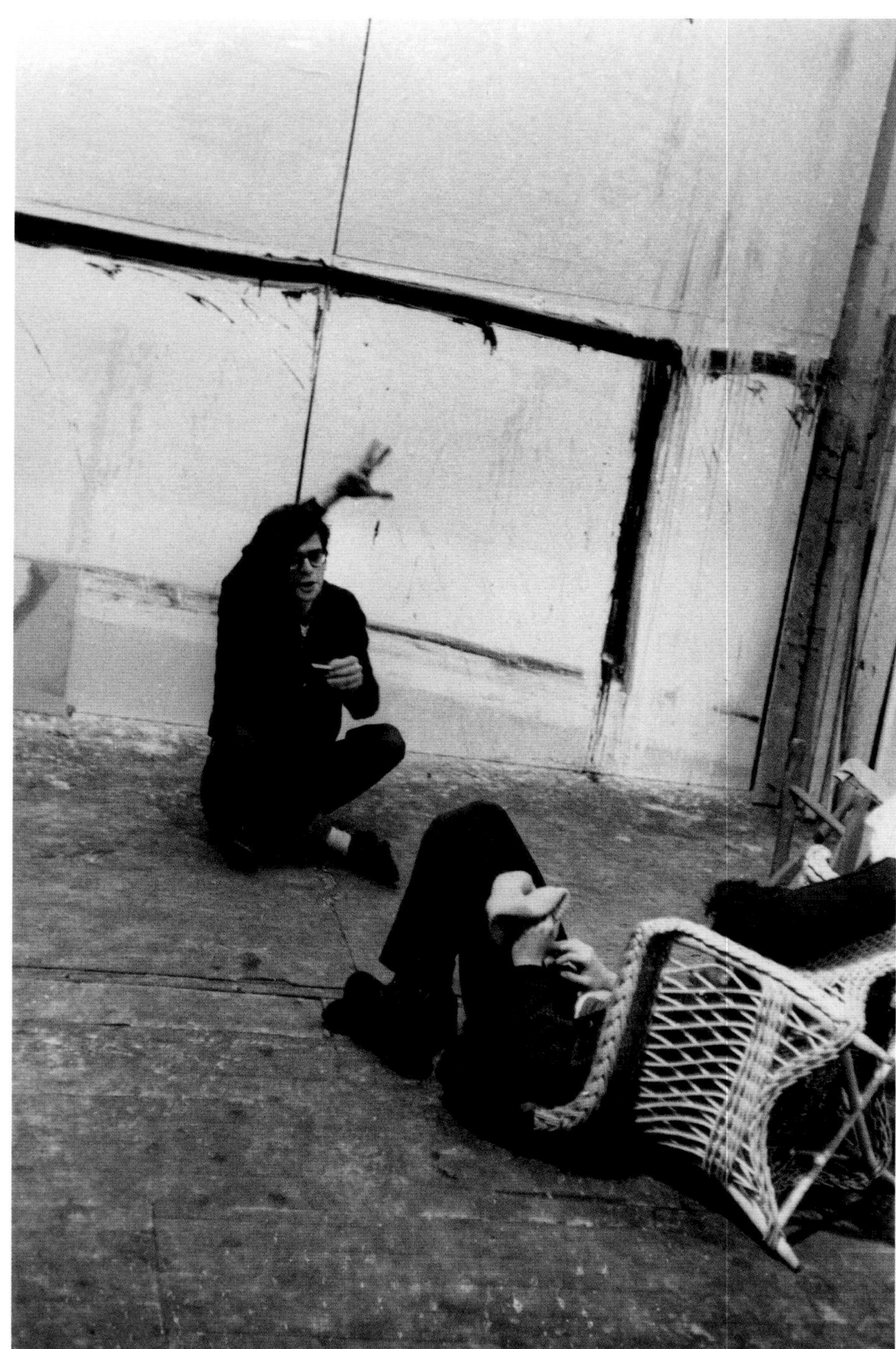

Allen Ginsberg, Gregory Corso

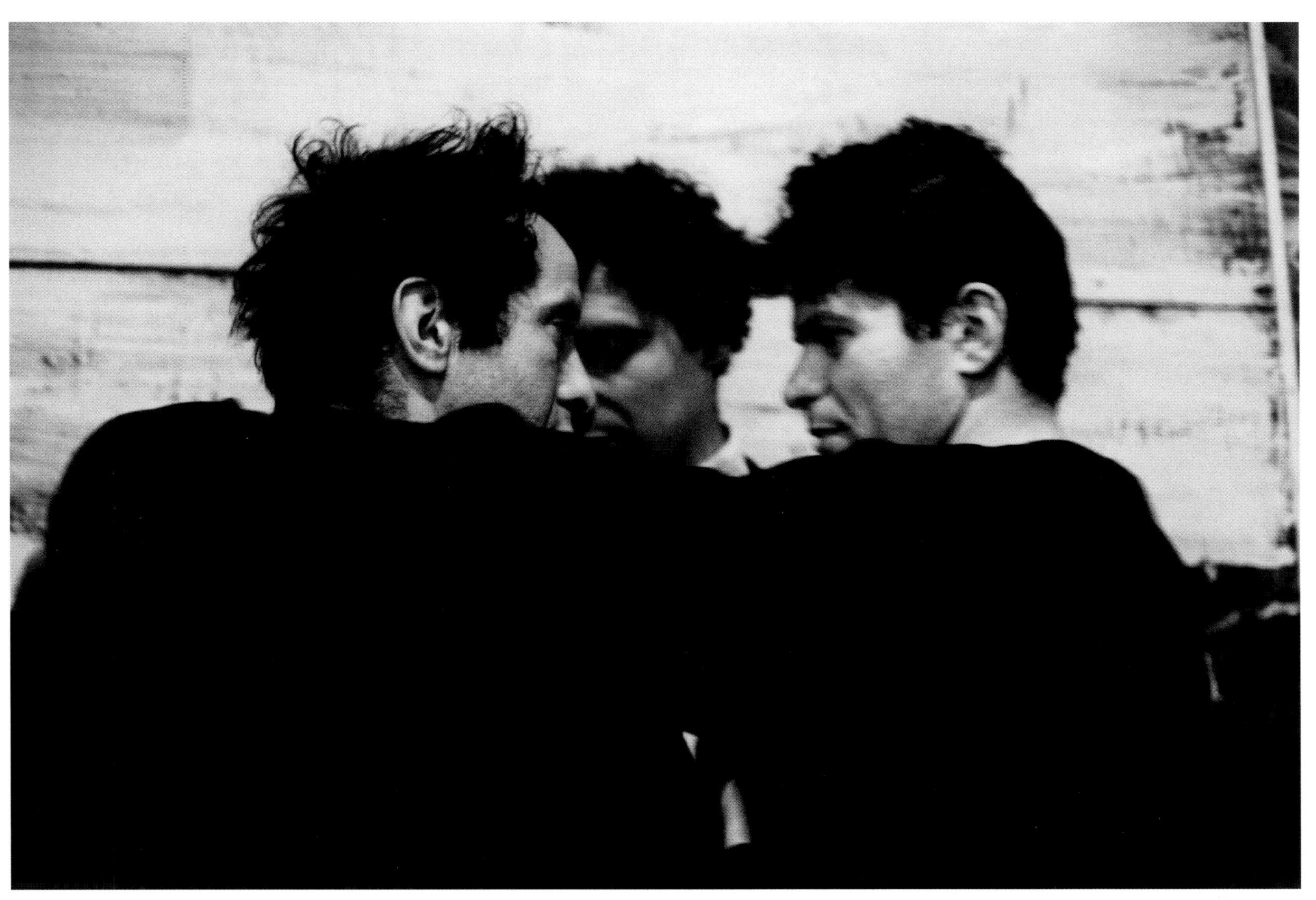

Robert Frank, Alfred Leslie, Gregory Corso

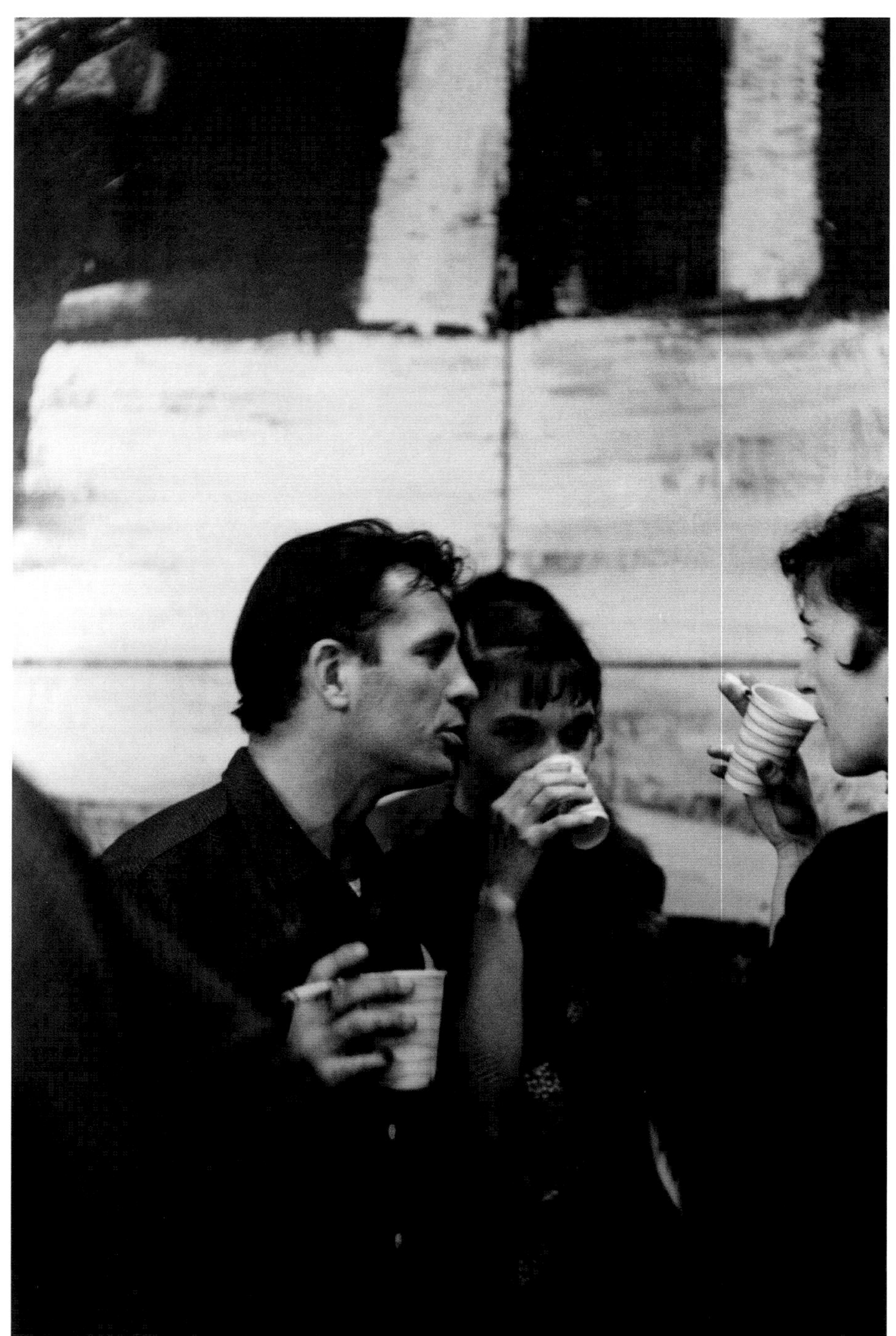

Jack Kerouac, Dody Müller, Cessa Carr

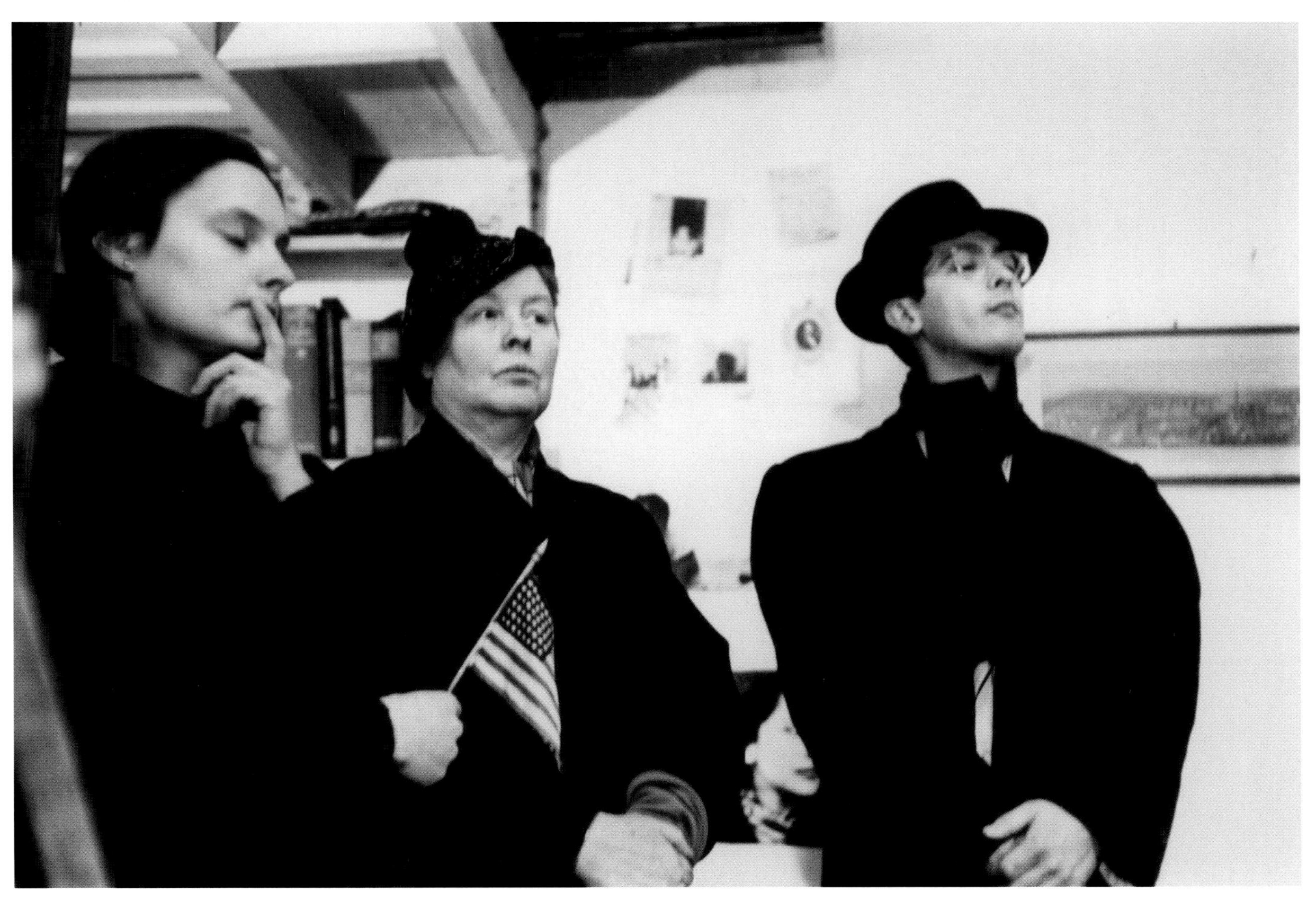

Sally Gross, Alice Neel, Richard Bellamy

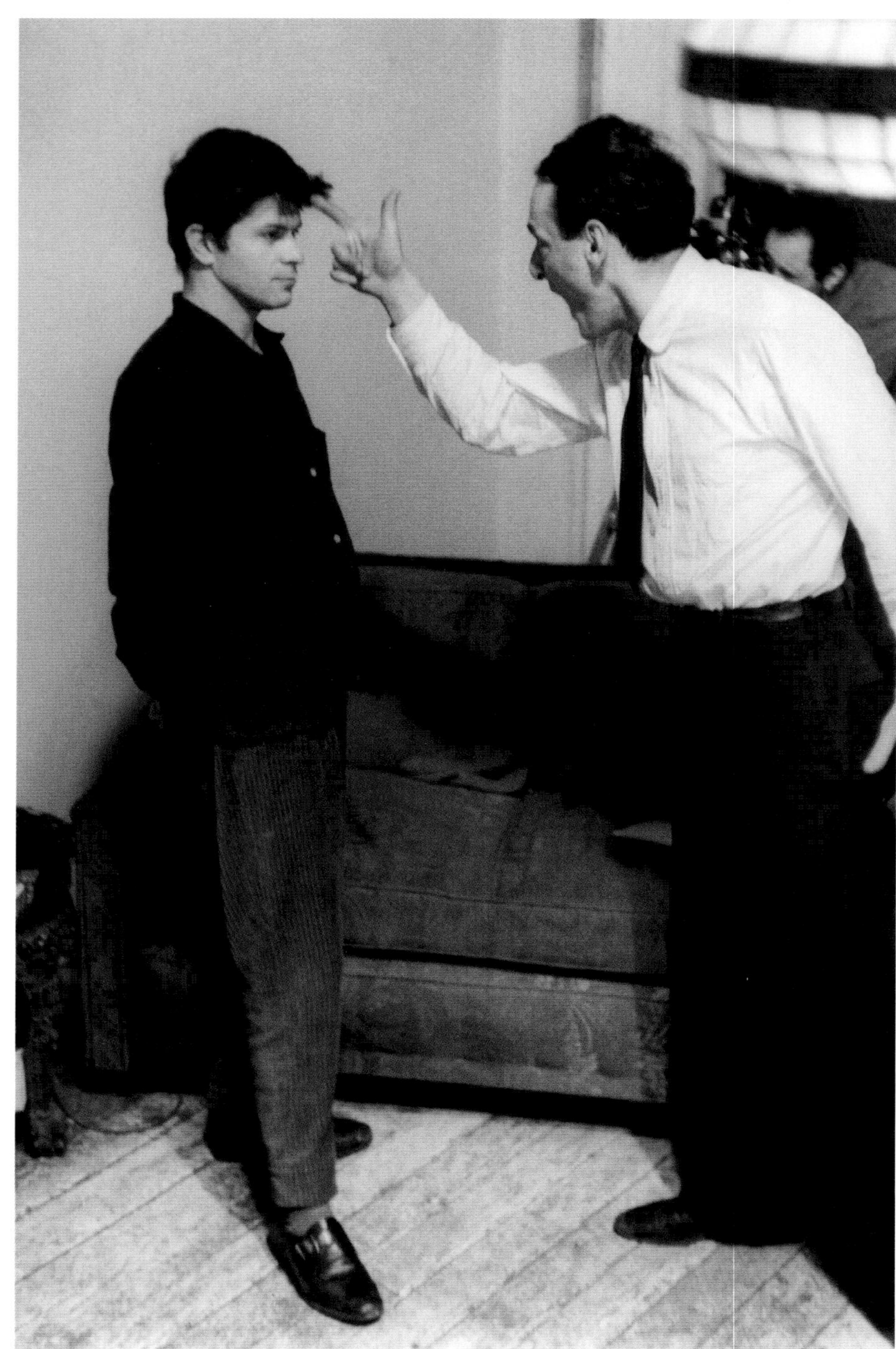

Gregory Corso, Larry Rivers

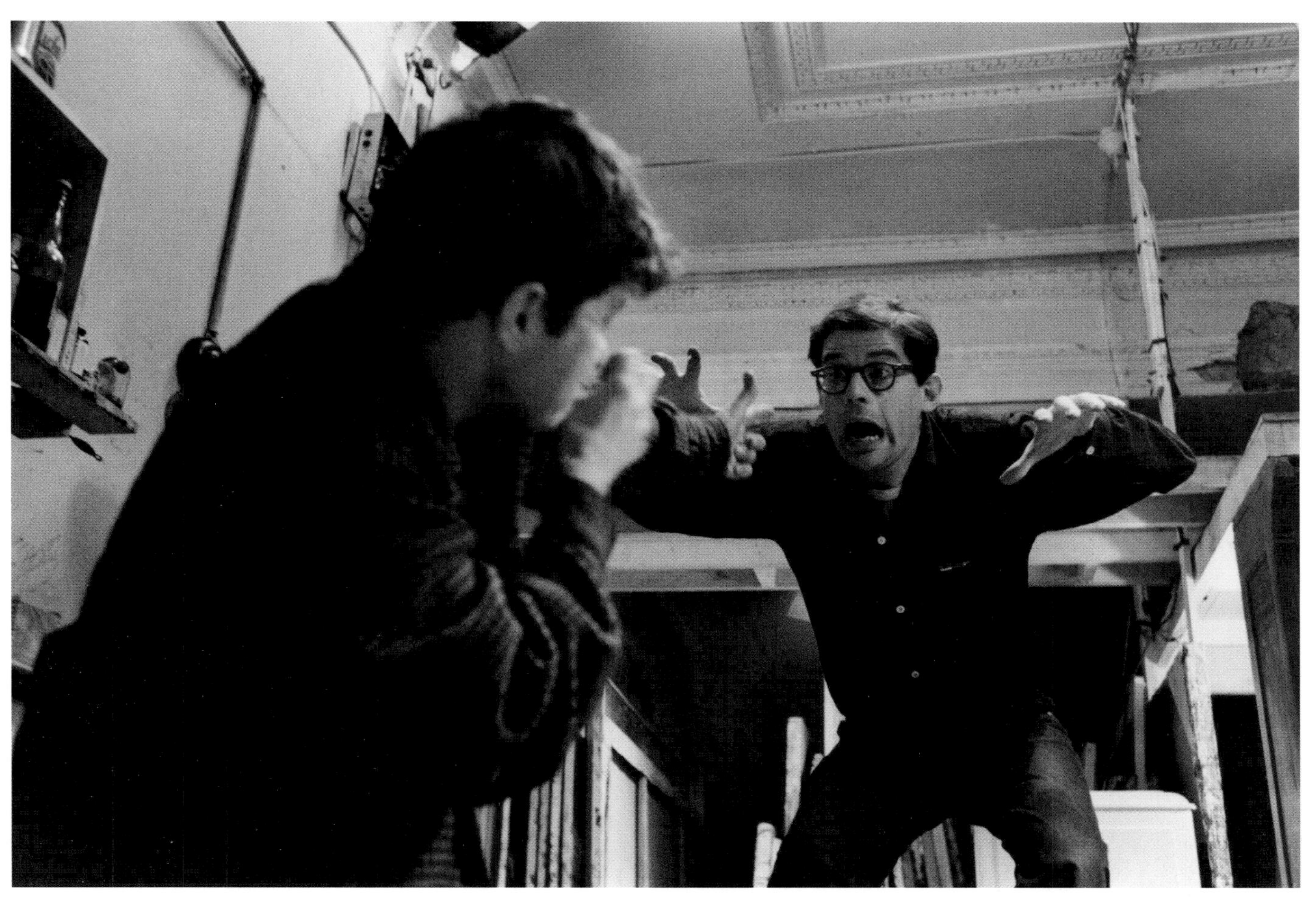

Gregory Corso, Allen Ginsberg

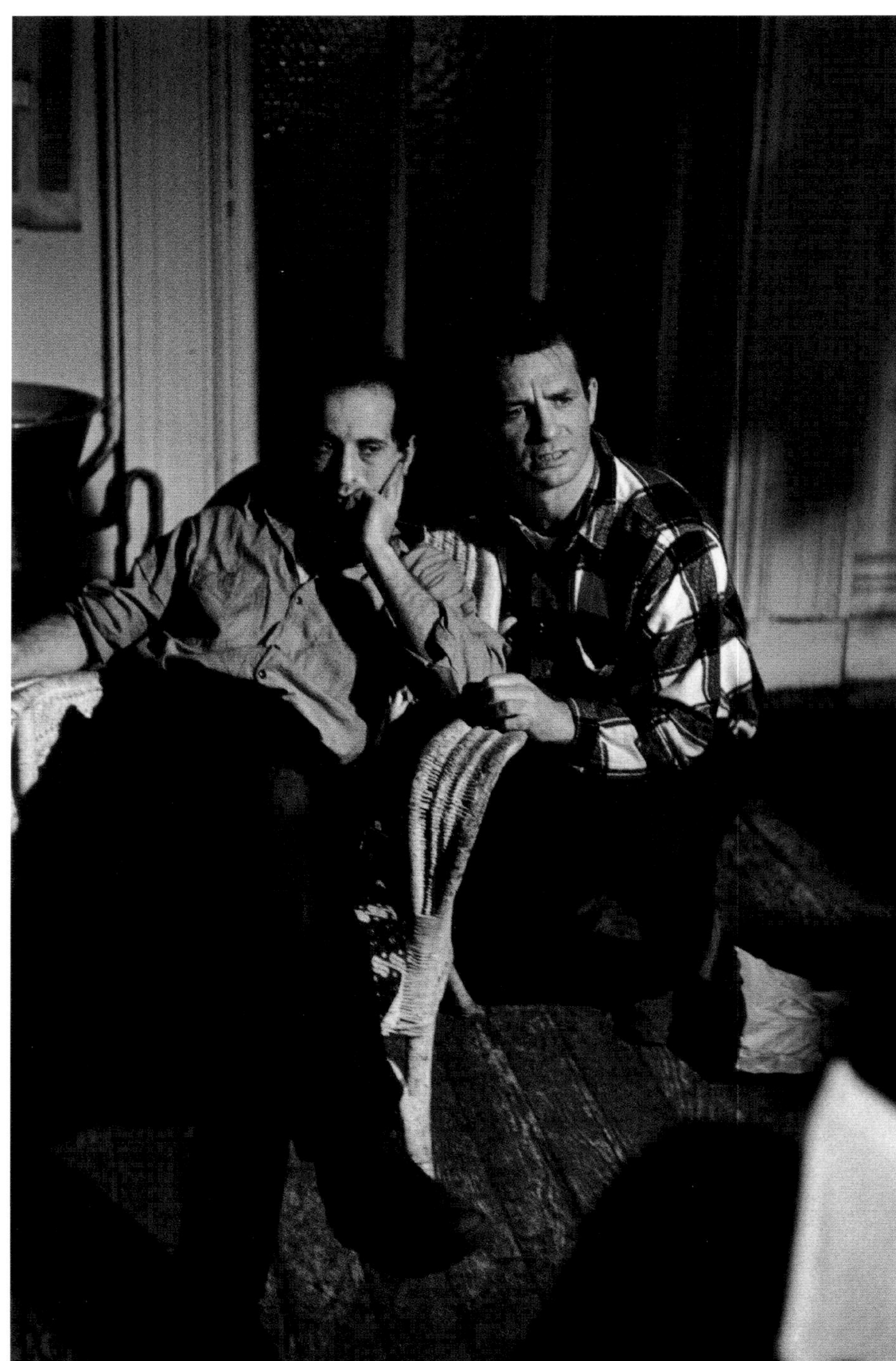

Robert Frank, Jack Kerouac

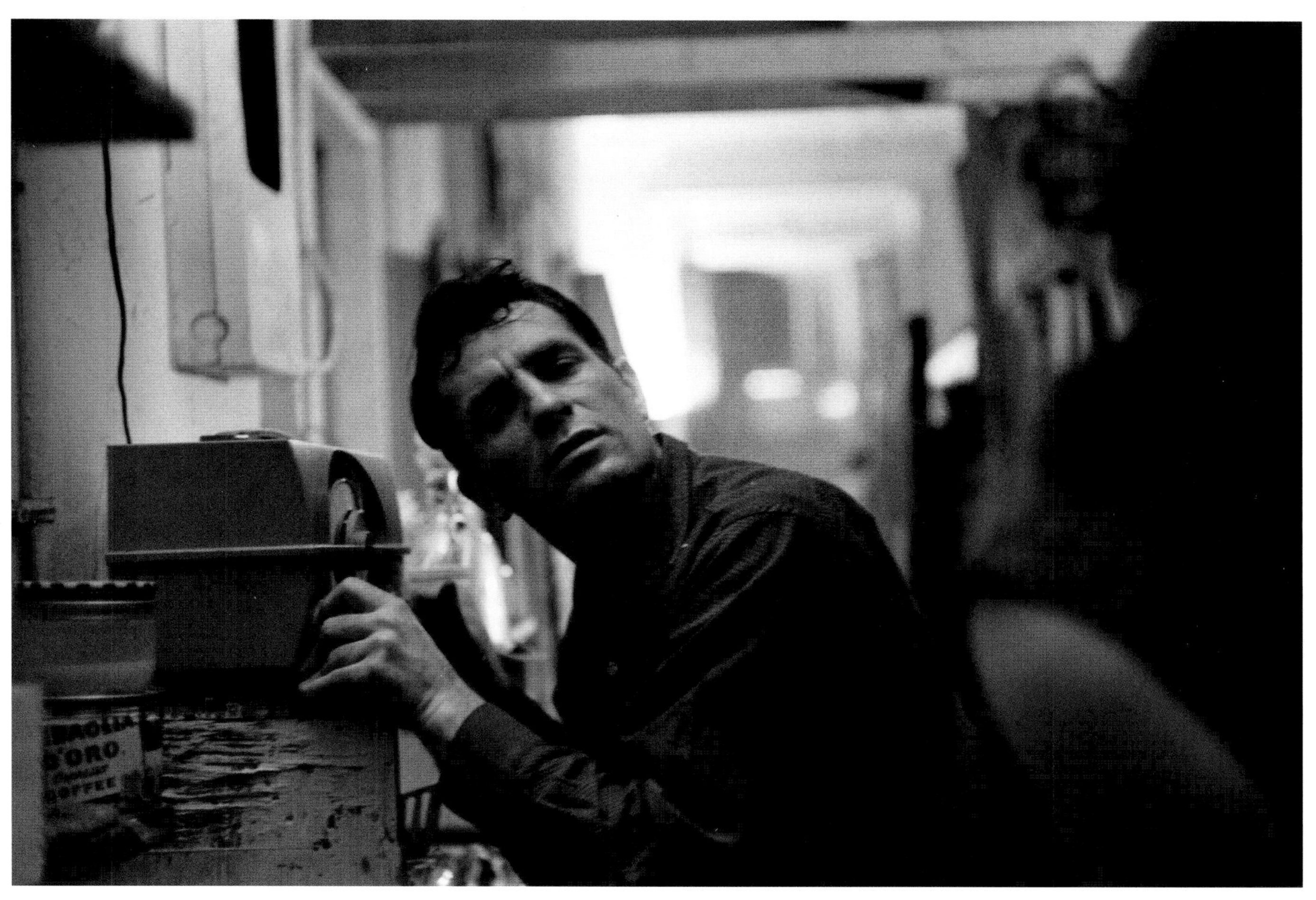

Jack Kerouac listening to himself on the radio

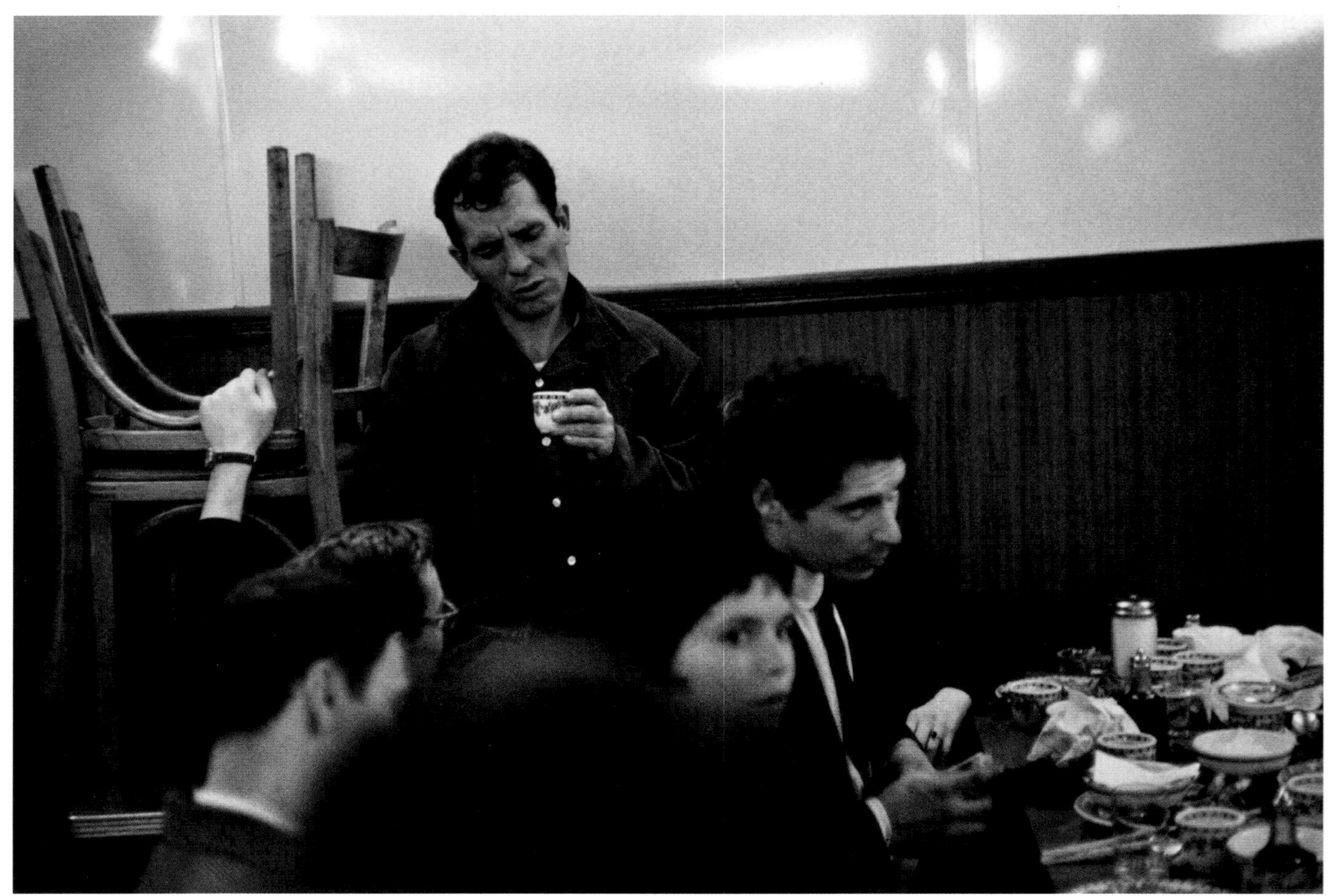

Jack Kerouac

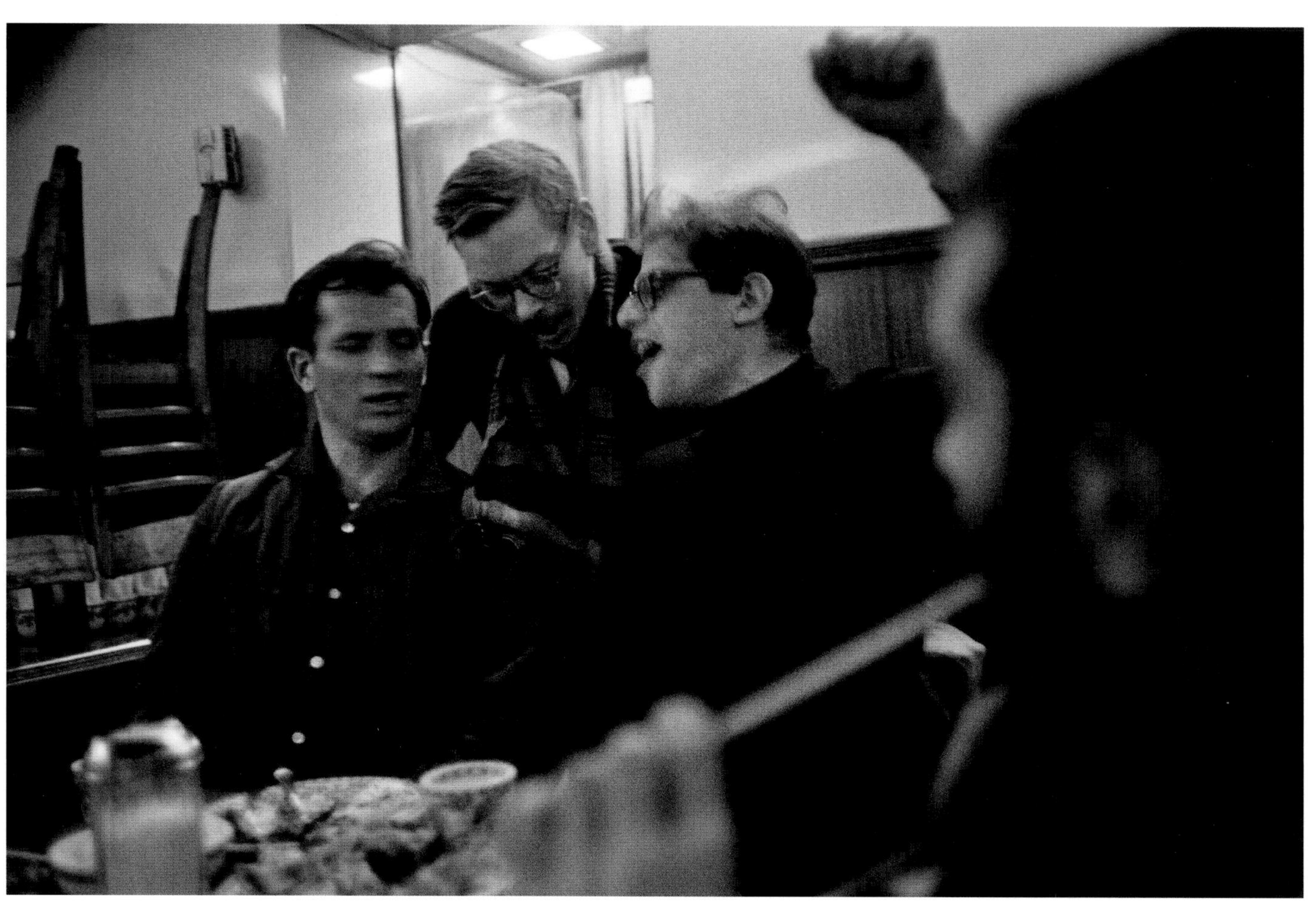

Jack Kerouac, Lucien Carr, Allen Ginsberg

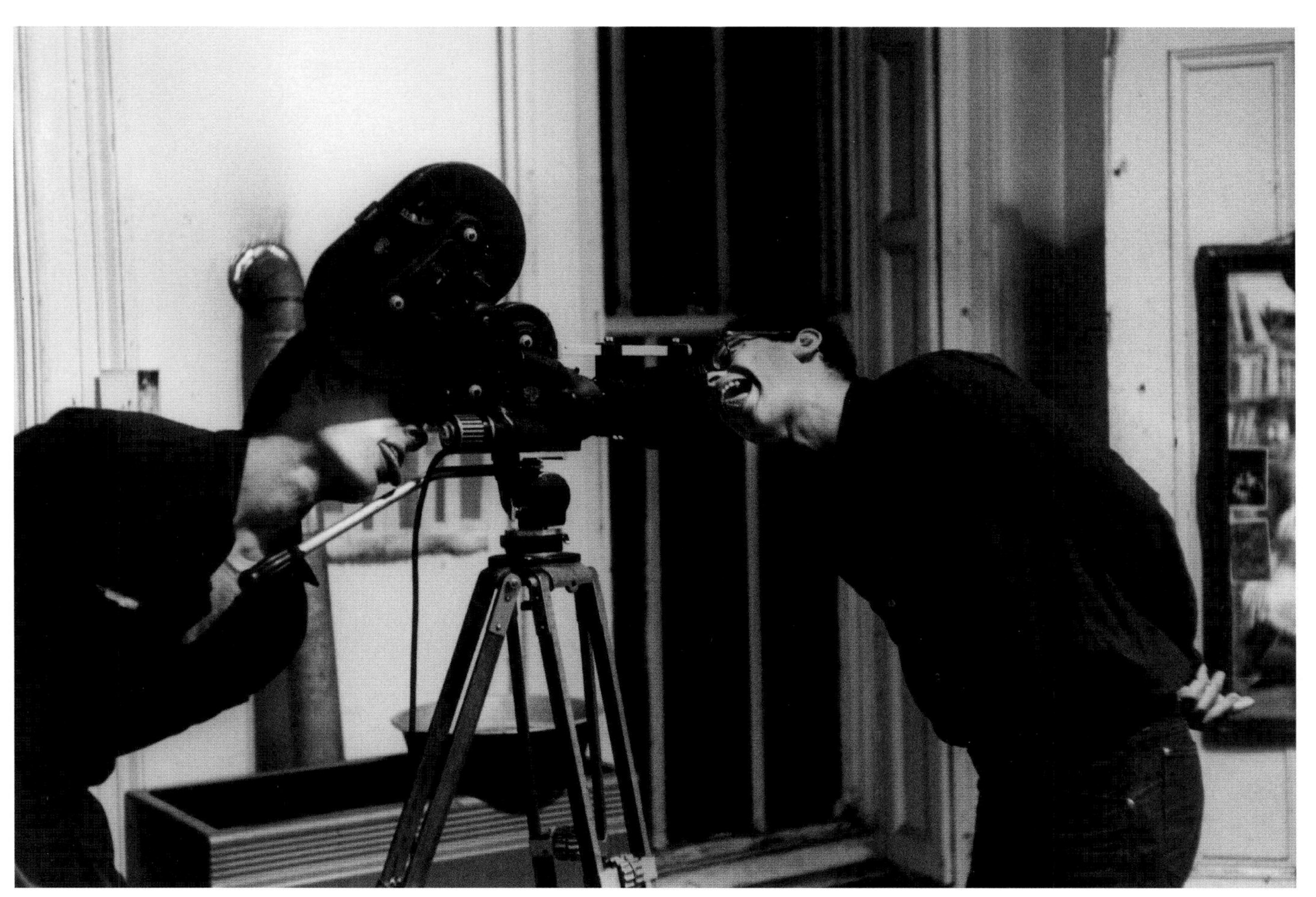

Peter Orlovsky, Allen Ginsberg

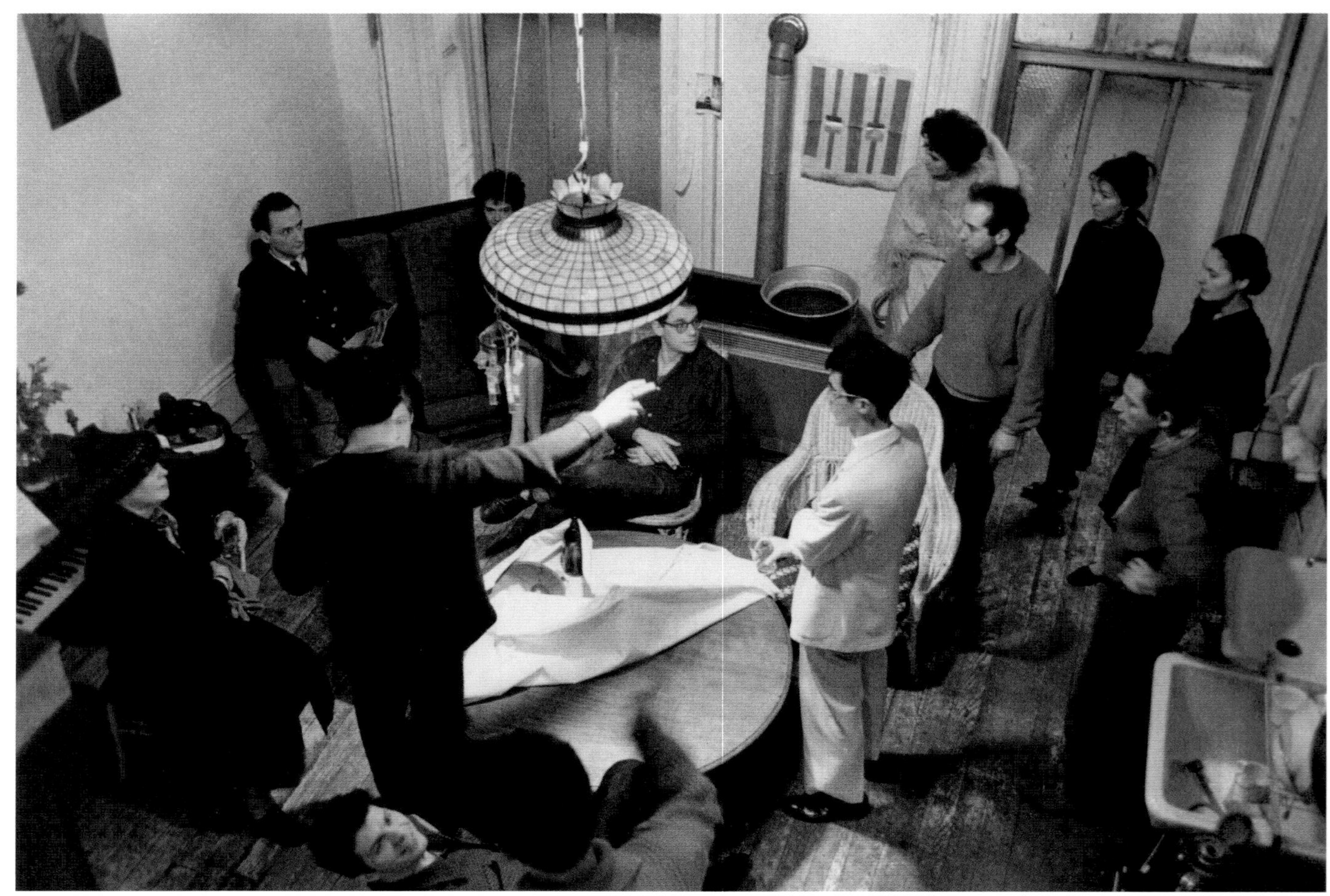

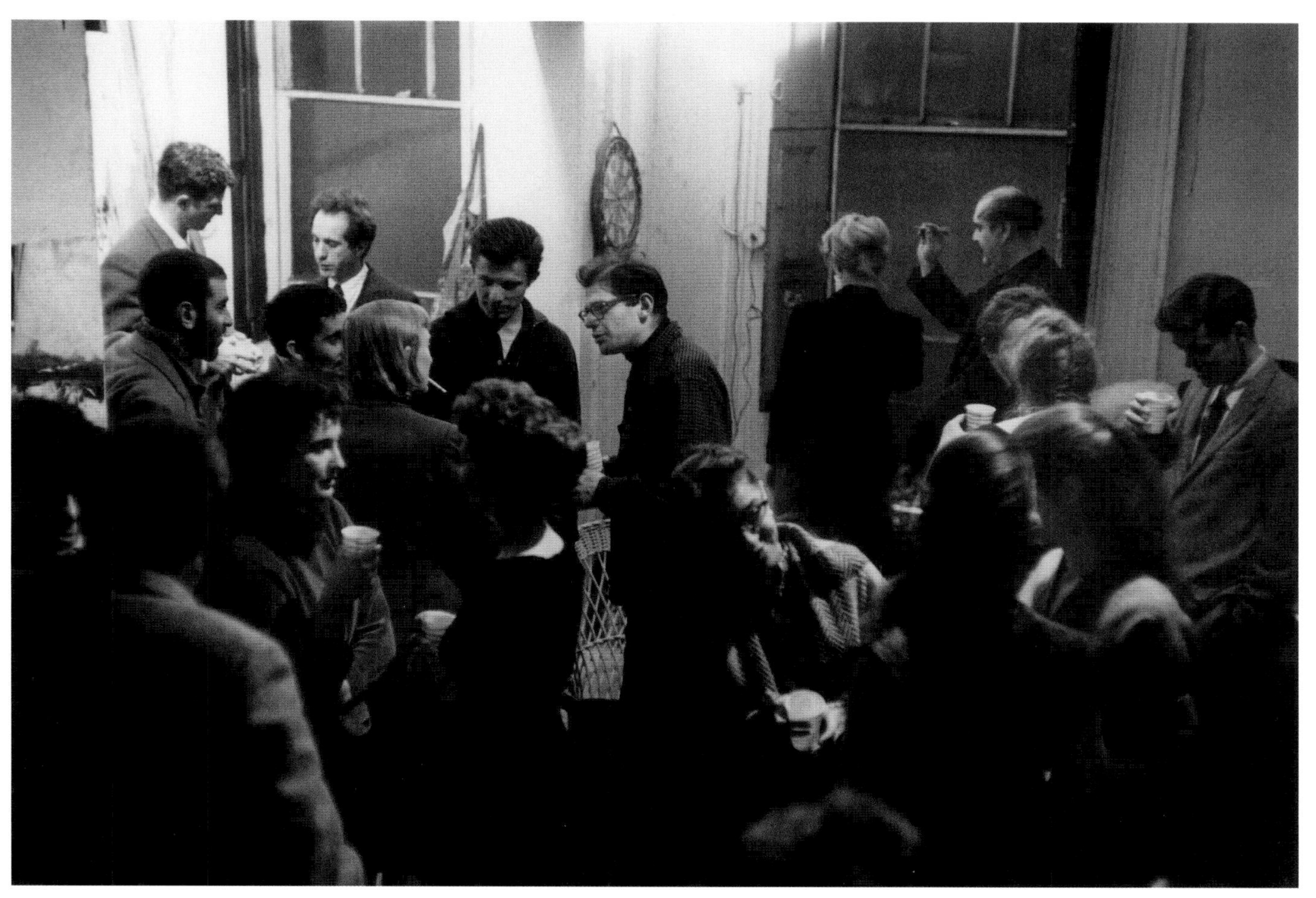

Zero Mostel (at right window)

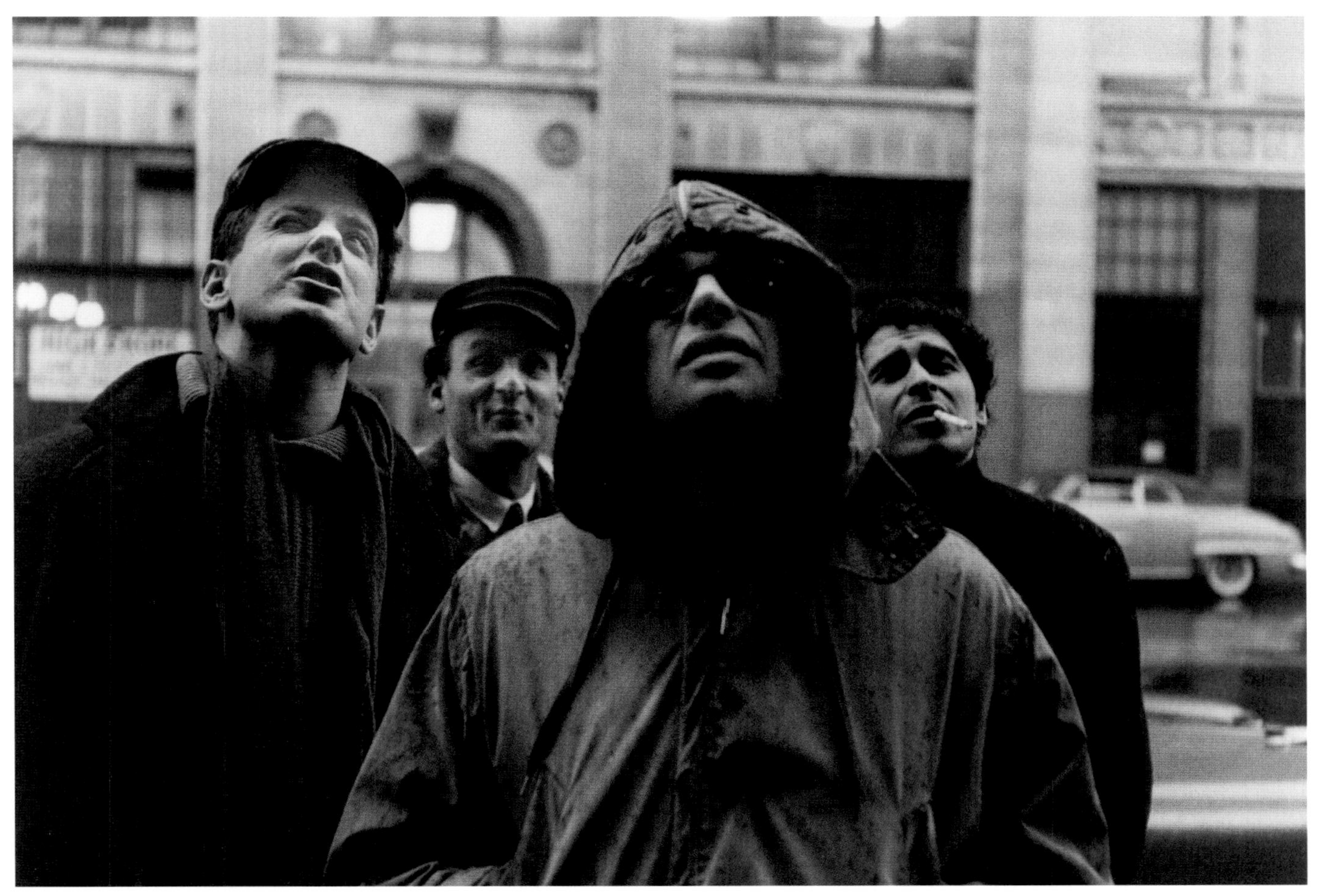

David Amram, Larry Rivers, Allen Ginsberg, Alfred Leslie

ART EVE
and HAP

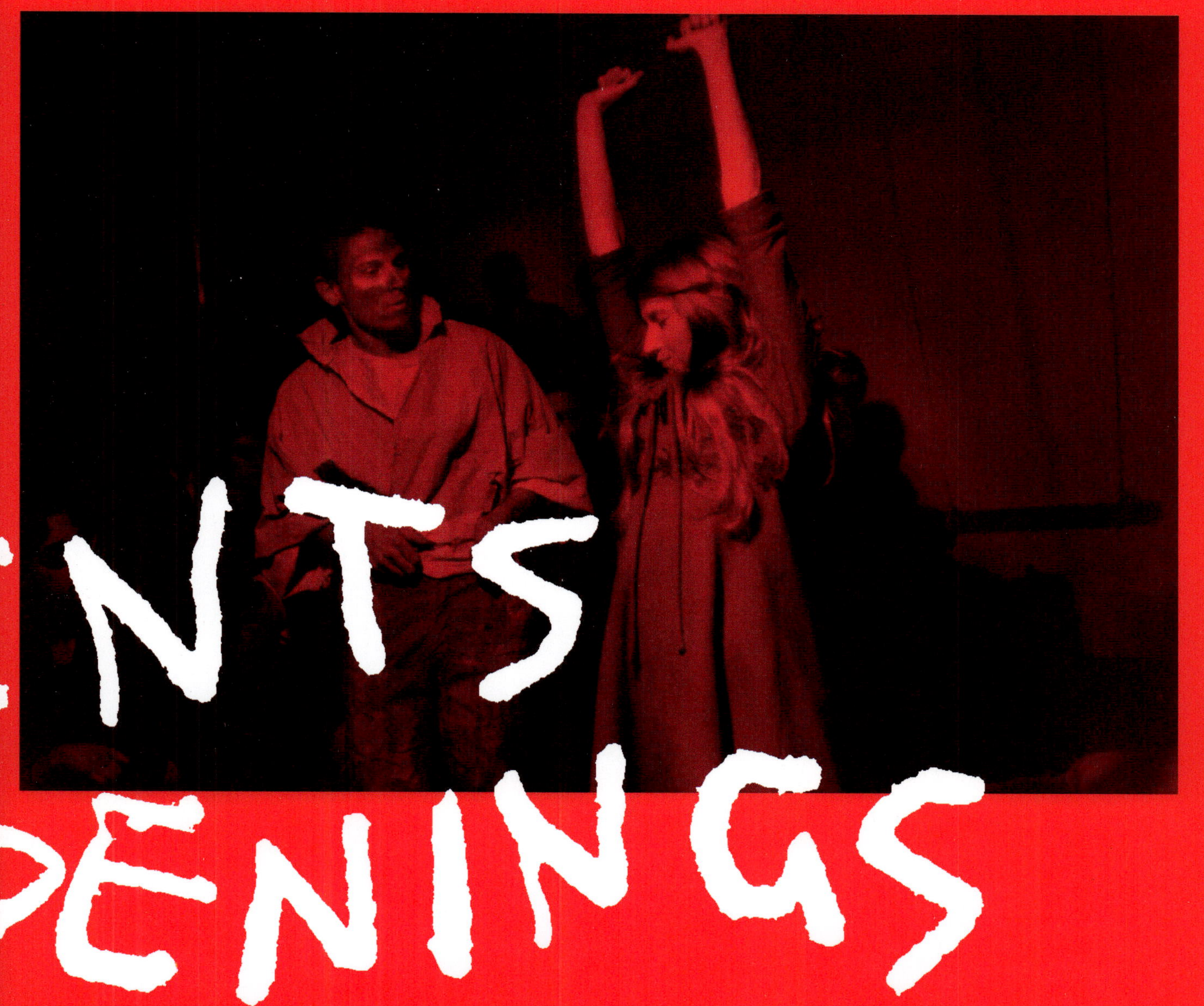
NTS
ENINGS

"It was lively, you couldn't tell a party from an opening from a happening."
   Mary Frank

Along with the paintings in the galleries, the block became the setting for new
performance art. Pop artist Claes Oldenburg opened his "store" on the Lower
East Side, Anita Ruben opened her gallery on Fourth Avenue, and presented
Allan Kaprow, Lucas Samaras and Jim Dine in "happenings." Red Grooms
wheeled his painting in a baby carriage for the "Magic Train Ride." This new
performance art was outflanking the 10th Street painters. It was surprising
to see an actual refrigerator door in a painting by Tom Wesselmann.
The happenings were more like events than paintings. Dada-inspired
performances were enlarged to include the audience. Red Grooms created
a more funky, down-to-earth kind of performance with his *Magic Train Ride*
and *The Burning Building*. They were like childhood plays with shadows on
bed sheets and cut-out cardboard costumes. The "action" in Action Painting
took place in the gallery space. Red Grooms' *Delancey Street Museum* was a
downtown response to upperclass museums.

At an artist's party going bonkers, people in bedsheets with lampshades over their heads were fighting mock battles with wooden swords. They were adult artists exploring a new wacky energy with serious intent, to be presented later in art spaces. At a happening, a series of connected rooms each had a different absurd performance, while the viewers moved from room to room along a narrow corridor, unable to ever take it all in. The effect was to produce unresolved anxiety under the title "art event."

Beside Allan Kaprow who was the theorist of the happenings, Claes Oldenberg, Jim Dine, Lucas Samaras and Robert Whitman created their own acts of art which appeared senseless but added up. As artists, they determined this work to be taken seriously.

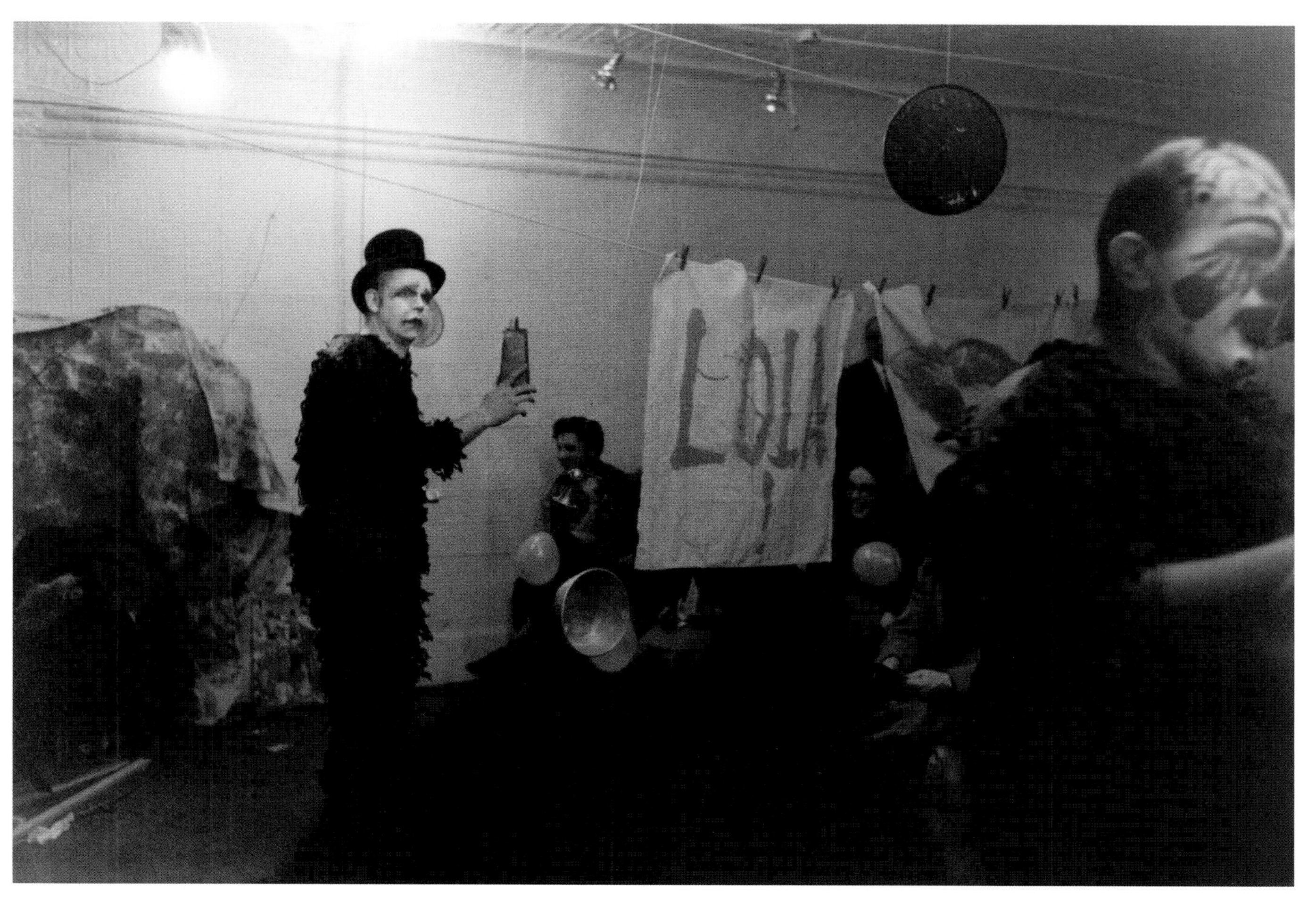

Claes Oldenburg, Jim Dine

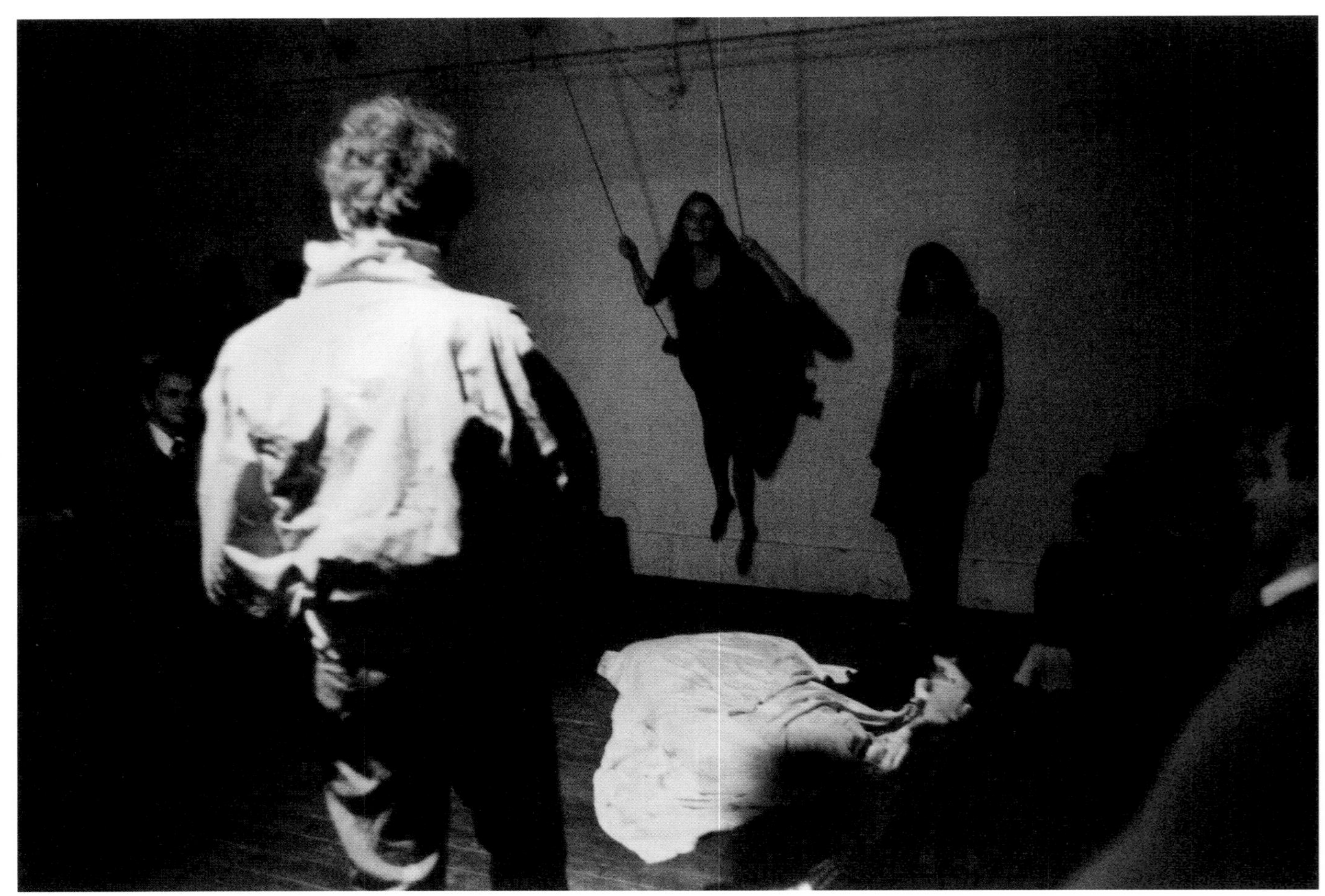

Lucas Samaras, Pat Oldenburg

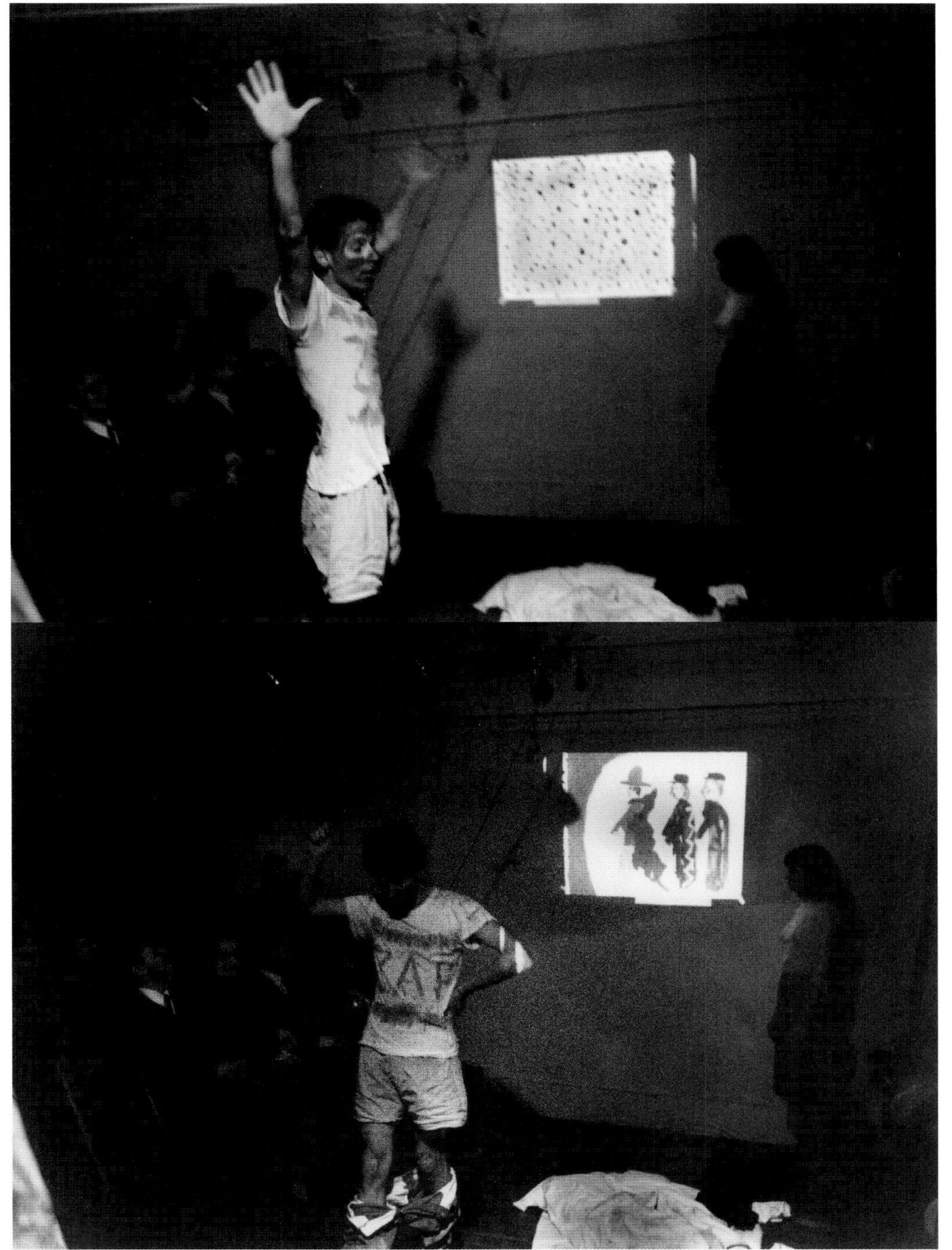

Lucas Samaras

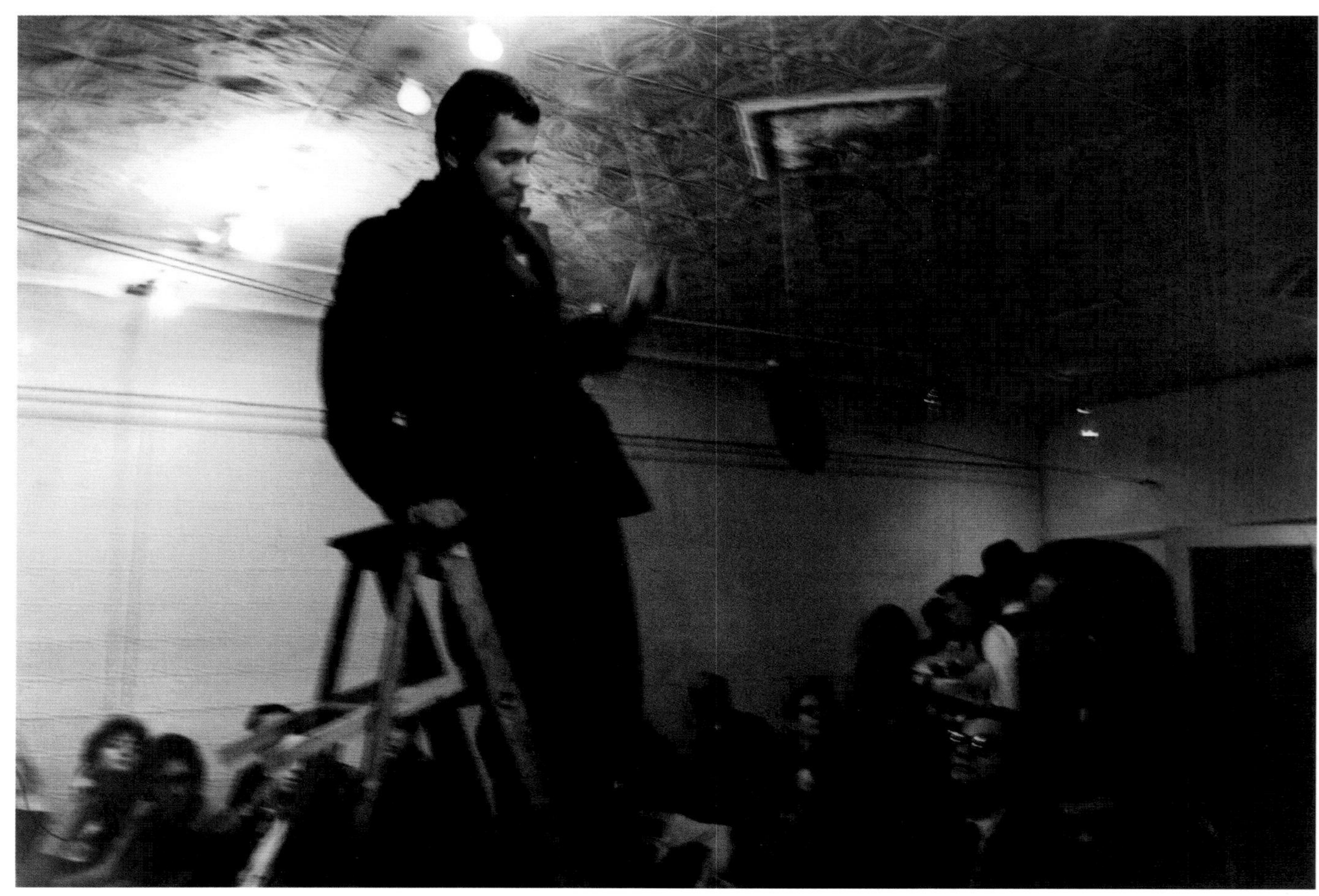

Allan Kaprow

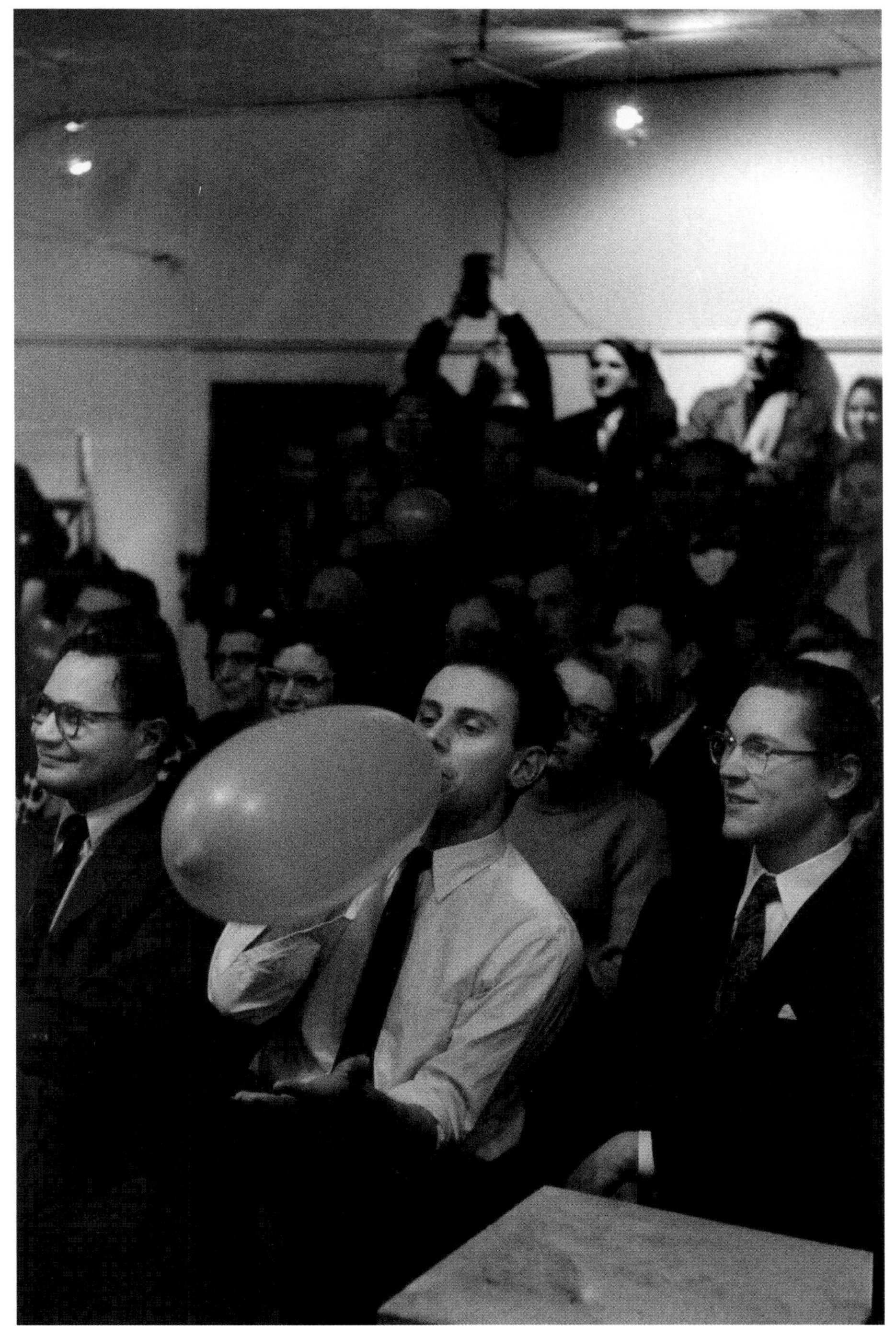

Lucas Samaras, Robert Whitman,
John Cage

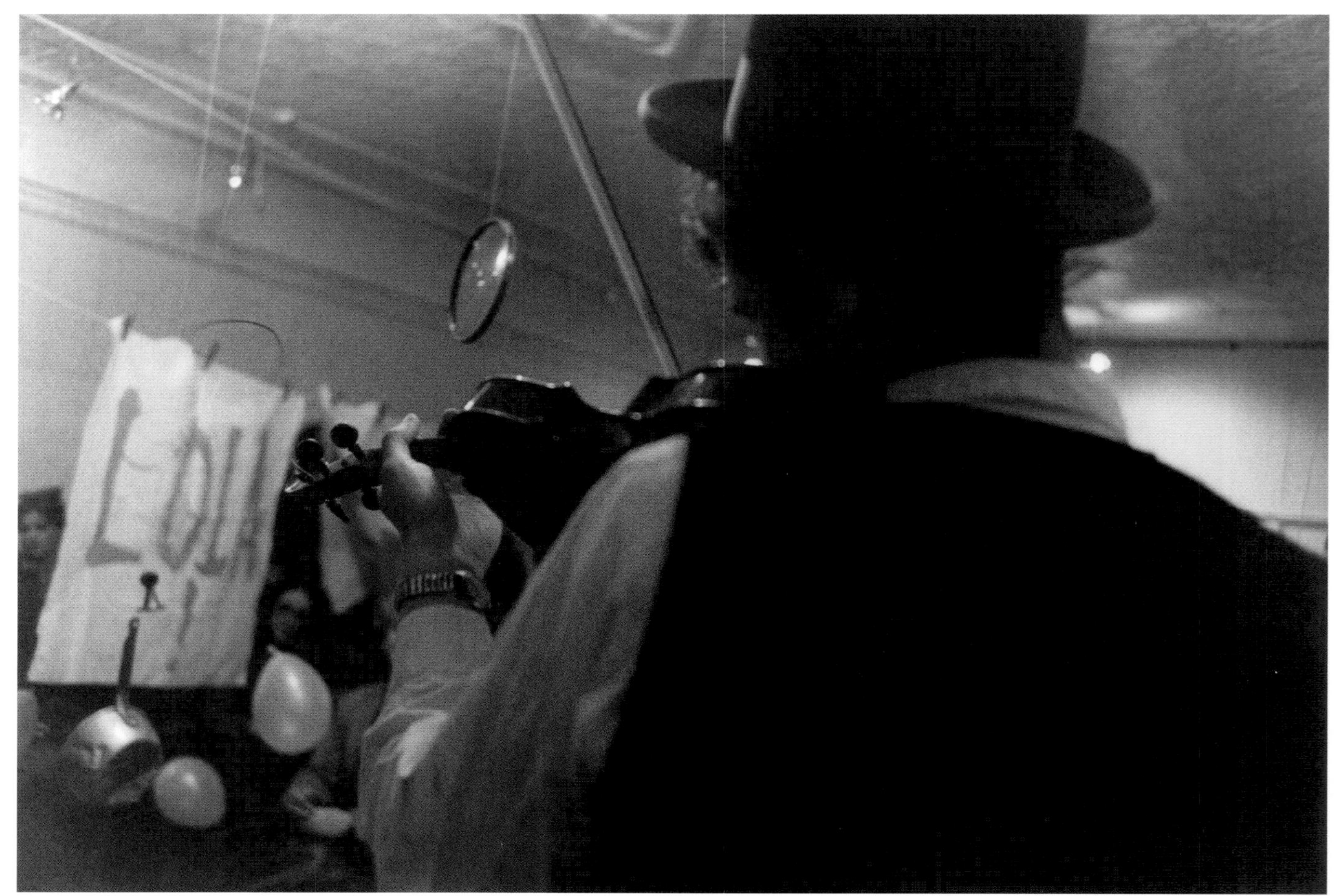

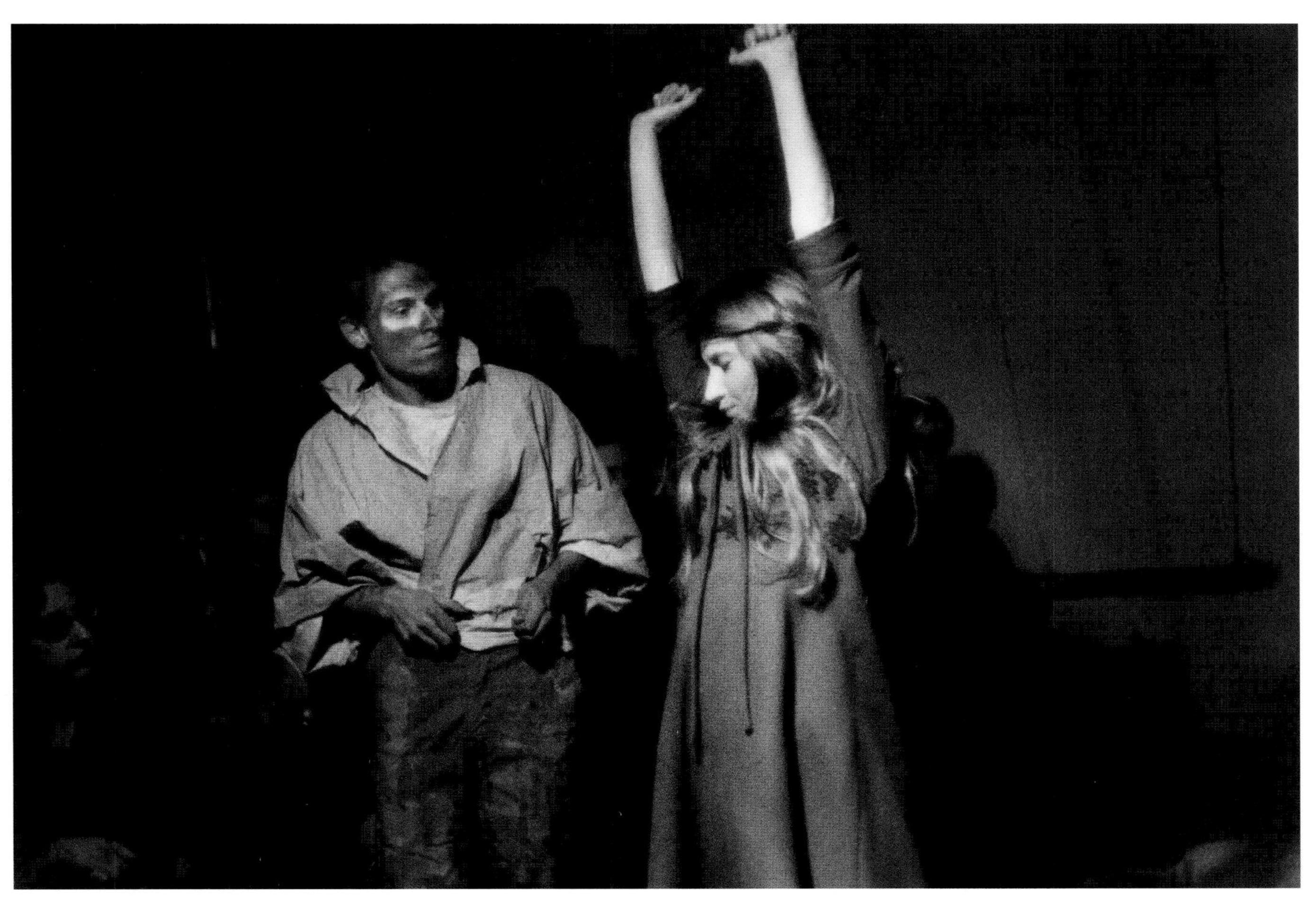

Lucas Samaras, Pat Oldenburg

Red Grooms' Performances

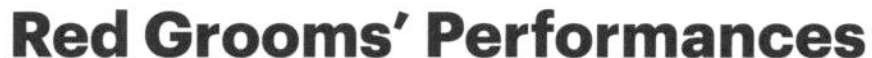

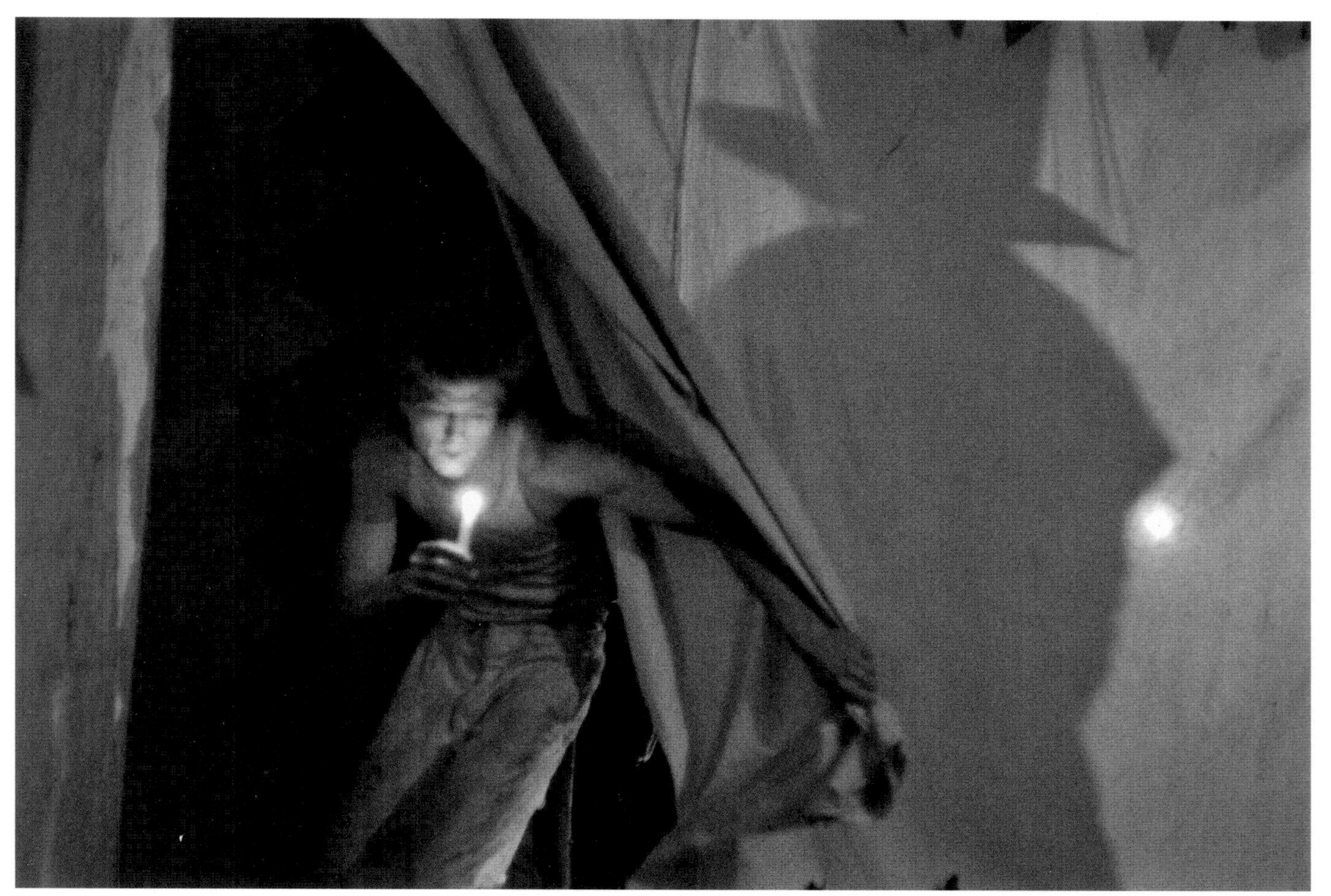

Red Grooms

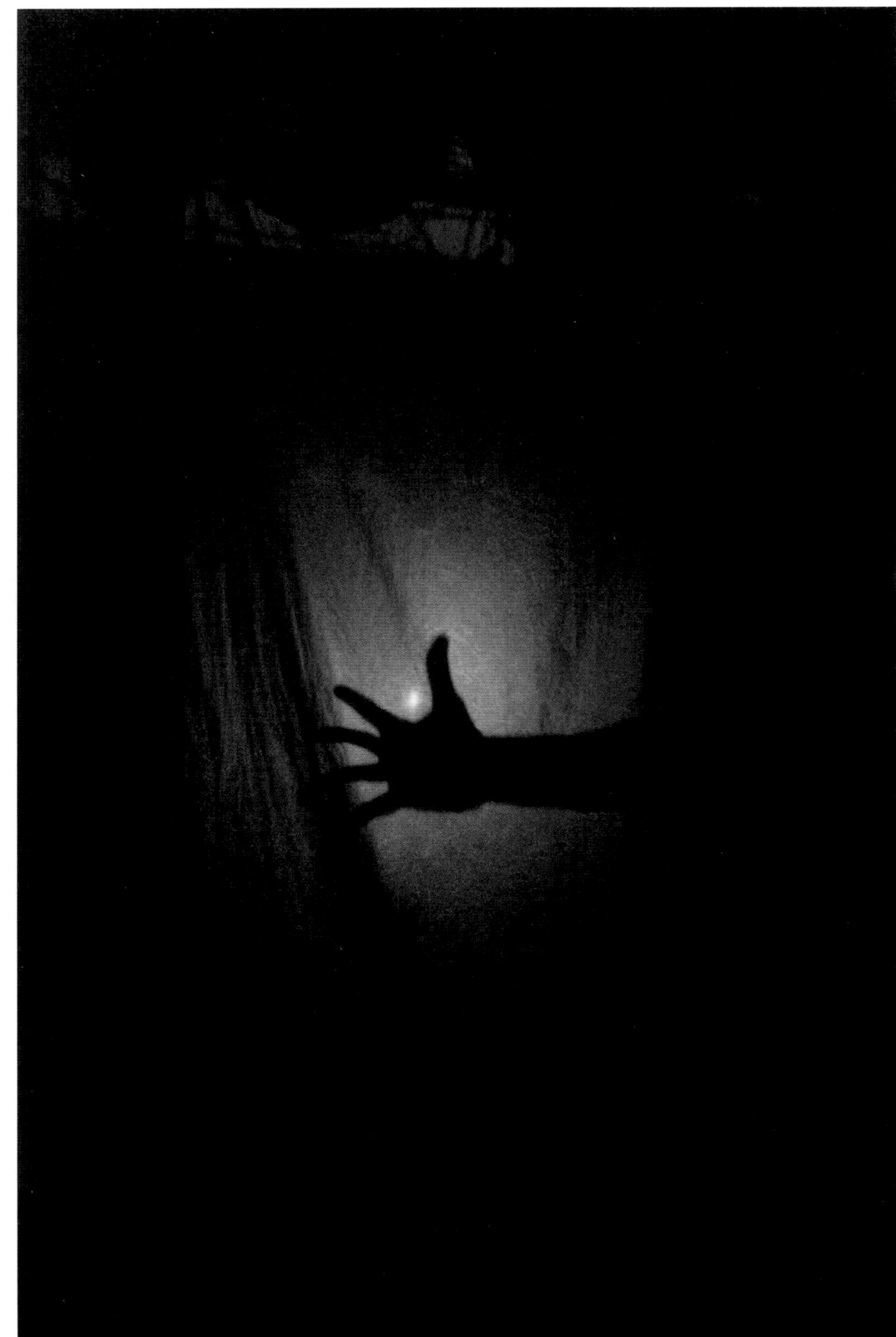

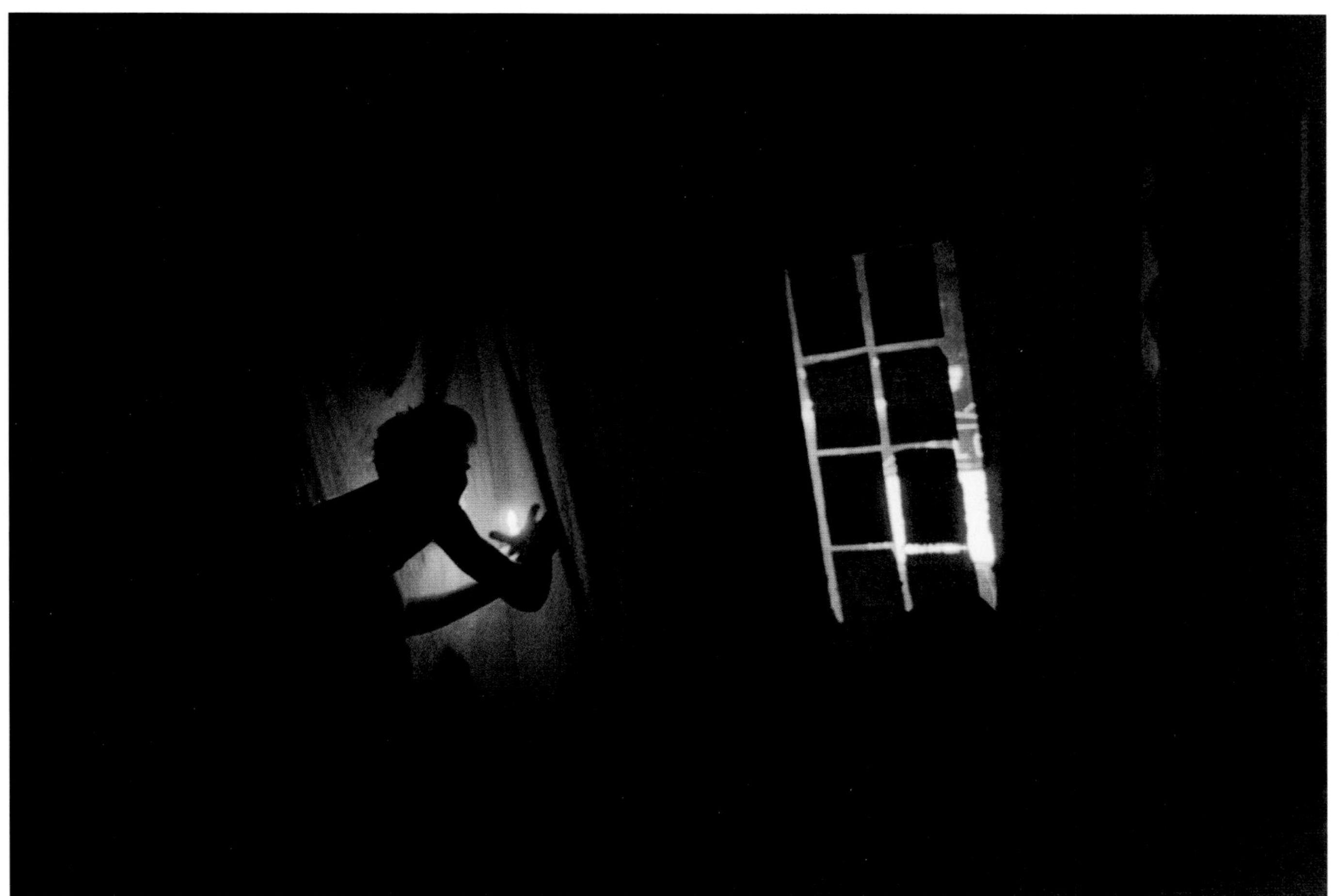

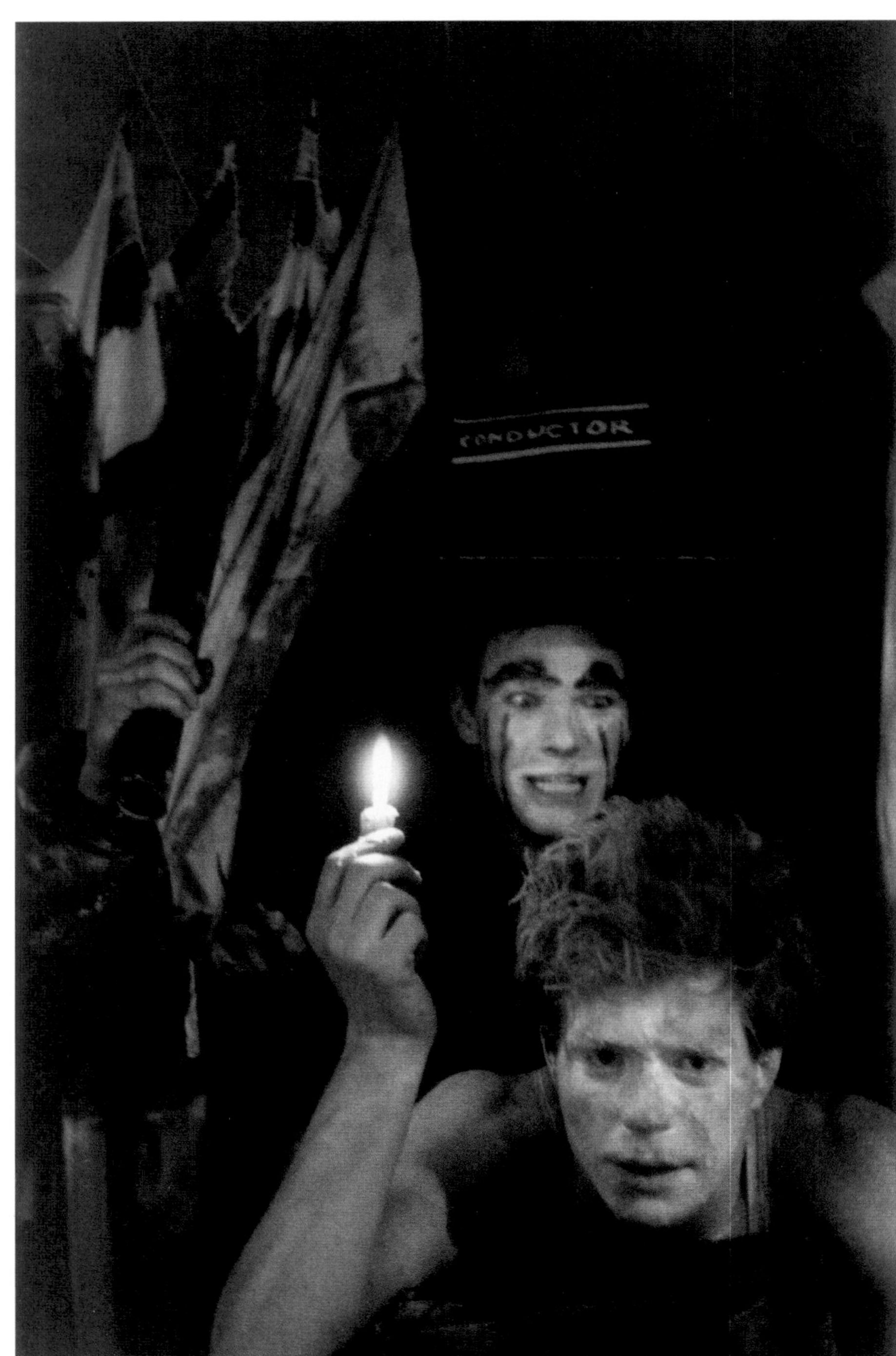

Terry Barrell, Red Grooms

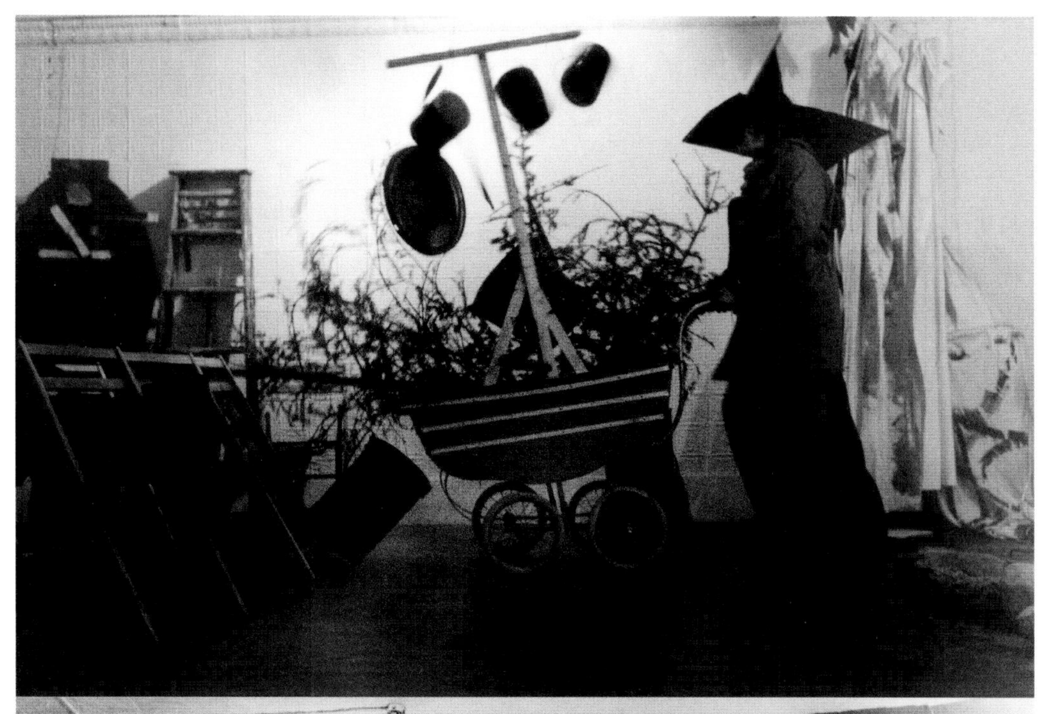

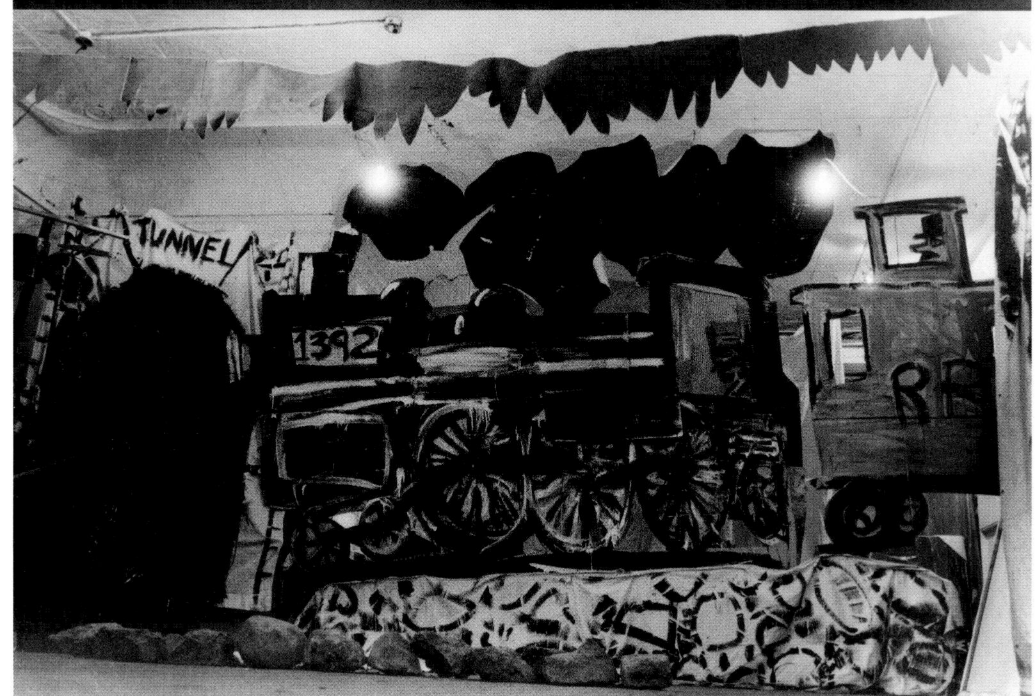
TUNNEL
1392
RR

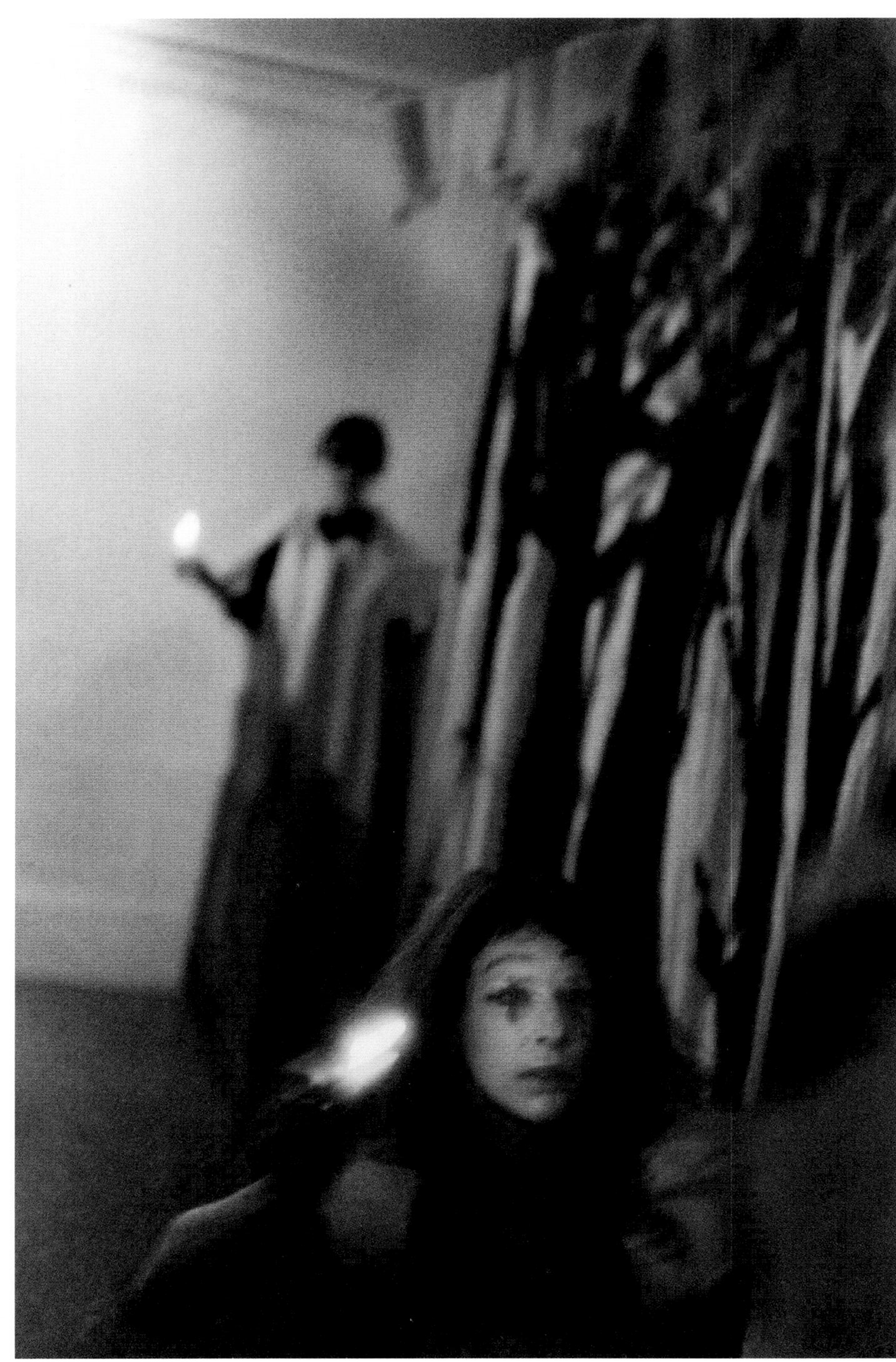

Mary Frank

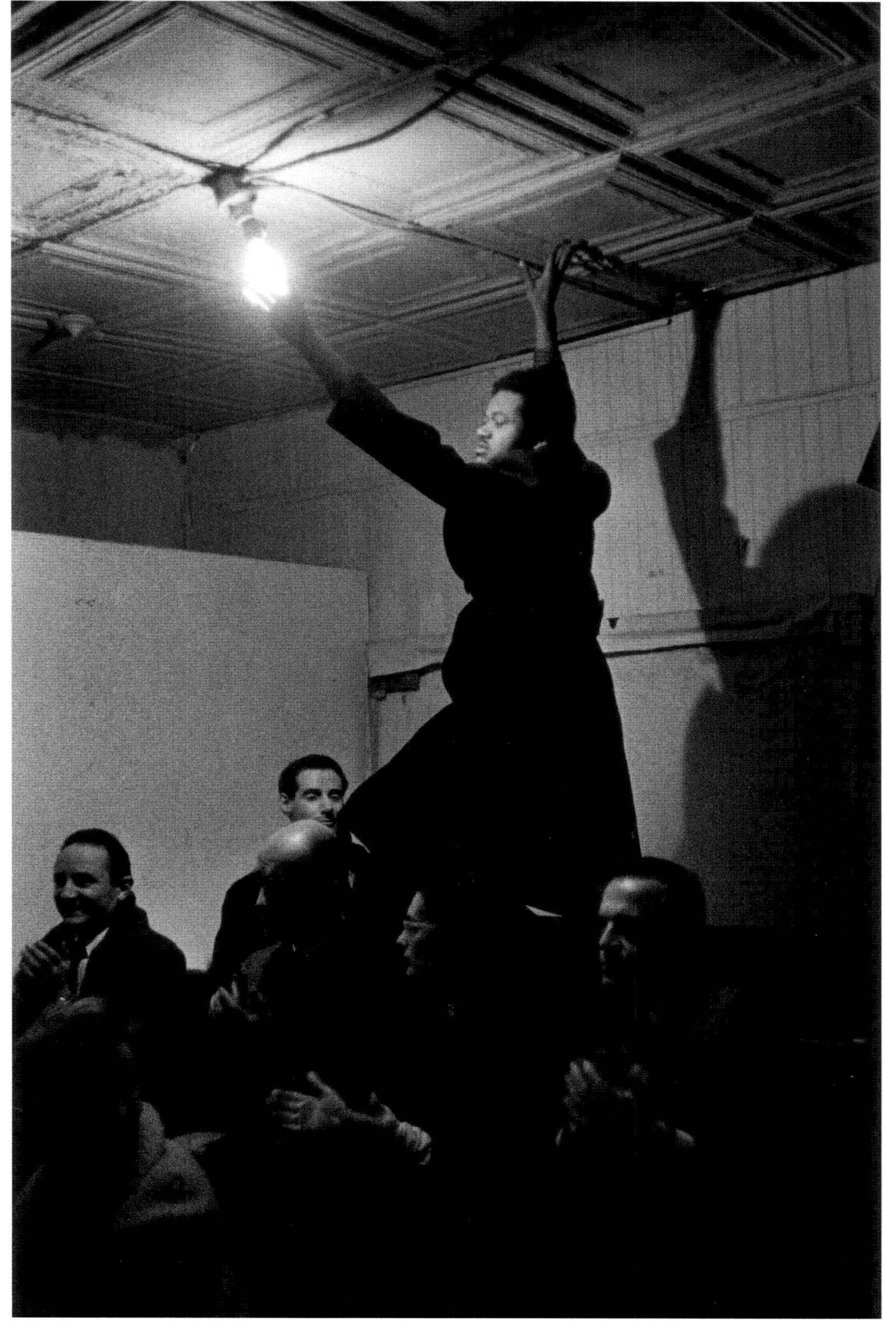

Bob Thompson

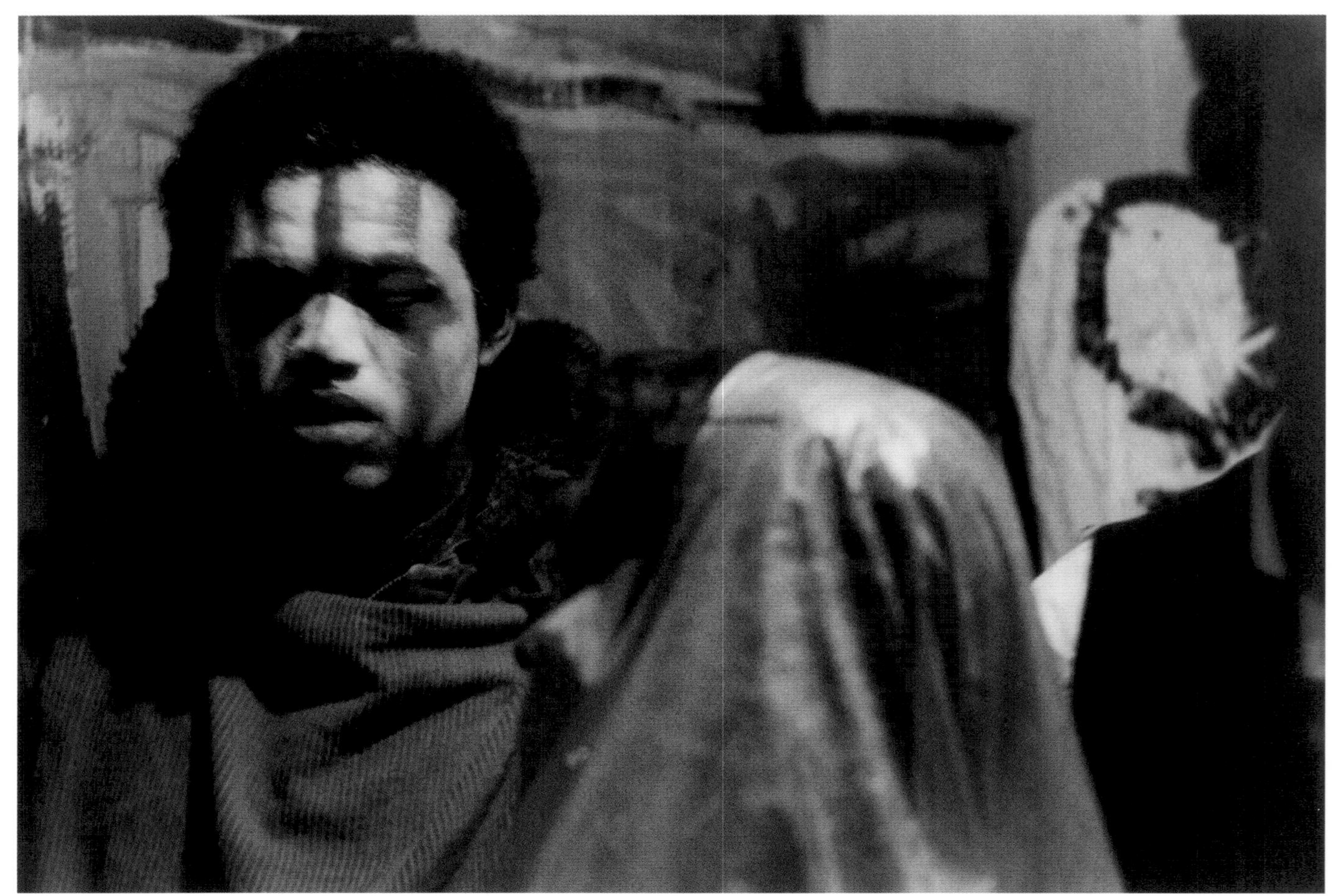

Bob Thompson

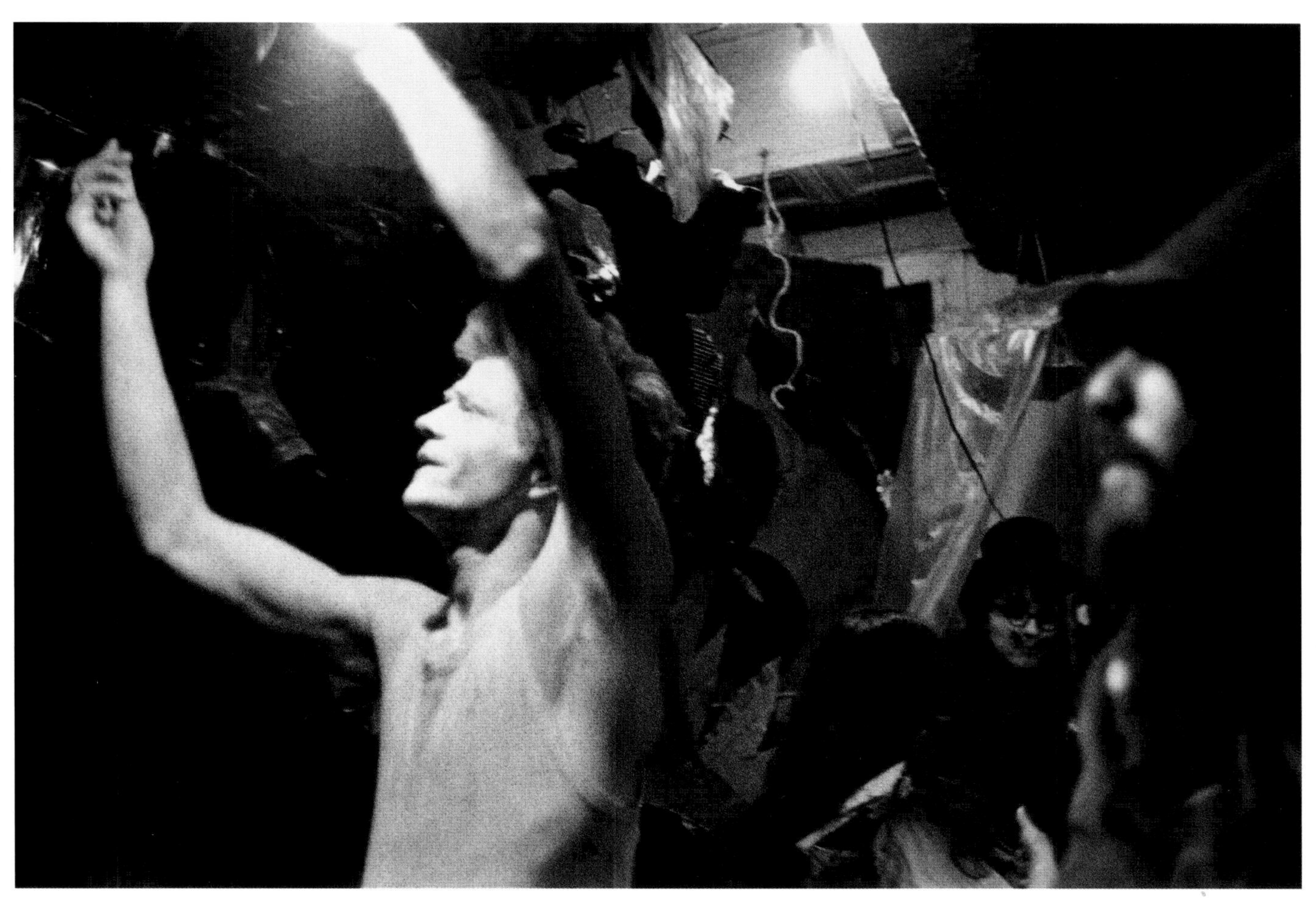

Red Grooms

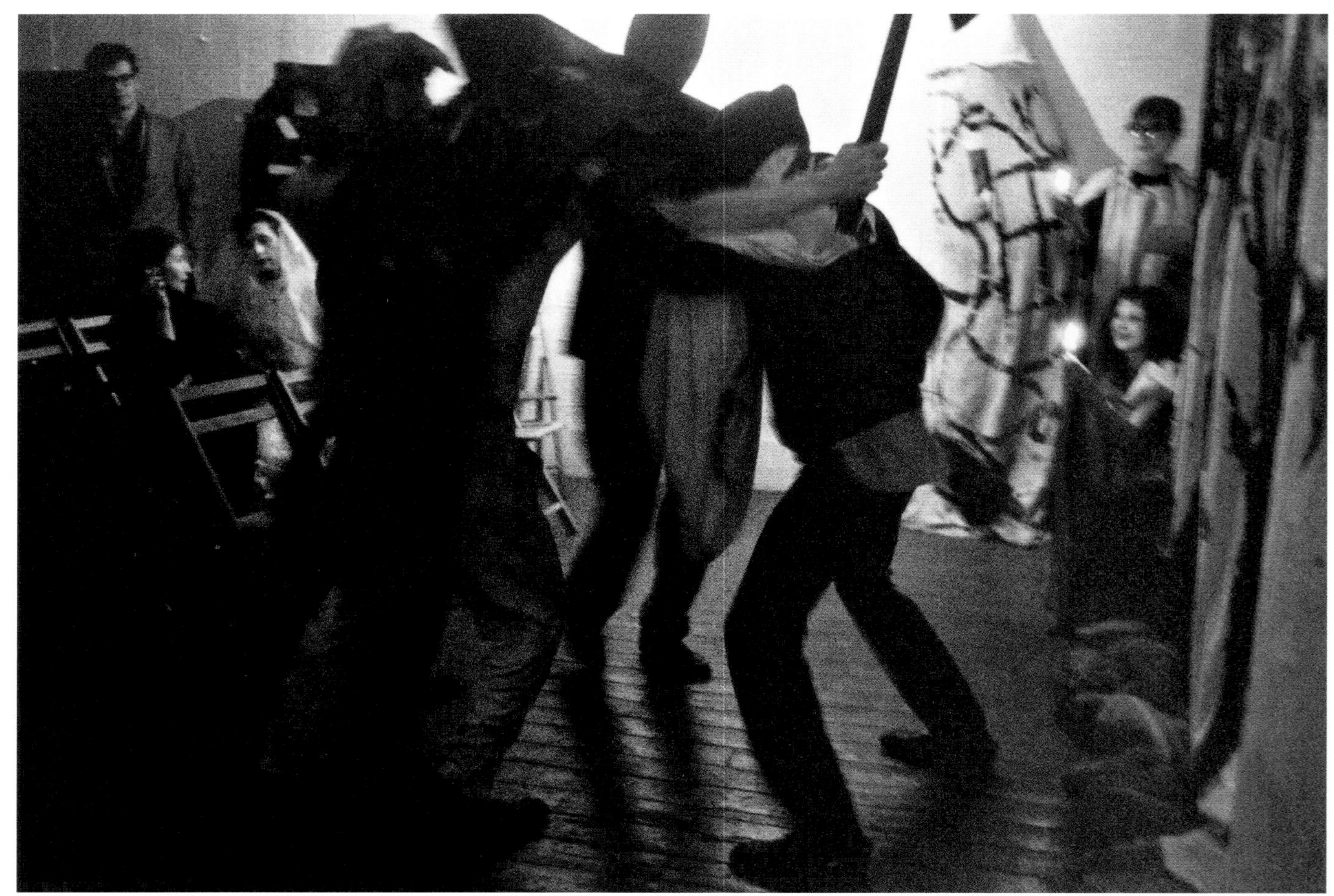

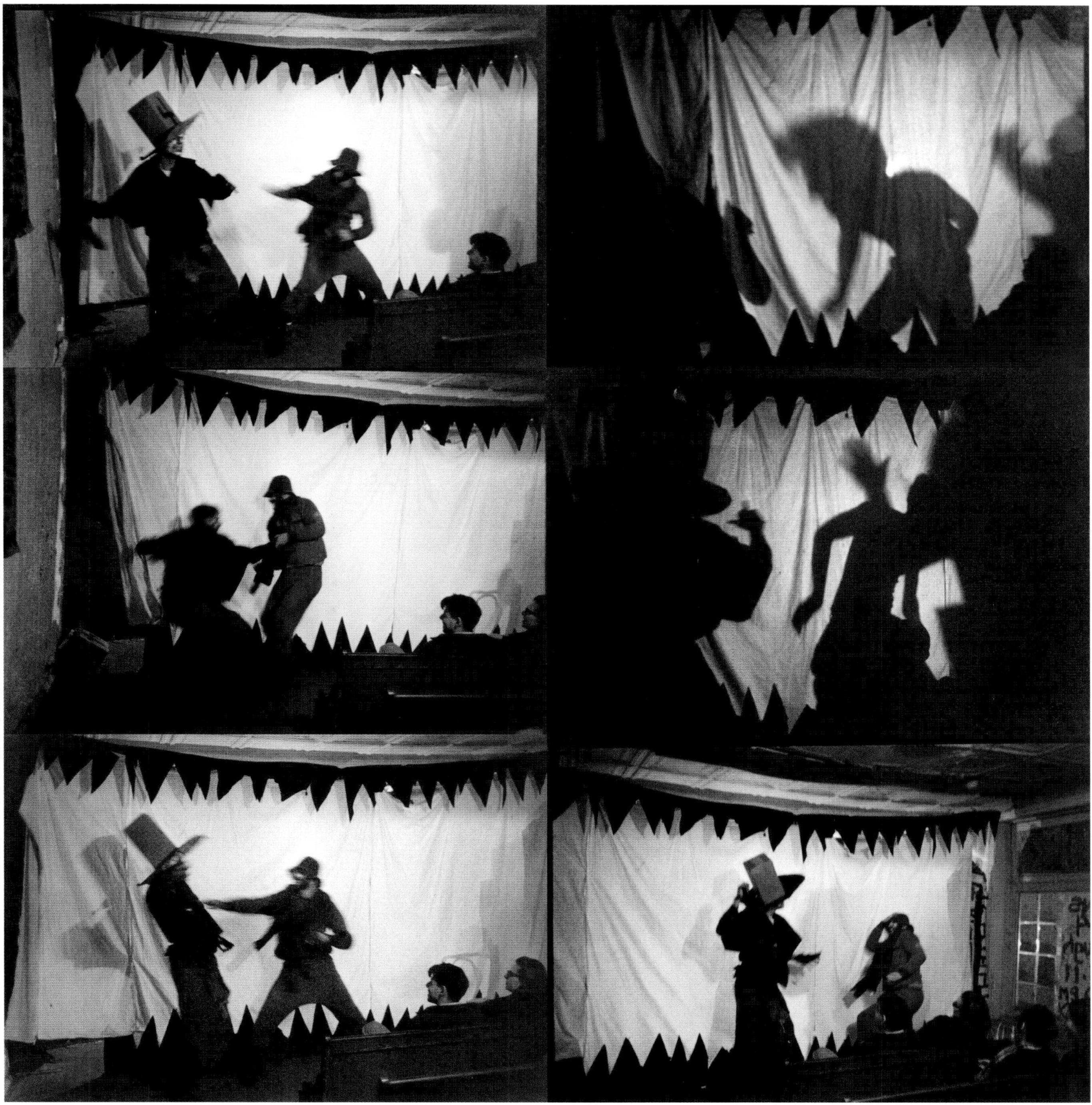

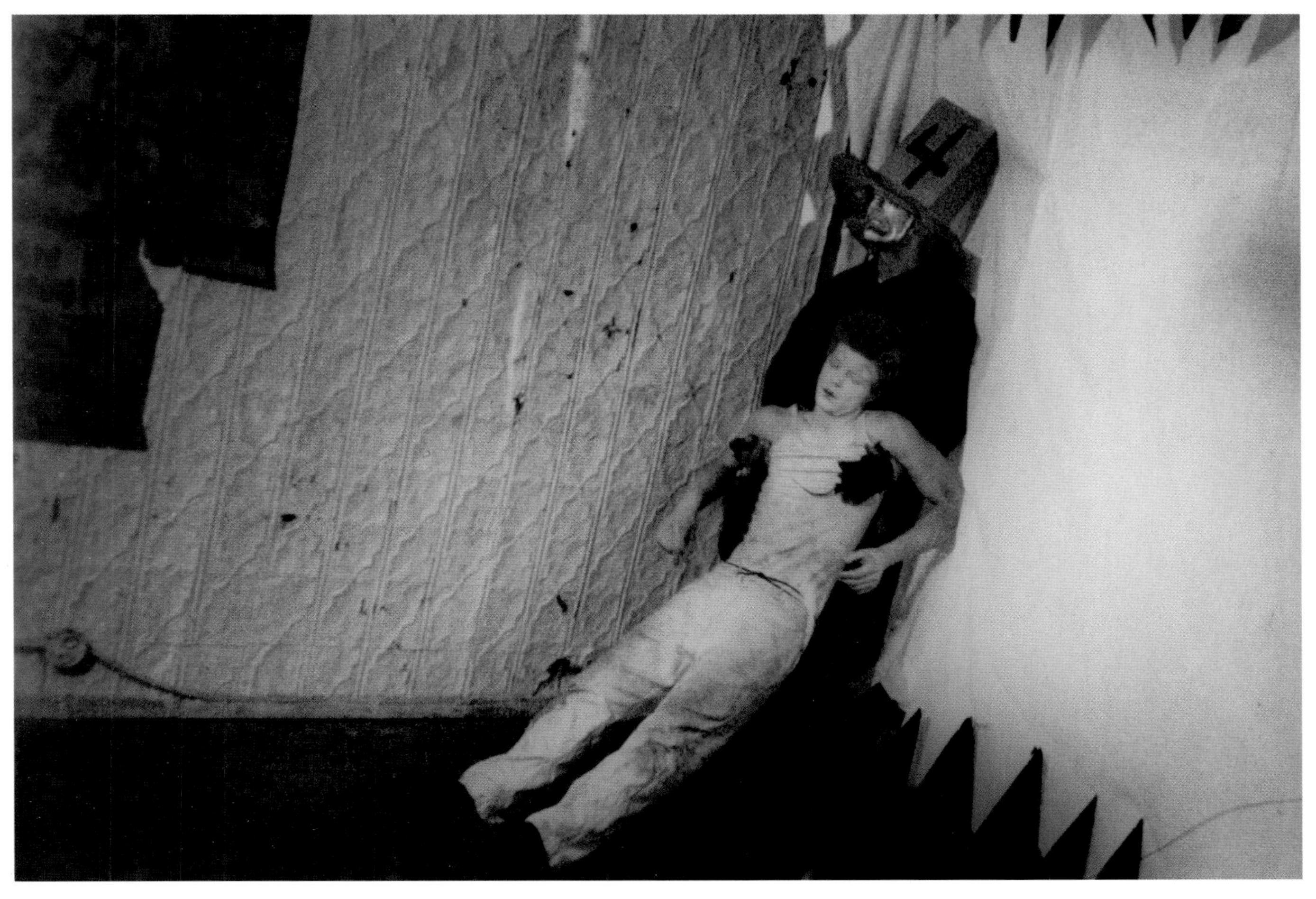

Red Grooms dragged off

PAINTIN

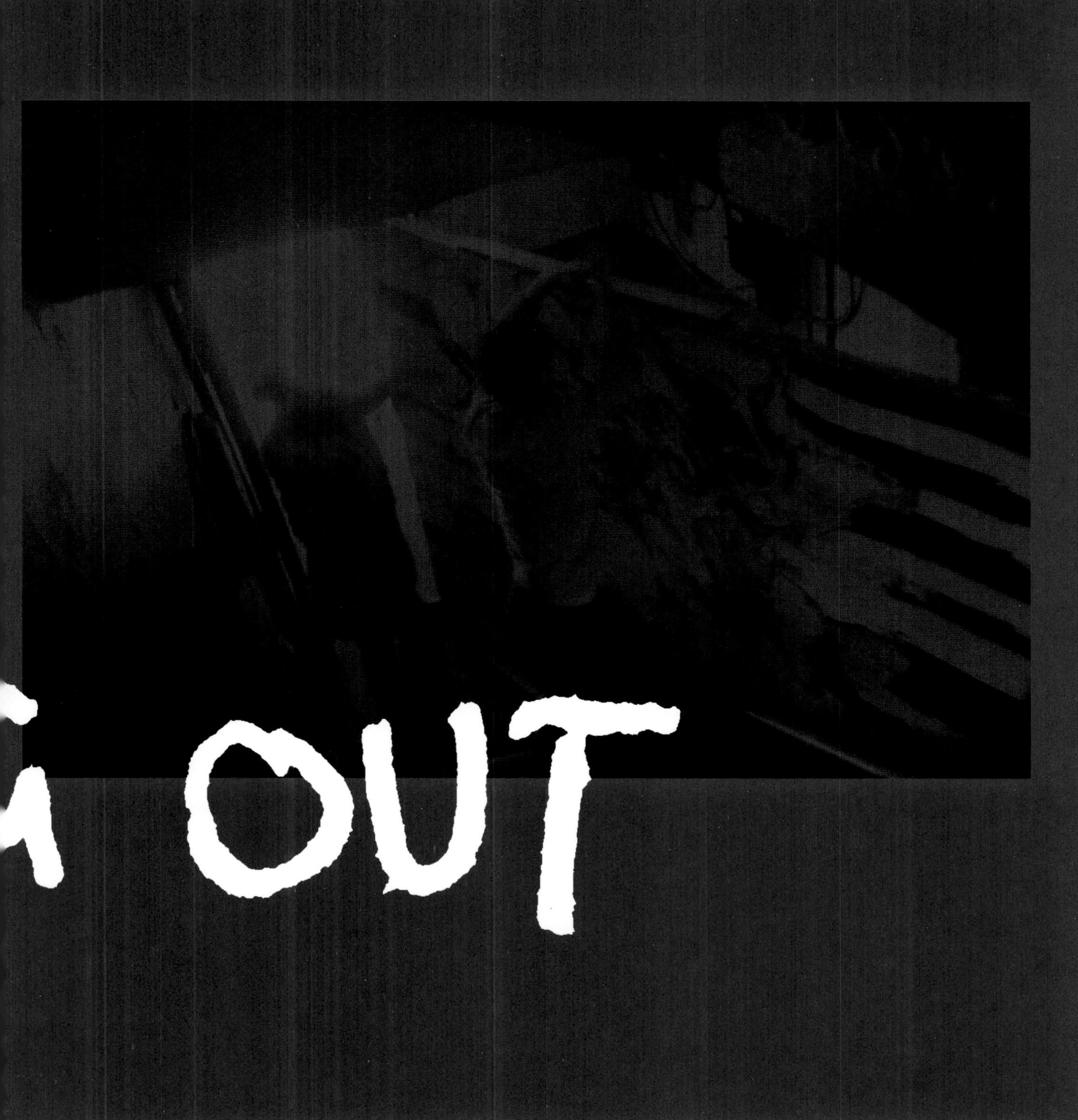
OUT

Larry Rivers and David Amram improvised a jazz performance for saxophone and French horn during *Pull My Daisy*. At that moment art movers arrived from the real world to carry off Alfred Leslie's large paintings. The musicians wouldn't stop their improvising and didn't lose a beat, shifting the focus of their music from the film to the painting. Allen Ginsberg crawled on all fours like a worshipper in front of the art movers who struggled to get the painting down the stairs and into their truck, for an exhibition in a distant place ... perhaps uptown ... elsewhere, outside of this raging downtown art scene.

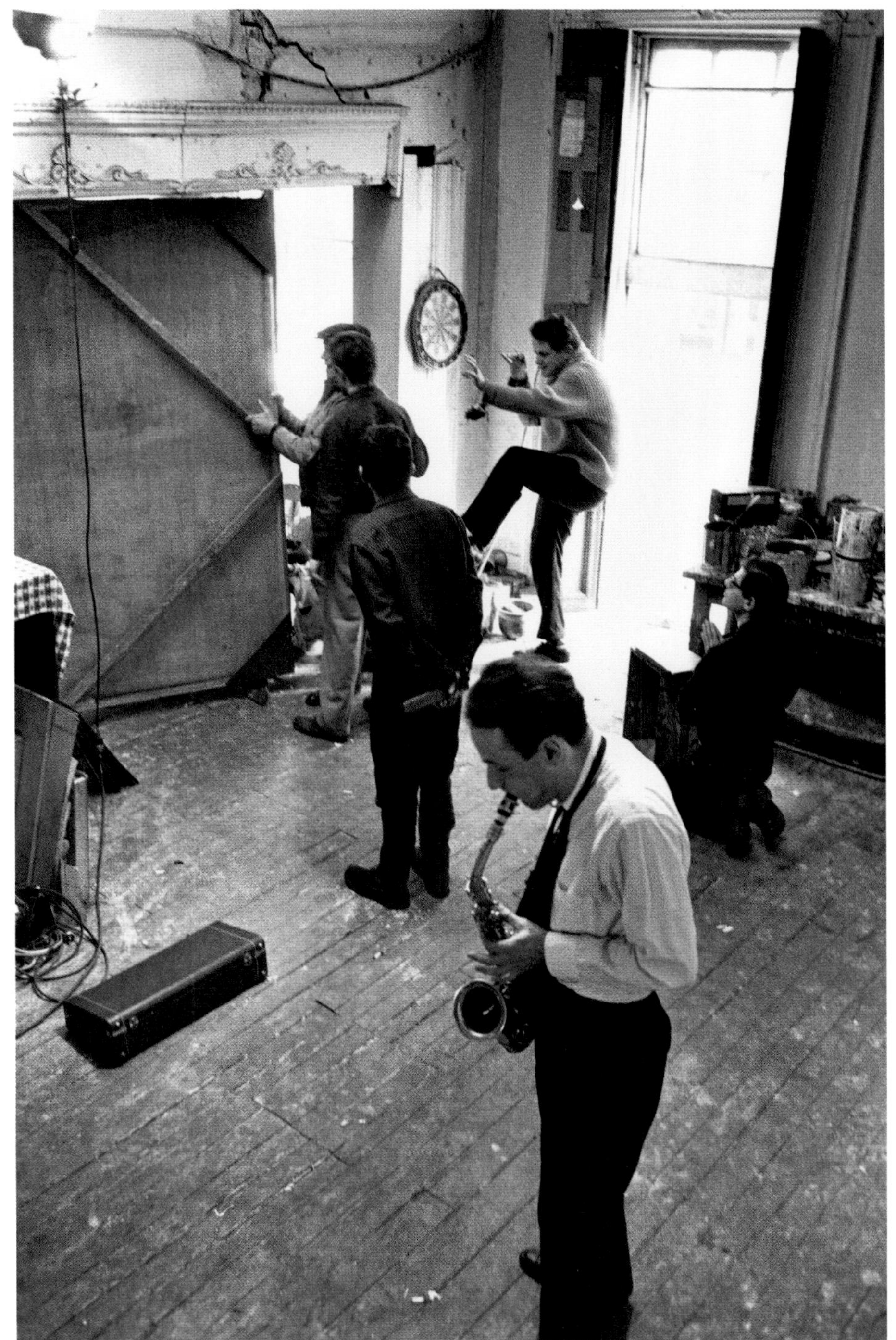

Larry Rivers (with saxophone),
Gregory Corso, David Amram (at window),
Allen Ginsberg

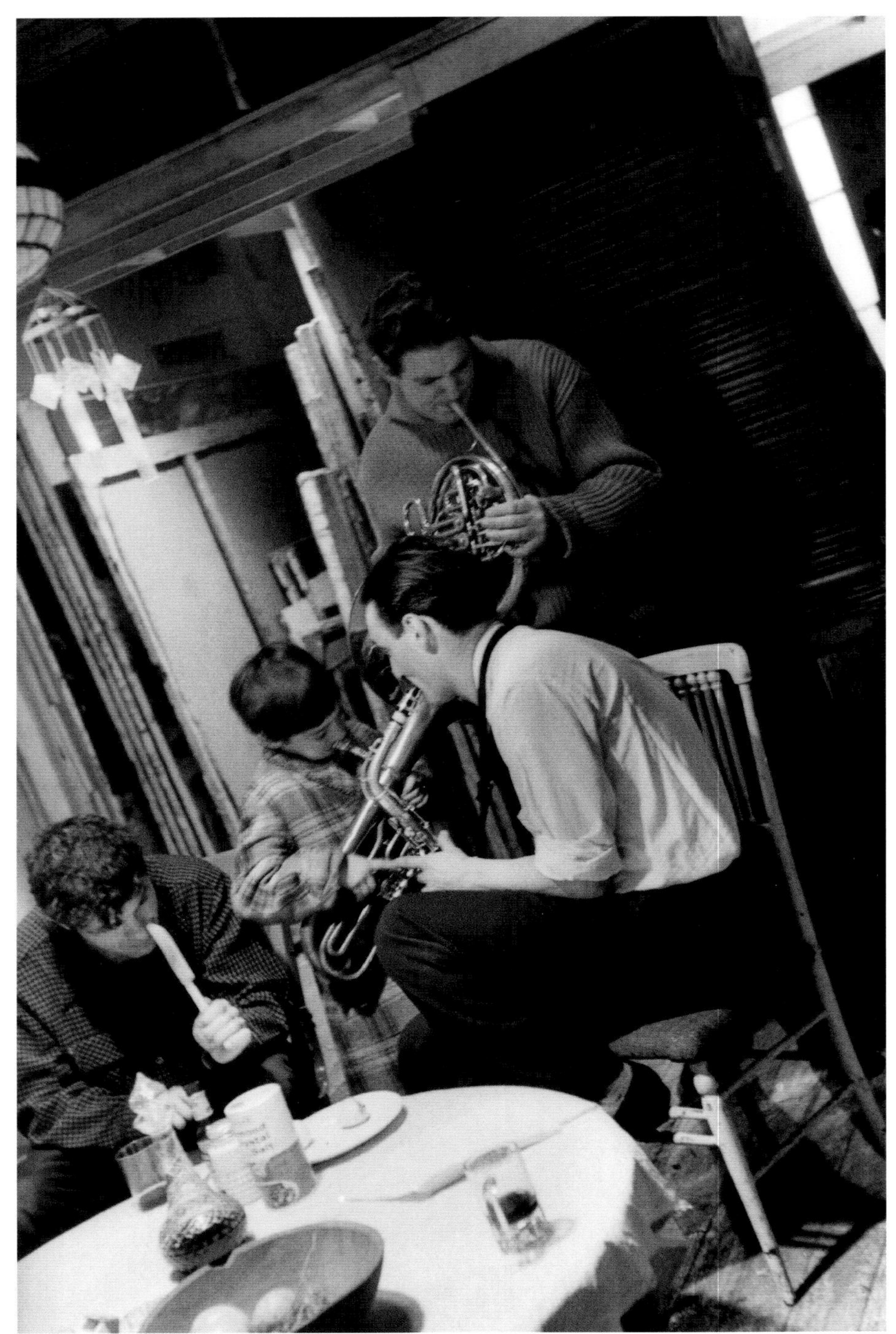

Gregory Corso, Pablo Frank, Larry Rivers,
David Amram

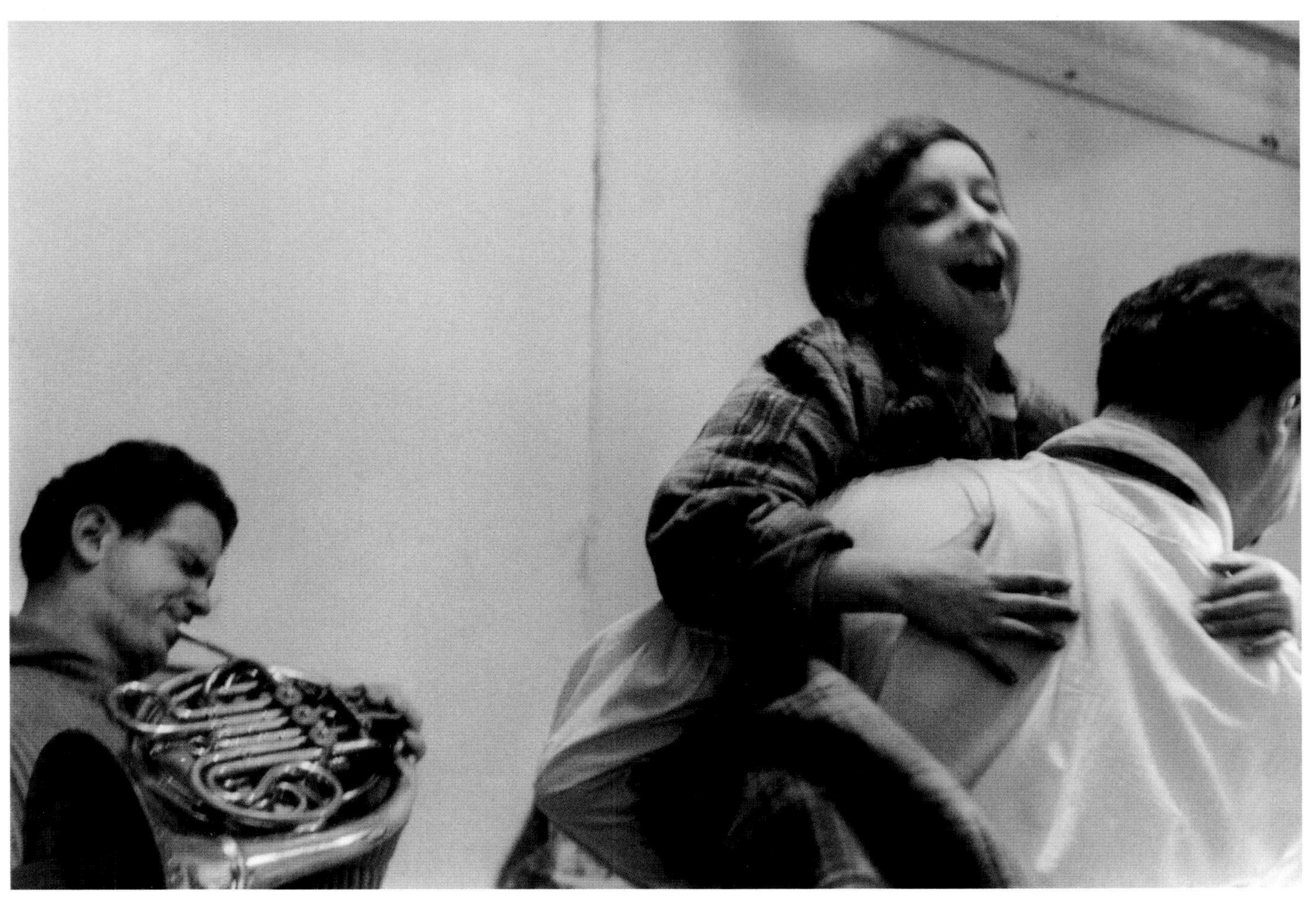

David Amram, Pablo Frank, Larry Rivers

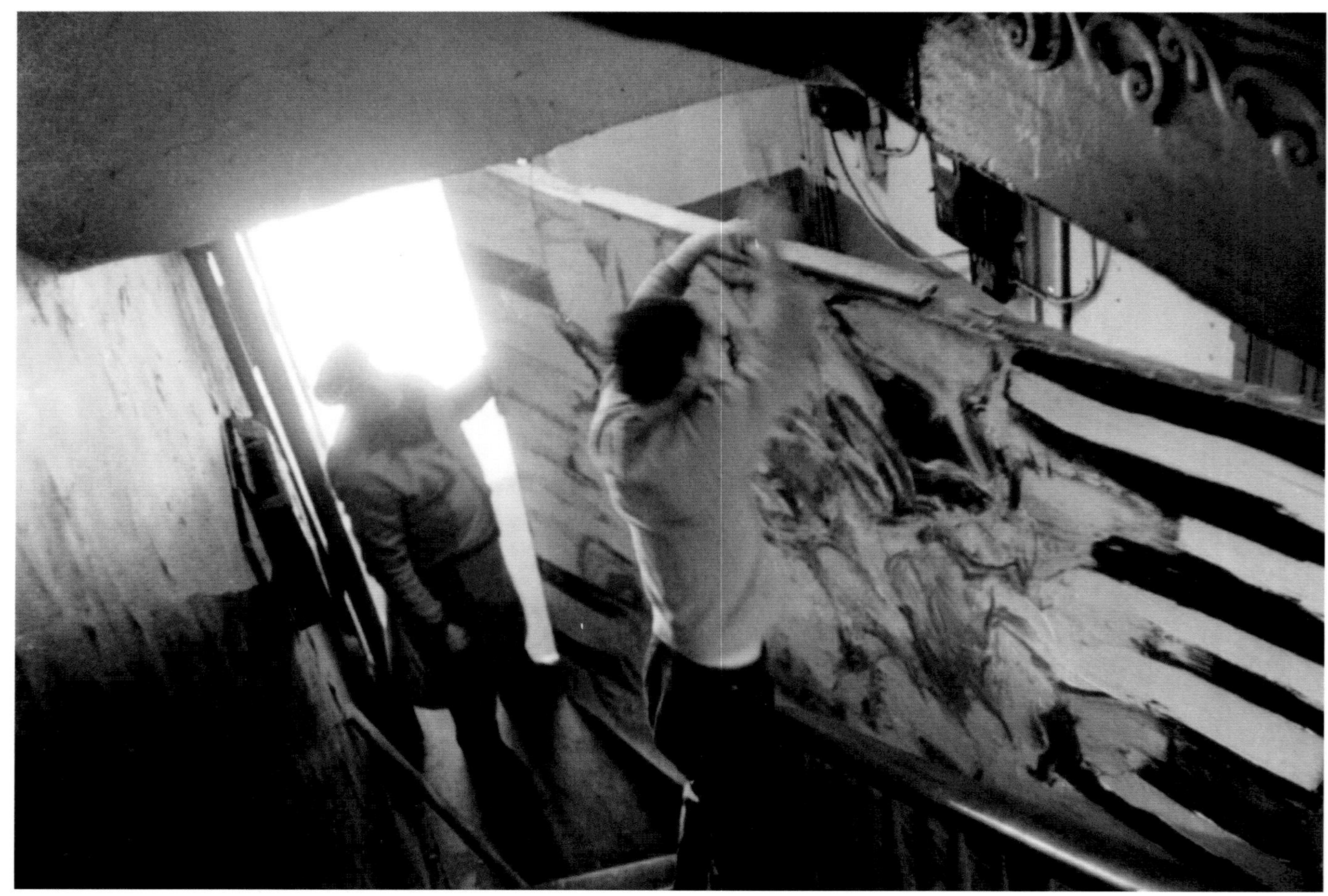

Alfred Leslie

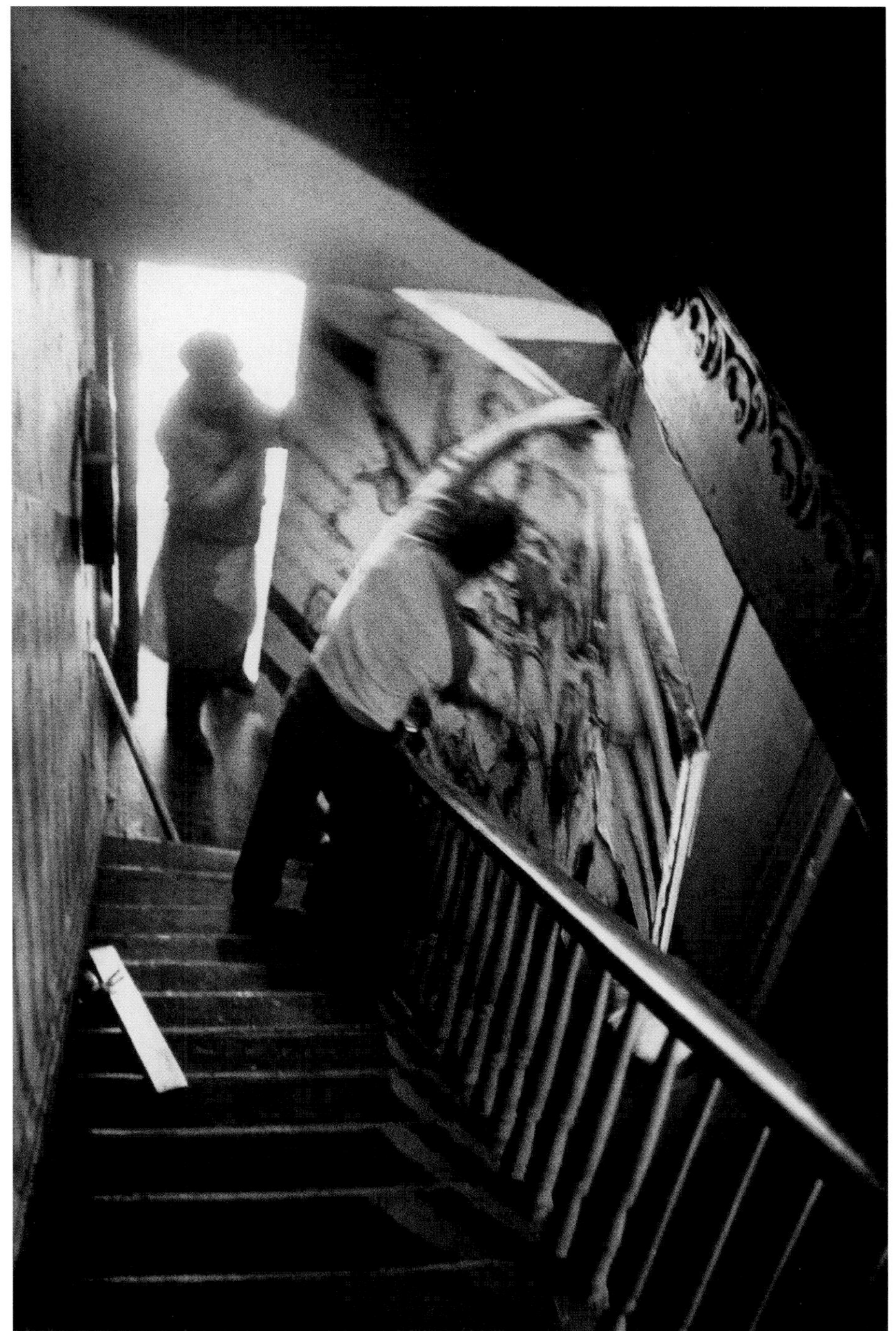

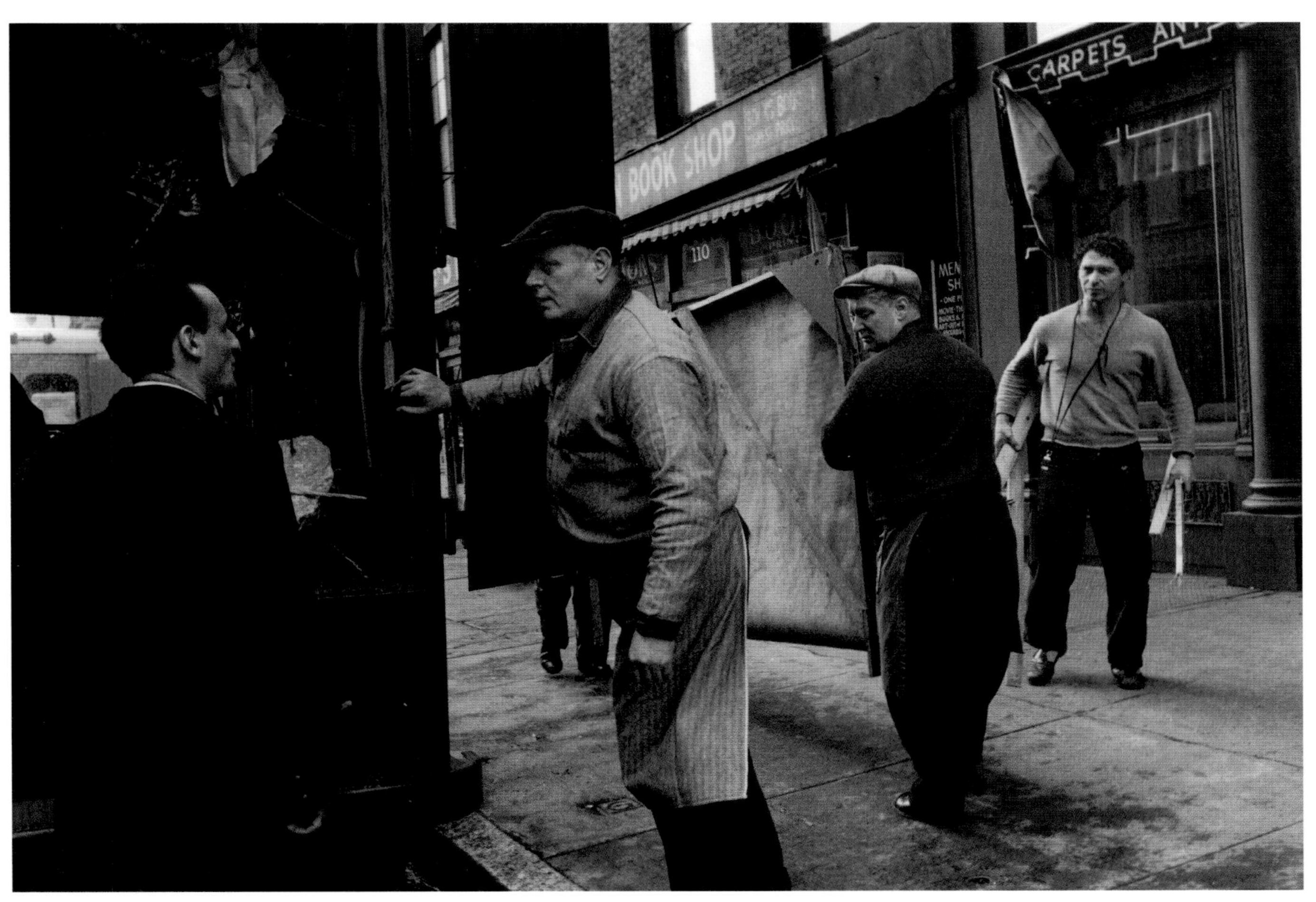

Larry Rivers, Alfred Leslie

In 1963 developers moved in, and the galleries moved out. Much of the block was torn down. The art world fractured into factions as Soho and Uptown flourished, and East Hampton beckoned. The artists continued their careers elsewhere. Evolutionary art movements eclipsed 10th Street. There was no need to put it together again. There is nothing like it today.

TENTH S

REMEMB

QUARE PAINTS
TREET
ERED

The buildings between 9th and 10th Streets on Third Avenue were old Civil War era structures with lofts which became artists' studios. Some artists lived here in illegal arrangements. This part of the city didn't have the "garrets and pretensions of Greenwich Village," neither was it the Lower East Side. It was a no man's land. The Third Avenue elevated train which had been in service for seventy years had recently been demolished, leaving behind layers of dirt which permeated everything.

The lofts had wood floors, splintered and deep in dirt. Cracked walls with layers of paint over plaster, embossed metal ceilings, iron bolts joining the shaky structures to the building next door. Large windows facing the avenue. Trucks rumbling by, day and night. Rent: fifty dollars a month.

—

With no idea of who else lived there, I was looking out the large window from my new loft to the street below, and saw a beautiful woman carrying her groceries, weaving between trucks across Third Avenue. She had the statuesque posture and graceful movement of a ballet dancer. I found out that she was Carolyn Brown, Merce Cunningham's lead dancer who lived a few doors down. Her husband, Earle Brown, was an avant-garde composer colleague of John Cage. Carolyn's passage through trucks with groceries became a dance of New York City for me: choreographed by traffic—a spontaneous solo performance in the street ... very Cagean.

Along 10th Street it was always a surprise to encounter the pristine white walls of the gallery spaces in the midst of the grimy street, which was occupied by Bowery derelicts and unfortunate homeless winos laying out on the sidewalks. Someone called them horizontal doormen. It was a sobering atmosphere.

There was an unused inner courtyard behind the galleries. City cats roamed there and a few untamed trees struggled toward the sky. De Kooning and Milton Resnick's studios faced the courtyard and my fire escape opened into it. I photographed it as a brick landscape. Robert Frank photographed Allen Ginsberg there hugging a tree and photographed my band, The New Lost City Ramblers against the bricks.

Soon after moving there (in 1957) I attended a memorial for the painter Jan Müller who had just died. His service was held at the nearby Grace Church which was filled with artists, and the speaker was art historian Meyer Shapiro. That's when I realized how large and cohesive this community of artists was.

—

The 10th Street galleries were always welcoming. They were owned and shared by the artists themselves who paid the rent. Lots of energy and exhibitions, an ever-changing museum of visions and ideas. Older artists challenged by younger innovations, the second wave of Abstract Expressionists made their mark while newer visual explorations emerged.

The dialog remained within the framework of painting on canvas. Established painters from the earlier years were always there: Kline, Guston, de Kooning, Vicente, Tworkov looking over the scene. Milton Resnick was seen everywhere.

Once a month, there would be a night of gallery openings, with one-person shows in the co-ops. The street was filled with painters, colleagues and visitors coming out to support each other. This was an art movement without a single direction, indicative of what was emerging after Abstract Expressionism: early Minimalist, Color Field, conceptual statements, painterly landscapes and photo-realism. No one label fit ... except perhaps the "downtown art scene."

The happenings and performances in art spaces weren't exactly welcomed by the older artists, whose art was challenged by these performance pieces. They were angered when uptown galleries started promoting Pop art. Robert Frank talked about the arrival of Pop art. He commented that Walker Evans was the first Pop artist in his photographs, celebrating the stuff of daily life and popular culture in the 1930s.

—

People on the block kept their eyes open for each other. Robert and Mary Frank were my neighbors. Mary said how difficult it was to make the choice between working in her studio or taking care of the children. Sometimes the kids, Pablo and Andrea, would come visit me via the fire escape, which opened into my loft.

De Kooning had phoned Mary to ask if she knew that her children were out on the fire escape … he could see them from his studio which looked out across the courtyard. Robert and Mary didn't have TV so the kids watched through other people's windows.

Mary recalls how artists would just drop into each other's studios, unannounced, and that many of the galleries had stairways and stoops where artists would sit and argue about who used more paint or bigger brushes, along with comments and criticisms.

Robert was editing and sequencing his book which became *The Americans*. He handed me a thick stack of 11×14 photo prints which were unlike his earlier work. I don't know what he thought of my silence.

Robert traveled to Paris in 1958 while Mary and the kids went to Provincetown. He left several boxes of his negatives with me, which I stored with my shoes. I received a letter from him asking me to bring certain filmstrips to Steichen's office at the Museum of Modern Art: They would be shipped to Paris. Robert had entrusted the negatives for *The Americans* with me rather than with the museum. It was either for the convenience of a neighbor, or his suspicion of uptown institutions. Whichever way, we looked out for each other.

My memory of those years is a composite of artists striving towards their
undefined, indefinable purposes. The silent images of paintings displayed
in bright galleries mix with the sounds of avant-garde, jazz and folk music.
I see the comics of Red Grooms, the colored geometry of Al Jensen, the
boldness of Norman Bluhm, the pained allegories of Mary Frank, and grainy
photographs of Robert Frank ... the products of lofts and studios churning
out works, breaking the surface of art, with little support other than their own
resources.

One winter night Red Grooms and myself walked into the Cedar Bar, and
placed snowballs in the coat racks in an effort to enliven things. Nobody
noticed.

At a restaurant celebrating the opening of a Mary Frank exhibition,
de Kooning shoveled spaghetti into my mouth. He was in joyous spirits.

Realizing reality. When starting to get my loft fit to live in ... I mopped it
several times but never got it clean enough. While cleaning the stone window

sill, a chip of stone fell to the street below, nearly hitting a wino who looked up, shook his fist at me and growled, "I'll sue you for everything you got." When the gas man came to hook up the heater he asked, "What are you going to do here?" I said I was going to do photography and make paintings. "You can't make a living that way, you better get a job." There was a similar conversation with the man from the electric company—with the same response.

I never had really considered how I was going to make a living, since I was so unthinking and committed to making my own art, and decided then to never buy anything on time. I figured if I didn't make the payments, anything would be taken away. My guiding economic principle became "If you can't afford something outright, don't buy it at all." Never borrow money – that way the banks wouldn't have money to loan and capitalism would collapse ... which at that time was not such a bad idea.

—

P.S. I always considered myself as an outsider on the block. I had come from five years at Yale Art School, where I studied with Josef Albers whose vision of art was quite different from the 10th Street painters, many of whom were former Hans Hofmann students. Yet Albers had introduced us to artists from NYC: de Kooning, James Brooks, Conrad Marca-Relli, Ad Reinhardt, Stuart Davis and Burgoyne Diller were visiting critics. At Yale I worked with Herbert

Matter who encouraged my photography, and when I arrived in NY he made me welcome in the art world of Pollack, de Kooning and Kline who were his friends. Herbert had also introduced me to Robert Frank ... both were Swiss.

During the years I lived on Third Avenue, I founded a musical group The New Lost City Ramblers, and photographed and filmed Bob Dylan on the roof of my loft building. I made my first film *The High Lonesome Sound* at that time. Dylan wrote (on *Highway 61 Revisited*), "In case you didn't know, your rooftop has been torn down."

David Budd

Norman Bluhm

Carolyn Brown

Jim Dine

Charlotte Brooks

Lucas Samaras

David Budd

Nick Marsicano

Miles Forst

John Krushenick

James Brooks

Charles Cajori

Peter Orlovsky

Landis Lewitin

Robert Whitman

Michaela

Giorgio Cavallon

Lionel Abel

Allan Kaprow

Ludwig Sander

A memory list of artists encountered around the block and at the Cedar Bar

Wilfrid Zogbaum

Barbara Forst

Lucien Carr

Al Jensen

Alice Neel

James Brooks

Shindy

Claes Oldenburg

Nicholas Krushenick

Sidney Geist

Tom Wesselmann

Emily Mason

Friedel Dzubas

Larry Rivers

Paul Georges

Arthur Trager

Ted Jones

Felix Pasilis

Michael Lowe

Alfred Leslie

Andrea Frank

Pablo Frank

Red Grooms

Terry Barrell

Lois Dodd

Delphine Seyrig

Hans Hofmann

Milton Resnick

Jackie Ferrara

Morton Feldman

Leo Castelli

Irving Sandler

Eli King

Jack Tworkov

John Cage

James Rosati

Al Kotin

Earle Brown

Bob Thompson

Aaron Siskind

Philip Guston

Michael Loew

Denise Parker

Pat Oldenburg

Phillip Pavia

Sally Gross

Alex Katz

Grace Hartigan

George Spaventa

Sally Hazelet

Reuben Kadish

Theo Stamos

Herman Cherry

Richard Bellamy

Aristodimos Kaldis

Cessa Carr

Harry Holtzman

Pat Passlof

Budd Hopkins

Tom Hess

Dody Müller

Gregory Corso

Howard Kanovitz

Zero Mostel

Jay Milder

Paul Jenkins

Allen Ginsberg

Lester Johnson

Rudy Burckhardt

Gert Berliner

Bob Beauchamp

Saul Leiter

Mark di Suvero

Max Spoerri

Jackie Ferrara

David Amram

Gabriel Kohn

Robert Rauschenberg

Ad Reinhardt

Franz Kline

Mary Frank

Robert Frank

Esteban Vicente

Mercedes Matter

Michael Goldberg

Wolf Kahn

Jack Kerouac

Angelo Ippolito

Al Held

Frank O'Hara

Herbert Crehan

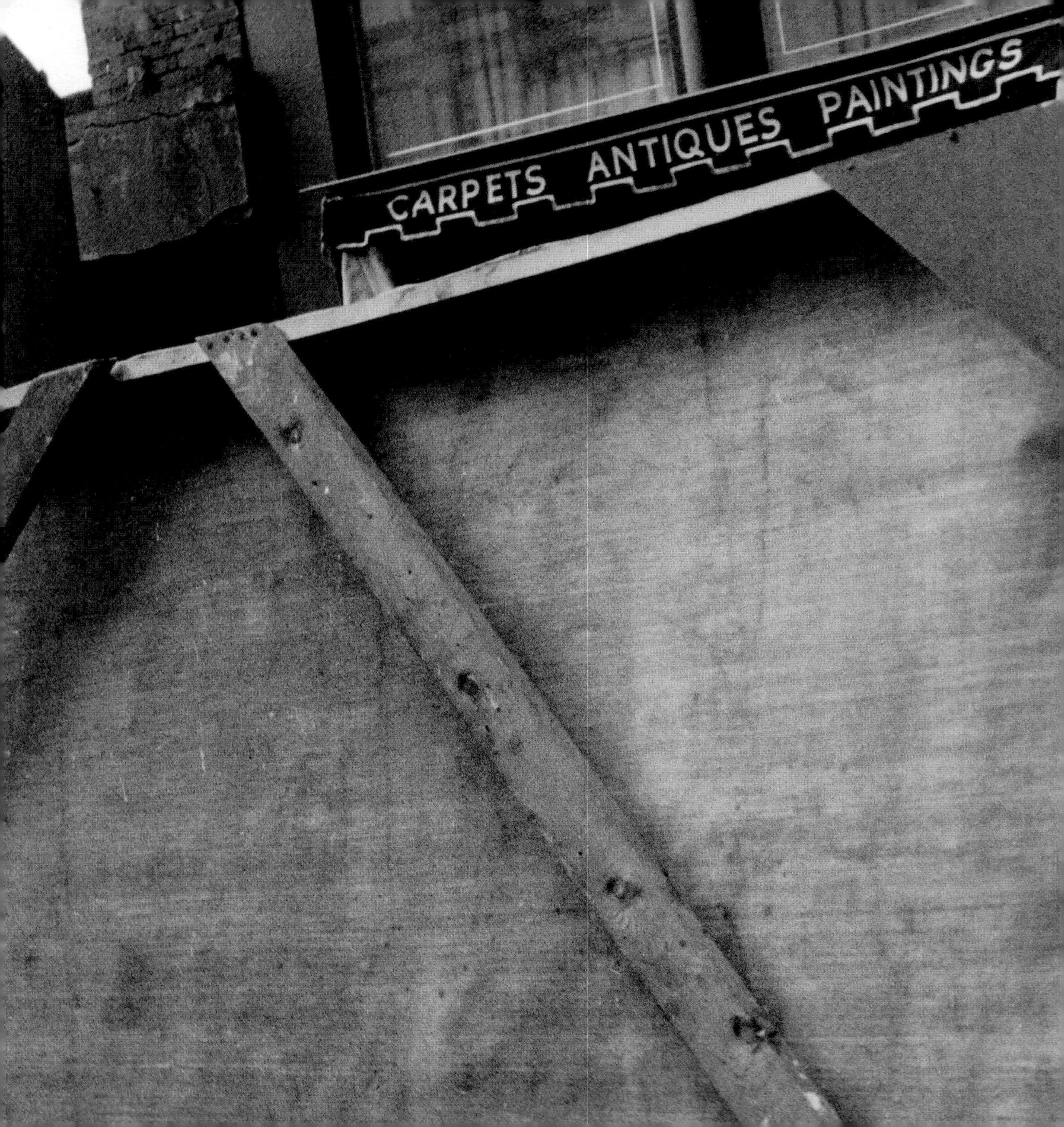

CARPETS ANTIQUES PAINTINGS

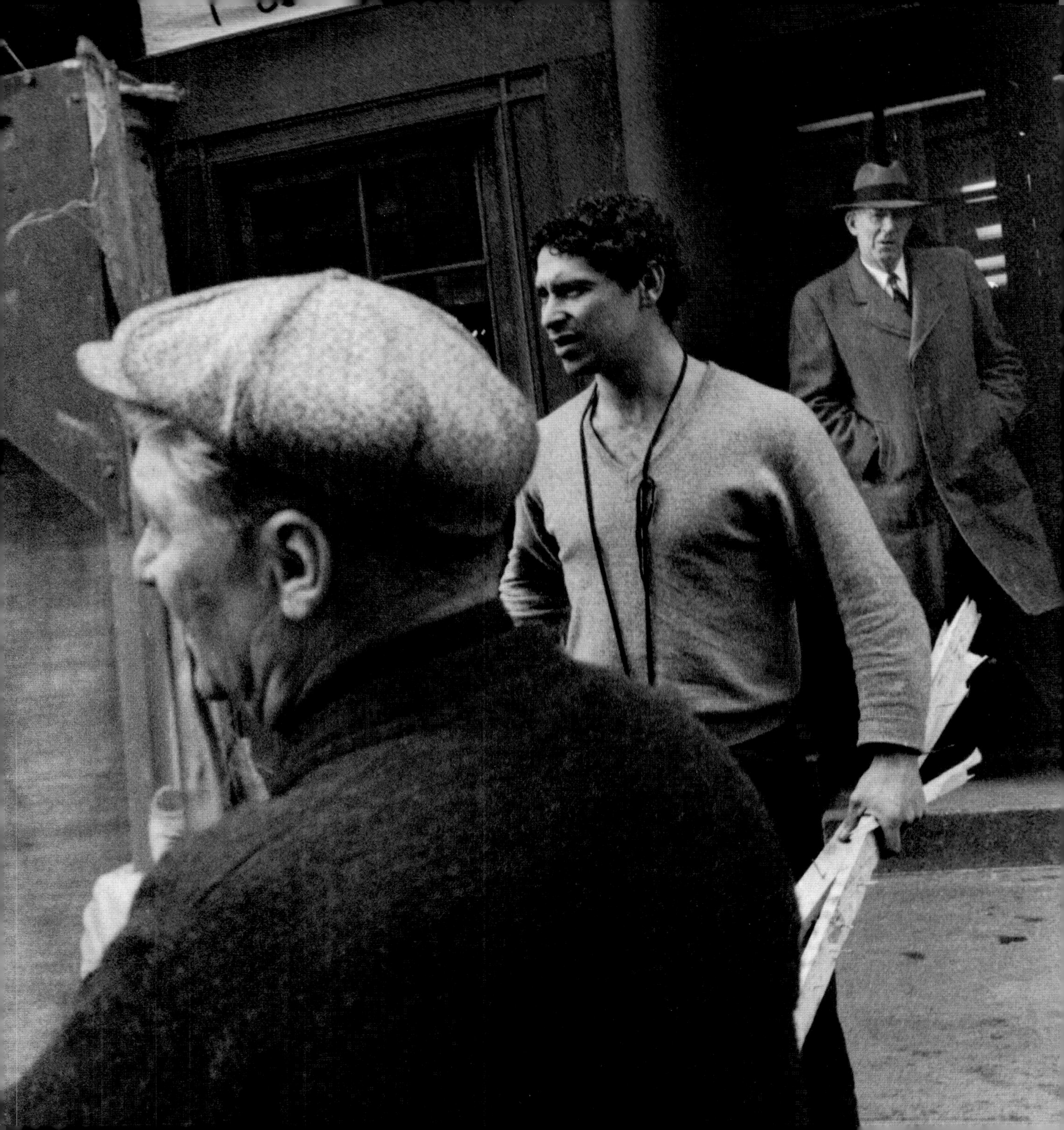

The information in this book is based on my own memory.

Thanks to:

Sonya Cohen Cramer for editorial insights both in texts and in shaping of the book.

Melissa Burt for creating the NYU Grey Art Gallery exhibition "Inventing Downtown: Artist-Run Galleries in New York City, 1952–1965."

Gerhard Steidl for encouraging the project early on. His delight in images suggested further inventions. As publisher, printer and designer, he sees with open eyes.

Sid Kaplan for making new prints.

Dealers Parker Stephenson and Deborah Bell who always see possibilities.

Mary Frank for sharing memories.

Robert and Mary Frank my neighbors who pointed to a way through the labyrinth.

Herbert Matter for spirit, friendship and encouragement.

Mercedes Matter who showed me a way to the early Abstract Expressionist painters and the Cedar Bar.

Ed Ruscha who suggested the dots in "Cheap Rents ... and de Kooning."

John Elderfield for writing the introduction: "It could have been longer, and if I had more time I probably could have made it shorter."

First edition published in 2015

© 2015 John Cohen for the images
© 2015 John Cohen and John Elderfield
for the texts
© 2015 Steidl Publishers for this edition

Book design: Victor Balko / Steidl Design
Scans and separations
by Steidl's digital darkroom

Production and printing: Steidl, Göttingen

Steidl
Düstere Straße 4
37073 Göttingen
Germany
Phone +49 551 49 60 60
Fax +49 551 49 60 649
mail@steidl.de
steidl.de

ISBN 978-3-86930-903-3
Printed in Germany by Steidl

Object information for fig. 1, p. 11:
Willem de Kooning (American, born
The Netherlands, 1904–1997)
Backyard on Tenth Street, 1956
Oil on canvas, 48 × 58½ in.
The Baltimore Museum of Art:
Frederic W. Cone Fund, BMA 1956.158
© 2015 The Willem de Kooning Foundation /
Artists Rights Society (ARS), New York
Photograph by Mitro Hood

Pages 6–7 and 176–7: Alfred Leslie